18 End-Time Bible Prophecies

Larry Wilson

P.O. Box 273
Bellbrook, Ohio 45305
(513) 848-3322

ISBN 0-945383-29-0

Cover Credit: Greg LaFever
Centerville, Ohio

printed by

TEACH Services
Donivan Road
Route 1, Box 182
Brushton, New York 12916

Acknowledgements

This book is dedicated to the glory of the best friend human beings have ever had. His earthly name is Jesus.

Special thanks is due a growing host of dedicated people who have generously given time and money to make this ministry a dynamic reality.

Wake Up America Seminars, Inc. is a non-profit, educational organization. WUAS is not affiliated, endorsed nor sponsored by any religious organization. Our single mission is to herald the imminent return of our Lord Jesus Christ through whatever means possible.

Christian Commitment

This text was written by an unknown African Pastor, and reprinted by the late evangelist, Paul Gelatt Sr., in his book, *Miracles Among the Pioneers*. It is included for it is worthy of memorization:

I'm a part of the fellowship of the unashamed. I have Holy Spirit Power. The dye has been cast. I have stepped over the line. The decision has been made. I'm a disciple of His. I won't look back, let up, slow down, back away or be still.

My past is redeemed, my present makes sense, my future is secure. I'm finished and done with low living, sight walking, small planning, smooth knees, colorless dreams, tamed visions, mundane talking, cheap living and dwarfed goals.

I no longer need pre-eminence, prosperity, position, promotions, plaudits or popularity. I don't have to be right, first, tops, recognized, praised, regarded or rewarded. I now live by faith, lean on His presence, walk by patience, lift by prayer and labor by power.

My face is set, my gait is fast, my goal is heaven, my road is narrow, my way rough, my companions few, my Guide reliable, my mission clear. I cannot be bought, compromised, detoured, lured away, turned back, deluded or delayed. I will not flinch in the face of sacrifice, hesitate in the presence of the adversary, negotiate at the table of the enemy, ponder at the pool of popularity or meander in the maze of mediocrity.

I won't give up, shut up or let up until I have stayed up, stored up, prayed up and preached up for the cause of Christ. I am a disciple of Jesus. I must go till He comes, give till I drop, preach all I know and work till He stops me.

And when He comes for His own, He will have no problem recognizing me – my banner will be clear. Amen.

18 End-Time Bible Prophecies

Table of Contents

continued

Table of Contents
continued

Introduction to Apocalyptic Prophecy

There are 18 prophecies in Daniel and Revelation that are apocalyptic in nature. In other words, these two books of the Bible contain 18 prophecies that deal with the end of the world. Some of these prophecies have been underway for more than 25 centuries and others have not yet begun to come to pass. However, these 18 prophecies lock together to form a comprehensive matrix so that we can be certain of our chronological position within them. In short, we can clearly determine which events are before us.

The word apocalyptic comes from the word apocalypse. According to Webster, an apocalypse is a divine or glorious revelation. For this reason, the last book of the Bible is often called *The Apocalypse* or *The Revelation.* The title of the book, Revelation, suggests a revealing of something that is otherwise unknown. However, in a larger sense, the other 65 books of the Bible also qualify as "revelations" for they reveal wonderful things about God and His works that would otherwise be unknown.

The books of Daniel and Revelation are unlike the other books of the Bible. These two books contain a special kind of prophecy not found elsewhere. There are 18 of these special prophecies and they are distinguished from the other prophecies of the Bible by their unusual operation. For this reason, these two books are often separated from the others as the apocalyptic books of the Bible.

Five types of predictions

The Bible contains a minimum of five distinct types of prediction. These include:

1. Messianic prophecies: These prophecies specifically relate to the person of Jesus in either His first or second coming. There are more than 450 Messianic statements or prophecies. Two excellent examples of first advent prophecies are found in Isaiah 53 and Psalm 22.

2. Judaic prophecies: These prophecies relate to promises of prosperity or destruction for the ancient nation of Israel. These prophecies have conditional elements in them most of the time. A good example of this type of prophecy is found in Ezekiel 37 through 48. Judaic prophecies contain important object lessons and principles for all generations of people, for God's unchanging interest in man is clearly revealed in these prophecies.

This prophetic group also presents a special challenge. The problem is that God gave ancient Israel a number of prophecies which were based on the contingency that certain conditions would be met by Israel. Because the conditions were not met by the people to whom they were given, these prophecies will not be fulfilled. This point is further discussed in Appendix A.

3. Day of the Lord prophecies: These prophecies are numerous and are scattered throughout Scripture. They relate to the vindication of God and/or His people. Elements within these prophecies are often general enough that they can have parallel applications at different times. Ultimately though, these prophecies predict the triumph of God and/or the vindication of His people in a contemporary setting. For example, Isaiah 24 and Ezekiel 7 contain parallels between the final days of Israel and the final days of earth's history. Sometimes, "Day of the Lord" prophecies have conditional elements embedded in them if they are given as a warning. Matthew 24 is a "Day of the Lord" prophecy. This prophecy applies both to the end of Jerusalem in A.D. 70 and the end of the world. Calamitous events from each are mingled together in one prophecy because there are ominous parallels.

4. Local prophecies: Local prophecies apply to specific people, places and times. For example, the prophecy concerning Nineveh (Jonah 1) was a local prophecy. Local prophecies require a messenger to explain or proclaim the prophecy. Before the flood, Noah was chosen as such a messenger. In the days of Nineveh, Jonah was called to be such a messenger. At the first advent of Christ, John the Baptist was appointed as a local messenger.

Even though the messages of local prophecies are specific to people at certain times, universal principles and/or conditions underlying their messages remain applicable as we approach the end of the age.

5. Apocalyptic prophecies: In this volume, the apocalyptic prophecies of Daniel and Revelation are defined as structural prophecies; that is, prophecies that outline a specific sequence of events. An apocalyptic prophecy is identified by the presence of a beginning and an ending point in time. Both the fulfillment and sequence of apocalyptic prophecy are unconditional. A clear-cut example of this type prophecy can be found in Daniel 2. There, Nebuchadnezzar's vision outlines a sequence of kingdoms which must occur in the order in which they were given.

Sometimes, the sequence or structure of apocalyptic prophecy is defined by numeric order. For example, the second trumpet in Revelation 8 occurs *after* the first trumpet. The critical point here is that chronological order is always maintained in an apocalyptic prophecy, otherwise we could not know which event would be next.

Distinctive treatment necessary

Each of the five prophecy types deserves distinctive treatment. Mixing the prophecies or merging their respective rules of interpretation makes understanding impossible.

Rules of interpretation

Rules of interpretation are inseparable from the study of prophecy, for conclusions are directly connected to the methods used for interpretation. If we interpret prophecy using faulty rules, we end up with faulty conclusions. It's that simple.

Rules are not biased toward any religious denomination. We must rely upon consistent rules to help solve the unknown. This is true in every science. For example, the simple equation $2x + 3 = 13$ can only be solved by using mathematical rules. Since rules of interpretation are not written down in the Bible, they must come from careful research and observation.

This is critical: *Rules of interpretation cannot be made up; rather, we can only discover the presence or operation of rules.* Rules are detected when we find consistent behavior within prophetic elements. Once consistency is recognized, we can then define the rule. In other words, if we observe certain things to always be true, only then can we identify the presence of a rule.

Consider this example. Sir Isaac Newton researched the effects of gravity. He studied the behavior of gravity using different experiments. After observing that gravity behaved in certain consistent ways, he wrote down a formula expressing its operation. *Sir Isaac Newton did not make up the rules governing gravity.* God did that. But, Sir Isaac Newton was able to discover the rules by which gravity operates and he was able to state the rules of gravity in such a way that the effect of gravity could be calculated and understood by others.

The study of apocalyptic prophecy is very similar to the study of gravity. We reason from the known to the unknown. Before we can interpret those parts of prophecy that are unknown, we have to discover the rules by which fulfillments occurred in the past. By carefully observing the behavior of apocalyptic prophecies that have been fulfilled, we can then discover the rules by which they work. After we understand how the rules apply to those prophetic elements that have been fulfilled, we can then begin to solve those portions of apocalyptic prophecy that are in the future by using rules of interpretation that are consistent.

World of difference between truth and faith

One more point. There is a world of difference between prophetic truth and prophetic faith. Prophetic truth refers to those prophecies or those portions of prophecy that qualify as fulfillments. Prophetic faith, on the other hand, refers to those prophecies that are yet to be fulfilled. Since no one can prove something that hasn't happened, our prophetic faith should be carefully built upon the truth that comes from solid principles of interpretation.

What is a prophetic fulfillment?

So, how can we know if an apocalyptic prophecy has been fulfilled? A fulfillment is a full-filling of the prophecy. In other words, a fulfillment occurs when all the specifications of a prophecy are met. Every detail of the prophecy must be satisfied before a fulfillment can be declared. This also means that the chronological order of the prophecy must also be satisfied. For example, some people may claim that the fourth trumpet of Revelation 8 has already been fulfilled. If their claim is true, they not only have to demonstrate that all of the details of the fourth trumpet have been met, they also have to demonstrate the orderly fulfillment of the first three trumpets.

The three rules

Three rules have been detected in the operation of apocalyptic prophecy. Keep in mind, there are different types of prophecy and each type has its own rules of interpretation. But, regarding the apocalyptic prophecies of Daniel and Revelation, these three rules appear to operate consistently:

1. Each apocalyptic story or sequence is identified by the presence of a beginning point and an ending point in time. Events within each story are given in chronological order.
2. A prophecy or prophetic element is not fulfilled until all the specifications of the prophecy are met. This includes the order of the sequence.
3. If some portion of a prophecy is declared symbolic, the Bible must clearly

interpret the meaning of the symbol with applicable scripture.

Supremacy of apocalyptic prophecy

Because apocalyptic prophecy is unconditional, all other prophecies of the Bible are subordinate to apocalyptic sequencing. This means that apocalyptic prophecy determines the chronological placement of non-apocalyptic prophecies. For example, Amos, Ezekiel, Joel, Obadiah and many New Testament prophets believed that the great and awful day of the Lord was "near" and plainly said so. (See Appendix B.) There's no question that what they saw in vision led them to conclude that the "Great Day of the Lord" was at hand. In Revelation, John also indicates that the fulfillment of the things he saw was *near or soon.* The problem is that the ancient prophets did not understand how their visions fit into the overall chronology of God's larger plan.

No one prophet was shown *everything* that God intends to bring about. No disciple of Jesus expected that time would last another 2,000 years. Paul sums up the process of prophetic revelations saying, **"In the past God spoke to our forefathers through the prophets at many times and in various ways... For we know in part and we prophesy in part."** (Hebrews 1:1, I Corinthians 13:9) So, each time God spoke to a prophet about the end of time, more detail was provided. But, without understanding the sequences of events, that is, the backbone of apocalyptic prophecy, prophecies about the "Great Day of the Lord" cannot be chronologically placed nor can their content be fully appreciated.

Is God restricted by His own word?

Some argue that God's sovereignty is restricted by imposing the fulfillment of certain prophetic events before the Second Coming can occur. This argument stands without merit when we understand that it was God who gave the prophecies in the first place. It was God who originally set the time-schedule according to His own authority. It was God who revealed the schedule to man. And, God will keep the schedule He has set. Acts 1:7 clearly says that the Father has *set* appointed times and seasons.

Some also argue that the words *near* and *soon* should be understood from God's perspective, that is, with God, a day is as a thousand years and a thousand years as a day. These will often show that a thousand years can exist between two verses because with God, time is nothing. Now think about this point. *What rule of interpretation consistently explains when a thousand years exists between two verses and when a thousand years does not exist between two verses?* If a thousand years can exist between verses that appear to be adjacent, then we are left without any means of knowing when the end of the world is due.

On the other hand, some claim that the last days began at Calvary. What sense does this make? If the past 2,000 years can be termed, "last days," then we would be justified in saying that another 2,000 years could also qualify as "last days." The reader is encouraged to read Appendix B for more discussion on these points.

The point here is that apocalyptic prophecy serves as a organizer for understanding God's timetable. Because His chronology has not been correctly understood in times past, a number of people across the centuries have declared prophecies to be fulfilled, when in reality fulfillment did not occur. Remember, fulfillment requires two affirming actions: first, all specifications of the prophecy must be met; and secondly, the event must happen in its chronological order. If this little system of checks and balances is ignored, the result will be nothing less than prophetic confusion and uncertainty.

Supporting information

The books of Daniel and Revelation also contain additional information that supports their apocalyptic prophecies. This information includes historical settings and apocalyptic parallels. For example, in the book of Daniel we learn how Daniel got to Babylon, how the three Hebrews were tested on the plain of Dura and a host of other things. Of course, there is discussion about the contents of the visions, but it is the visions themselves that declare the order of events. For this reason it is important that we establish where each vision begins its story and where it ends its story. For example, apocalyptic story one begins in Daniel 2:29 and ends with verse 35.

In the book of Revelation, we find some information that is not apocalyptic. For example, there is historical data, some information about Jesus in heaven, why John was on the isle of Patmos, the condition of the seven churches in Asia Minor at the time of John's vision, and some commentary. In fact, Revelation 17 is entirely devoted to commentary and Revelation 22:6 begins an epilogue. Even though there is more to Daniel and Revelation than their prophetic content, only those portions of Daniel and Revelation that lay out a sequence of events qualify as apocalyptic prophecy.

Supporting doctrines

The reader must understand that apocalyptic prophecy requires a clear understanding of five major doctrines. If these doctrines are not correctly understood, the climax of Revelation's story makes no sense. In fact, the major reasons for prophetic divergence between denominations today is doctrine not rules of interpretation! For example, if a person holds to the doctrine of an eternally burning hell, then Revelation 20 makes no sense whatsoever. In short, here's the problem. Suppose Julius Caesar went to hell at his death in 44 B.C. Why would God resurrect him at the end of the millennium only to burn him up in the lake of fire that follows? To make matters worse, how could Julius Caesar already be in hell when the judgment of human beings takes place at a *specific* point in time? Even more, if the wages of sin is burning in hell for eternity, then Jesus didn't pay the penalty for sin. He was only dead for about three days. My point is this: a correct interpretation of Revelation requires a sound doctrinal position on five eternal truths. They are:

The authority of God
The appearing of God
The temple of God
The salvation of God
The condition of man in life and death

These wonderful themes are closely examined in my book, *The Revelation of Jesus*. (See details inside back cover.)

Start and stop

It is most important that we identify when in time each apocalyptic prophecy begins and ends. For this reason, all 18 apocalyptic prophecies of Daniel and Revelation are chronologically presented in the chart on pages 335-336.

The reader is reminded that the original manuscripts of Daniel and Revelation did not include chapter and verse designations. These "helps" were added centuries after the manuscripts were written, to facilitate the study of the Bible. By using chapter and verse notation, students can quickly find a sentence or group of sentences for further investigation. These well-intentioned helps can create a minor problem. Since we normally think of a chapter in the Bible as a complete unit, it is easy to overlook the 18 prophecies because they are grouped differently than chapter units. So, do not be confused by the fact that prophecies can begin and end anywhere within a chapter.

Watch for the signs

Read this sentence twice: One prophecy ends and another begins when the next event chronologically occurs before the previous event. For example, suppose you are reading about the six seals in Revelation 6. As you read verses 12-17, the sixth seal is described. This seal describes the second advent of Jesus and this prophecy ends with verse 17. After you finish reading verse 17, the following verse begins talking about four angels holding back the four winds. See

Revelation 7:1. Since the four angels hold back the four winds *before* the second coming of Jesus, the beginning of a new prophecy is detected. (It just so happens in this case that a chapter break also occurs at the end of the six seals prophecy.) Remember though, a story does not begin because a new chapter ends or begins. *A new story only begins when the next event chronologically occurs before the previous event.* This simple process never fails.

Here is another essential point: The elements of each prophecy happen in the order in which they are given. This means that each prophecy progresses from its beginning point to its ending point just as it was written. On a few rare occasions, the order of a prophecy is momentarily broken so important details can be given to the reader. However, these momentary breaks do not affect the obvious sequence of the prophecy.

Big points and little points

This writer cannot accurately explain every detail in Daniel and Revelation. And I will not be surprised if I wrongfully interpret some of the prophetic elements. No one human can know everything there is to know about the Bible. But, I also believe it is possible to come close to understanding the truth by careful investigation. Prophetic truth has several dimensions. For example, we may correctly place the occurrence of the fifth trumpet but wrongfully interpret the event. Or, we may correctly interpret the fifth trumpet and wrongfully calculate the time of its occurrence.

But the most exciting point for me as a student of Bible prophecy is that I don't have to wait long to see how my conclusions compare with reality. I believe events of global consequence are soon to take place. Obscure prophetic matters will soon become clear as events unfold. But, the essential matters will be understood in advance, for the purpose of apocalyptic prophecy is this: God desires that His people understand His actions in advance so that when fulfillments occur, our faith might be strengthened.

Plan on frustration

Every student of prophecy experiences frustration at first. This frustration may be compared to learning to play the piano. At first, the sounds are not very beautiful. However, persistence pays off. In time, melodious music (more or less) will come from all who practice and put effort into their music. The same is true of the study of prophecy. It takes considerable time and effort to find and understand the harmony of the sum of all the parts. But, harmony and beauty will be found if you persist.

For those who have closely studied my teachings over the years, you will notice a few minor changes. I mention this because many people are unwilling to update their prophetic views. This is sad, because truth is ever unfolding and if we are unmovable, we shall be left behind. In short, truth is eternal and unchanging, for God is both eternal and unchanging. But, man's perception of truth is finite and faulty and there is no greater joy than climbing a little higher in understanding the truths of God. If we become content with what we know, we are left with no other alternative than to become stagnant. Stagnation leads to fermentation and mental fermentation leads to stupidity.

Given the diversity of minds and beliefs, many will disagree with my conclusions. And, it is not necessary that the reader agree with me. But, those who seek truth go through a very fascinating experience. The closer people get to correctly understanding truth, the more similar their views. There is a sequence of events that shall bring us to the end of the world and there is only one correct explanation of the events that shall come to pass. The prophecies within Daniel and Revelation have the answers.

Let your interpretations be your own

Therefore, I ask the reader to consider my conclusions – not to accept my interpretations. Let your interpretations be your own – after all, you've got to face the events ahead by yourself. Remember, the prophetic equation is not complete until all the pieces of the puzzle are correctly placed. This is perhaps the most difficult part of prophetic study: *You have to understand the whole thing before you can be certain about the elements of your conclusion.* For this reason, I am often accused of saying things without substantiation. I freely confess to doing this because some subjects are substantiated by other facts not involved with the matters at hand. Given the breadth of some themes, it is not helpful to explore supporting tangents at the time of presentation because the matter becomes so tedious or expansive that it can be overwhelming. But, there are two ways to comprehend. First, the determined student can read and reread this book. The second and third reading of this volume will be more helpful than the first reading because the threshold for understanding the harmony of these things is quite high. Secondly, if the student is not able to comprehend the material presented in this volume, there is solace knowing that time is going to fully reveal the truth anyway. And given the events before us, some exposure to the prophecies of God right now is better than hysteria and terror then. Anticipating *what* God is about to do, understanding *why* He is going to do it and timely preparation for His actions is our privilege. These are the profound functions of Bible prophecy.

The interlaced column

According to Webster, a paraphrase is an attempt to clarify the meaning of the author's words by restating his original idea in different words. On the other hand, a translation is quite different from a paraphrase in that a translation is a direct conversion of the equivalent sense from one language to another.

This book is neither a paraphrase nor a translation. The purpose of this book is to explain the 18 prophecies of Daniel and Revelation as I currently understand them. So, I have taken the liberty of interlacing the verses of the Bible with my own words and thoughts so that the student might quickly grasp the comprehensive story that comes from the 18 prophecies. I realize that some will heartily disagree with this practice. But, whether my opponents will admit it or not, *all* students of the Bible practice interlacing. What scholar ever presented an exegesis without interlacing his own thoughts or findings into the meaning of a text?

The better we understand the Bible, the more clearly we comprehend the larger meaning of its verses. Even though it is not common practice to present Bible texts with our own words interlaced within them, such a process may have some merit—for what appreciable difference is there between thinking interlaced thoughts and writing down interlaced thoughts?

I certainly don't intend to corrupt the true meaning of the Bible. In fact, I read in Revelation 22:18,19 that if any of us corrupt the message of Revelation by adding to it or taking away from it, God will deal accordingly with us. I've thought about these verses for a long time and I understand them to mean that if we *willingly* alter the true message in the book, God will hold us responsible.

As a minimum, there are three ways to interpret the meaning of Revelation 22:18,19. First, the text could be applied to ancient scribes. Since there were no duplicating machines back then, the warning could be interpreted as a threat to those who made copies of the original document. Secondly, the warning could be applied to translators of the original text. However, every bilingual person knows that it is not possible to translate directly from language to language. For example, the English translation of Revelation has more words than the original Greek. Perhaps the best application of these verses can be understood in this sense: When the prophecy of Revelation is fully understood, its testimony must not be muted or altered by any person. Penalties and consequences aside, let the truth say what it must.

I also find in Revelation 1:3, a special blessing for everyone who will study and try to understand what Revelation means. So, consider this volume a stepping stone toward your understanding. This little book is by no means, the final word on the meaning of Daniel and Revelation.

Inherent danger

The greatest danger with interlacing is that some of my interlaced verses will either say things contrary to what you already believe to be true or things you don't yet understand. Because people rarely explore things they believe to be full of error, I'm sure many copies of this book will end up in the trash. However, to those who are open minded enough to read this volume through, I would like to share a secret. The second time you read this volume through, you will appreciate the content much more. You will be amazed at the harmony within the 18 prophecies. You will also understand so much more about each prophecy and its role in the larger picture. The third time you read this book through, you will be amazed at how tiny details in one prophecy align with little elements in other prophecies to form the prophetic matrix. This matrix will then enable you to understand things which can not be seen otherwise. Thereafter, each time you study the 18 prophecies, you will be amazed at how the 18 prophecies of Daniel and Revelation are dependent and integral to the *entire* Bible. No pleasure on earth compares with understanding God's great love and His purposes for His children.

Additive nature

The study of apocalyptic prophecy is additive in nature. This means that you have to accept some things *as possibilities* before you can proceed to understand the matter at hand. For this reason, I highly encourage the reader to read this book in a chronological fashion. Don't succumb to the temptation to jump around looking for this or that until you clearly understand the operation of the rules of interpretation and the chronological placement of essential elements. When you find something disagreeable or different than what you have believed, go to the apocalyptic chart in the back of the book and notice the chronological location of the event under discussion. Compare my conclusion with other items that are occurring at the same time. In fact, you should often refer to the apocalyptic chart so you can see the chronological progression of each story. Even more, you will behold the intricate relationships between the prophecies. For example, see if you can locate the opening of the fourth seal in Prophecy 7 and the casting down of the censer in Prophecy 9.

By reading this volume in a sequential manner, the reader should be able to see how the rules are applied in simple prophecies before trying to understand how the rules apply in more difficult situations.

If you disagree with my conclusions, don't waste time arguing with me. Direct your energy into the ultimate prophetic challenge: Draw *your own* prophetic chart and then, clearly outline *your* prophetic conclusions in a book. Properly identify where every prophetic element belongs. Most who disagree with my conclusions refuse to do this and I am quite puzzled by their eagerness to condemn my views and their reluctance to openly reveal their position. As my sales manager, Court McLeod, used to say, "The proof is in the pudding." So, if you have a better conclusion, tell everyone what you believe. Distribute several hundred copies of your findings. Time will then reveal, by the absence or presence of the things we predict, the truth-full-ness of every prophetic position. In fact, this book is my response to you as required by the challenge.

Larry Wilson

December 1991

P.S. If you have a better chart, please send me a copy.

Prophecy 1

Daniel 2:29-35

Beginning point in time: About 605 B.C.
Ending point in time: When Jesus sets up His kingdom
Synopsis: This prophecy forms the foundation of all other apocalyptic prophecies. The chronology of seven world empires is laid out in very simple but forceful terms. The seven kingdoms suggest this is a complete story. If the reader is watchful, he will notice the operation of the three rules of interpretation mentioned on page 4. Even though the vision says nothing about the amount of time required for fulfillment, we now know that almost 26 centuries have passed since it was given.

NIV

{29} "As you were lying there, O king, your mind turned to things to come, and the revealer of mysteries showed you what is going to happen.

{30} As for me, this mystery has been revealed to me, not because I have greater wisdom than other living men, but so that you, O king, may know the interpretation and that you may understand what went through your mind."

{31} "You looked, O king, and there before you stood a large statue – an enormous, dazzling statue, awesome in appearance. {32} The head of the statue was made of pure gold, its chest and arms of silver, its belly and thighs of bronze, {33} its legs of iron, its feet partly of iron and partly of baked clay.

{34} While you were watching, a rock was cut out, but not by human hands. It struck the statue on its

Interlaced thoughts

{29} "As you were lying there, O king, your mind turned to things to come, and the Revealer of mysteries showed you, in one great sweep, what the future holds.

{30} As for me, this mystery has been revealed to me, not because I have greater wisdom than other living men, but so that you, O king, may know the interpretation and that you may understand what you saw in vision."

{31} "You looked, O king, and there before you stood a large statue – an enormous, dazzling statue of a man, awesome in appearance. {32} The head of the statue was made of pure gold, its chest and arms of silver, its belly and thighs of bronze, {33} its legs of iron, its feet partly of iron and partly of baked clay.

{34} While you were watching, a rock was cut out of a holy mountain[1], but not by human hands.[2] It came out of heaven and

Interlaced thoughts

struck the statue on its feet of iron and clay and smashed them.

{35} Then the iron, the clay, the bronze, the silver and the gold were broken to pieces at the *same* time and became like chaff on a threshing floor in the summer. The wind swept them away without leaving a trace. But the rock that struck the statue became a huge mountain[3] that filled the whole earth."

End of Sequence

Note: To king Nebuchadnezzar, a holy mountain was a familiar symbol. The ancients worshiped on the highest hills or mountains for they believed that the gods dwelt in the lofty grandeur and beauty there. Using the king's knowledge, the God of Heaven revealed that a time was coming when the Son (the rock) of the Most High God (the mountain) would set up His kingdom on earth and in so doing, destroy the kingdoms of man. It is fair to say that the representations within the dream were easily understood by the king once the dream itself was recalled.

{36} "This was the dream, and now we will interpret it to the king.
{37} You, O king, are the present king of kings. You may think that you are the successful ruler of earth because you are brilliant and skillful, but recognize, O king, the God of

NIV

feet of iron and clay and smashed them.

{35} Then the iron, the clay, the bronze, the silver and the gold were broken to pieces at the same time and became like chaff on a threshing floor in the summer. The wind swept them away without leaving a trace. But the rock that struck the statue became a huge mountain and filled the whole earth.

{36} This was the dream, and now we will interpret it to the king.
{37} You, O king, are the king of kings. The God of heaven has given you dominion and power and might and glory;

NIV

{38} in your hands he has placed mankind and the beasts of the field and the birds of the air. Wherever they live, he has made you ruler over them all. You are that head of gold."

{39} "After you, another kingdom will rise, inferior to yours. Next, a third kingdom, one of bronze, will rule over the whole earth.

{40} Finally, there will be a fourth kingdom, strong as iron—for iron breaks and smashes everything—and as iron breaks things to pieces, so it will crush and break all the others.

{41} Just as you saw that the feet and toes were partly of baked clay and partly of iron, so this will be a divided kingdom; yet it will have some of the strength of iron in it, even as you saw iron mixed with clay.

Interlaced thoughts

heaven has given you dominion and power and might and glory; {38} in your hands He has placed mankind and the beasts of the field and the birds of the air. Wherever they live, He has made you ruler over them all. Your dominion, the great Babylon, is represented by the head of gold."

{39} "After you pass away, the Medo-Persian kingdom will rise and their kingdom will be inferior to yours. Next, a third kingdom will arise and be known as the kingdom of Grecia. It was represented in the dream by thighs of bronze, and just like previous kingdoms, it too shall rule over the whole earth.

{40} Finally, there will be a fourth kingdom that rules over the whole world as one empire. It will be known as Rome. It will be as strong as iron—for iron breaks and smashes everything—and as iron breaks things to pieces, so it will crush and subdue those that existed before it.

{41} Then, there will be a fifth kingdom. Just as you saw that the feet and toes were partly of baked clay and partly of iron, so the world in the time period of the feet will be divided. A few nations will have the strength of iron and the rest will be weaker, but like brittle clay. The weaker nations will, like brittle clay, have strong convictions about their sovereignty, but they shall be

Interlaced thoughts

dominated by the stronger nations nonetheless.

{42} Then you saw a sixth kingdom. As the toes were partly iron and partly clay just like the fifth kingdom, so the world in those final days will be partly strong and partly brittle when ten kings, represented by the ten toes, shall rule over the world.

{43} And just as you saw the iron mixed with baked clay, so the people of the fifth and sixth kingdoms will be a mixture of nations and will not remain united, any more than iron mixes with clay."

{44} "In the days of the ten toes, the Son of God will set up the seventh and final kingdom.[4] His kingdom will never be destroyed, nor will any part of earth be left to another people. When Jesus sets up His kingdom, He will crush all the kingdoms of man at *one* time and bring them and their offspring to an end, but the kingdom of God's Son will itself endure forever.

{45} This is the meaning of the vision of the Rock which was cut out of a holy mountain, but remember, O king, the kingdom represented by the rock is not of human origin, in fact, human hands will have nothing to do with the establishment of God's kingdom. The Rock of Ages will crush the iron, the bronze, the clay, the silver

NIV

{42} As the toes were partly iron and partly clay, so this kingdom will be partly strong and partly brittle.

{43} And just as you saw the iron mixed with baked clay, so the people will be a mixture and will not remain united, any more than iron mixes with clay."

{44} "In the time of those kings, the God of heaven will set up a kingdom that will never be destroyed, nor will it be left to another people. It will crush all those kingdoms and bring them to an end, but it will itself endure forever.

{45} This is the meaning of the vision of the rock cut out of a mountain, but not by human hands—a rock that broke the iron, the bronze, the clay, the silver and the gold to pieces." "The great God has shown the king what will take place in the future. The dream is true and the interpretation is trustworthy."

NIV

References

1. Psalms 43:3, 48:1, 68:16, 87:1
2. Deuteronomy 32:4, 15, 18; 1 Corinthians 10:4; Joshua 8:30,31
3. Daniel 7:14
4. Revelation 17:12-17

Interlaced thoughts

and the gold to pieces." "The great God has shown king Nebuchadnezzar what will take place in the future. The dream is true and the interpretation is certain."

Prophecy 2

Daniel 7:1-11

Beginning point in time: About 600 B.C.
Ending point in time: Second coming of Jesus
Synopsis: This prophecy builds upon the foundation laid in Daniel 2. This prophecy confirms the progression of kingdoms as predicted in Daniel 2 so that a clear historical footing can be found. A historical footing is essential, for without it, we could not find our chronological position in any prophecy. The reader will also notice that this prophecy introduces a few new elements which neatly fit into the broad picture established in the first prophecy of Daniel 2.

NIV	Interlaced thoughts
{1} In the first year of Belshazzar king of Babylon, Daniel had a dream, and visions passed through his mind as he was lying on his bed. He wrote down the substance of his dream.	{1} "In the first year of Belshazzar, the last king of Babylon, I, Daniel, was nearing 70 years of age. I received a vision one night as I was lying on my bed. I wrote down the substance of the dream and recorded it in a book.
{2} Daniel said: "In my vision at night I looked, and there before me were the four winds of heaven churning up the great sea.	{2} In my vision at night I looked, and there before me were the four winds of heaven churning up the great sea of the Mediterranean.
{3} Four great beasts, each different from the others, came up out of the sea. {4} The first was like a lion, and it had the wings of an eagle. I watched until its wings were torn off and it was lifted from the ground so that it stood on two feet like a man, and the heart of a man was given to it.	{3} Four enormous beasts, each different from the other, came up out of the sea. {4} The first was like a lion, and it had powerful wings like an eagle that allowed it to swoop down upon its prey. I watched until its wings were torn off so that it could no longer overtake other nations and it was transformed so that it no longer walked upon the ground as a beast of prey but, it stood on two feet like a man and it was given a mind to comprehend its accountability to the Most High God.

Interlaced thoughts

{5} And there before me was a second beast, which looked like a bear. One of its shoulders was higher than the other because one side of this kingdom would rise to greater authority than the other. It also had three ribs in its mouth between its teeth, which represents the last three provinces of the previous empire that impeded its progress to world dominion. These provinces are Lydia, Egypt and Babylon. It was told by the Most High God, 'Get up and eat your fill of flesh and rule the world!'

{6} After that, I looked, and there before me was a third beast, one that looked like a leopard. And, it had four great wings like a bird so that it could quickly fly over the face of the earth and catch its prey. This beast had four heads because this world empire would eventually divide into four sectors, and it was given authority to rule over the earth by the Most High God.

{7} After these things, I looked, and there before me was a fourth beast – terrifying and frightening and very powerful. This monster beast did not resemble any animal I had seen before. It had large iron teeth that crushed and devoured its victims and whatever it conquered, it proceeded to utterly destroy so that nothing remained. The monster beast was different from all the former beasts in appearance and severity, and it had ten horns.

NIV

{5} And there before me was a second beast, which looked like a bear. It was raised up on one of its sides, and it had three ribs in its mouth between its teeth. It was told, 'Get up and eat your fill of flesh!'

{6} After that, I looked, and there before me was another beast, one that looked like a leopard. And on its back it had four wings like those of a bird. This beast had four heads, and it was given authority to rule.

{7} After that, in my vision at night I looked, and there before me was a fourth beast – terrifying and frightening and very powerful. It had large iron teeth; it crushed and devoured its victims and trampled underfoot whatever was left. It was different from all the former beasts, and it had ten horns.

NIV

{8} While I was thinking about the horns, there before me was another horn, a little one, which came up among them; and three of the first horns were uprooted before it. This horn had eyes like the eyes of a man and a mouth that spoke boastfully.

{9} As I looked, thrones were set in place, and the Ancient of Days took his seat. His clothing was as white as snow; the hair of his head was white like wool. His throne was flaming with fire, and its wheels were all ablaze.

{10} A river of fire was flowing, coming out from before him. Thousands upon thousands attended him; ten thousand times ten thousand stood before him. The court was seated, and the books were opened.

Interlaced thoughts

{8} While I was watching the monster and wondering about the ten horns, I saw another horn, a little one, which grew up among the ten horns and three of the ten horns were uprooted as the new horn grew up. The little horn had eyes like the eyes of a man indicating that it could comprehend things that the other horns could not understand and the little horn had a mouth that spoke boastfully claiming to possess certain privileges and authority from God which it didn't have.

{9} As I continued to watch this vision, my gaze was directed from earthly events to an even more impressive scene in heaven. I looked, and several thrones were brought into an enormous courtroom and the thrones were arranged in a circular fashion. Then, the Ancient of Days, the Most High God, came into the courtroom and took His seat on His throne which was in the center of the other thrones. His clothing was brilliant, as white as snow; the hair of his head was gloriously bright—white like wool. His throne was flaming like fire, and brilliant angels surrounded the thrones in concentric rings like wheels all ablaze. {10} I saw a brilliant procession of thousands of angels moving into positions, they looked like a river of fire. They entered the courtroom and took positions surrounding the Father's throne on every side. Thousands

Interlaced thoughts

upon thousands attended the Most High God; ten thousand times ten thousand stood reverently while awaiting His arrival. Then, when everyone was in place, the Father came and took His seat. The court was then seated. Some business was conducted before the official record books of heaven, which contain all the recorded deeds of men, were opened for investigation.

{11} Then my view was directed away from heaven and back to earth. My attention was directed at the little horn because of the boastful words the horn was speaking against the Most High God. I kept watching the little horn and the monster beast until the Second Coming when the monster and the little horn were slain. They were thrown into a lake of fire that is created at the Second Coming of Jesus. {12} I also saw that when the other three beasts were stripped of their authority, they were allowed to live until the end of time just like the monster and the little horn.

{13} Later, I was shown that when the courtroom scene in heaven took place, One like us, a human being, played an important role. It seemed that the business of the court could not begin until someone was found qualified to conduct the judgment. Eventually, the Son of Man was found worthy to perform this solemn work. Then, Jesus was carried

NIV

{11} Then I continued to watch because of the boastful words the horn was speaking. I kept looking until the beast was slain and its body destroyed and thrown into the blazing fire.

End of Sequence

{12} (The other beasts had been stripped of their authority, but were allowed to live for a period of time.)

{13} In my vision at night I looked, and there before me was one like a son of man, coming with the clouds of heaven. He approached the Ancient of Days and was led into his presence.

NIV

{14} He was given authority, glory and sovereign power; all peoples, nations and men of every language worshiped him. His dominion is an everlasting dominion that will not pass away, and his kingdom is one that will never be destroyed.

{15} I, Daniel, was troubled in spirit, and the visions that passed through my mind disturbed me.

{16} I approached one of those standing there and asked him the true meaning of all this. So he told me and gave me the interpretation of these things:

{17} 'The four great beasts are four kingdoms that will rise from the earth.

Interlaced thoughts

before the Father and many angels attended Him.

{14} After the coronation of Jesus was finished, the Father granted Him complete authority, all glory and sovereign power. The promotion of Jesus was unanimously agreed upon by the hosts of heaven. Everyone agreed that He alone was uniquely qualified to judge the human race. At the end of earth's drama, all peoples, nations and men of every language from the nations of earth shall confirm that His judgment is fair and true, and all peoples shall worship Him – every knee shall bow. His kingdom will be an everlasting dominion that will not pass away, and His kingdom is the only kingdom on earth that will never be destroyed.

{15} I, Daniel, was troubled in spirit, and the visions that passed through my mind disturbed me. I wondered, what do these things mean?

{16} I approached one of the angels who was standing in the heavenly courtroom and asked him the meaning of all these things. He gave me this interpretation:

{17} 'The four great beasts are four world empires that will rise from the earth. The sea represents multitudes of nations, languages and people that live upon the earth[1] and the four winds represent God's

Interlaced thoughts

methods of removing one kingdom and raising up another.[2]

{18} But Daniel, be of good courage, because the saints of the Most High God will be given the whole earth at the appointed time and they will possess it forever—yes, for ever and ever.'

{19} But, I wanted to know the true meaning of the fourth beast, the monster which was different from all the others and most terrifying, with its unbreakable iron teeth and indestructible bronze claws—the beast that crushed and devoured its victims and trampled underfoot whatever was left.
{20} I also wanted to know about the ten horns on its head and about the new horn that came up, before which three fell—the horn that was greater than the others and that had eyes and a mouth that spoke boastfully.

{21} The reason I wanted to know about the fourth beast and the new horn, is that I became afraid when I saw this horn waging war against the people of God. I saw this horn power defeating the saints for a long time— {22} until the courtroom scene took place and the Ancient of Days pronounced a temporary restraining order in favor of His people. I recognized that the little horn would regain its authority at the end of time and that it would again wage war against the saints just before the Second

NIV

{18} But the saints of the Most High will receive the kingdom and will possess it forever—yes, for ever and ever.'

{19} Then I wanted to know the true meaning of the fourth beast, which was different from all the others and most terrifying, with its iron teeth and bronze claws—the beast that crushed and devoured its victims and trampled underfoot whatever was left.

{20} I also wanted to know about the ten horns on its head and about the other horn that came up, before which three of them fell—the horn that looked more imposing than the others and that had eyes and a mouth that spoke boastfully.

{21} As I watched, this horn was waging war against the saints and defeating them,

{22} until the Ancient of Days came and pronounced judgment in favor of the saints of the Most High, and the time came when they possessed the kingdom.

NIV

Interlaced thoughts

Coming of Jesus. I also saw that the monster and the little horn, and the other three beasts lived until the end when they were finally thrown into a lake of fire.

{23} He gave me this explanation: 'The fourth beast is a fourth kingdom that will appear on earth. It will be different from all the other kingdoms and will devour the whole earth, trampling it down and crushing it.

{23} The angel gave me this explanation: 'The fourth beast is the fourth world kingdom that shall be called Rome. Rome will be different from the earlier kingdoms because it will devour the whole earth, trampling it down and crushing any people it desires. In fact, after conquering smaller nations and peoples, it will totally destroy some of them because of their rebellion against it.

{24} The ten horns are ten kings who will come from this kingdom. After them another king will arise, different from the earlier ones; he will subdue three kings.

{24} The ten horns are ten kings who will eventually rise in rebellion against Rome. These ten kings will break-up the Roman empire. These kings will lead tribes known as the Goths, Ostrogoths, Vandals, Burgundians, Franks, Lombards, Alameni, Suevi, Anglo-Saxons and Heruli. After they have broken the consolidated power of Rome into many pieces, another king will arise. Because he will be a religious king, he will be different than the ten political kings that overcome Rome, and when the time is right, the little horn will subdue the Heruli, Ostrogoths and Vandals, three of the ten kings, over a religious argument on the deity of Christ.

{25} He will speak against the Most High and oppress his saints and try

{25} The little horn will speak against the Most High and oppress

Interlaced thoughts

his saints and try to change the time for worship which the Most High God has set, and this religious king will replace some of the laws of the Most High God with his own. The Most High God has determined that His people shall be persecuted by the little horn for a time, times and half a time. This time period, in Jubilee units is 1,260 days which equals 1,260 years.[3]

{26} But the court in heaven will convene and the Father will temporarily stay the persecution of the little horn power. The little horn will be severely wounded. Later, this little horn power will regain strength and will lead others in persecuting the people of God at the end of time.[4] But, understand, all who oppose the truth of God will be completely destroyed when they are thrown into the lake of fire at the second coming of Jesus.

{27} Then everything that belonged to the rulers of earth will be given to the saints, the people of the Most High. The kingdom that follows will be an everlasting kingdom, and all of God's rulers in the earth made new will worship and obey Jesus.'

{28} This is the end of the matter. I, Daniel, was deeply troubled by my thoughts because I had never heard or seen anything like this. This was so different from what I expected about the future that my face turned pale. I kept the matter

NIV

to change the set times and the laws. The saints will be handed over to him for a time, times and half a time.

{26} But the court will sit, and his power will be taken away and completely destroyed forever.

{27} Then the sovereignty, power and greatness of the kingdoms under the whole heaven will be handed over to the saints, the people of the Most High. His kingdom will be an everlasting kingdom, and all rulers will worship and obey him.'

{28} This is the end of the matter. I, Daniel, was deeply troubled by my thoughts, and my face turned pale, but I kept the matter to myself."

NIV

References

1. Revelation 17:15
2. Ezekiel 14:12-21; Revelation 7:1-3, 6:8; Leviticus 26:14-35
3. See Appendix D.
4. Revelation 13:1-8

Interlaced thoughts

to myself for I didn't want my friends to think I had lost my mind.

Prophecy 3

Daniel 8:1-12

Beginning point in time: 538 B.C.
Ending point in time: Just before the Second Coming
Synopsis: This prophecy builds directly upon Daniel 7. The Ram and the Goat in this prophecy correspond to the Bear and Leopard in the previous vision. This vision establishes historical footings so that the dating of end-time events can be determined. For example, the 2,300-day period foretold in Prophecy 4 can only be determined by linking Prophecies 2, 4, and 5 together. And when this is done, the timing within Prophecy 6 can then be determined.

NIV	Interlaced thoughts
{1} "In the third year of King Belshazzar's reign, I, Daniel, had a vision, after the one that had already appeared to me. {2} In my vision I saw myself in the citadel of Susa in the province of Elam; in the vision I was beside the Ulai Canal. {3} I looked up, and there before me was a ram with two horns, standing beside the canal, and the horns were long. One of the horns was longer than the other but grew up later.	{1} In the third year of King Belshazzar's reign, I, Daniel received a second vision. {2} In my vision I saw myself in the beautiful citadel of Susa in the province of Elam; in the vision I was beside the Ulai Canal. {3} I looked up, and there before me was a ram with two horns, standing beside the canal, and the reach of its horns was long. One of the horns grew more slowly than the other but it eventually reached out farther than the first.
{4} I watched the ram as he charged toward the west and the north and the south. No animal could stand against him, and none could rescue from his power. He did as he pleased and became great.	{4} I watched the ram as he came out of the east and charged toward the west and the north and the south. No animal could stand against him, and none could escape his power. He did as he pleased and became great.
{5} As I was thinking about this, suddenly a goat with a prominent horn between his eyes came from the west, crossing the whole earth without touching the ground.	{5} As I was thinking about this, suddenly a goat with a prominent horn between his eyes came from the west, he was traveling so fast across the whole earth that he did

Interlaced thoughts

not seem to touch the ground. {6} He came toward the two-horned ram I had seen standing beside the canal and charged at him in great rage. {7} I saw him attack the ram furiously, striking the ram and shattering his two great horns. The ram was powerless to stand against him; the goat knocked him to the ground and trampled on him, and none could rescue the ram from his power. {8} Then, the goat became very great, but at the height of his power an unusual thing happened, the mighty horn was broken off, and in its place four strong horns grew up toward the north, south, east and west.

{9} Later, I saw another scene. Out of the four winds, specifically, the north, came another horn, which started small but grew in power as it traveled toward the south and to the east and toward my homeland in the west.

{10} This horn grew in popularity around the world until it acquired a following as large as the host of the heavens, and it threw many sacred beliefs, which many take to be God's will, down to the earth and he trampled on them claiming that he knew the truth about God. He confirmed his claim of being God before Moslems, Jews, Catholics, Heathen, Agnostics, Protestants and Eastern Mystics by miracles he had power to do and he denounced

NIV

{6} He came toward the two-horned ram I had seen standing beside the canal and charged at him in great rage. {7} I saw him attack the ram furiously, striking the ram and shattering his two horns. The ram was powerless to stand against him; the goat knocked him to the ground and trampled on him, and none could rescue the ram from his power. {8} The goat became very great, but at the height of his power his large horn was broken off, and in its place four prominent horns grew up toward the four winds of heaven.

{9} Out of one of them[1] came another horn[2], which started small but grew in power to the south and to the east and toward the Beautiful Land.[3.]

{10} It grew until it reached the host of the heavens, and it threw some of the starry host[4] down to the earth and trampled on them.

NIV

{11} It set itself up to be as great as the Prince of the host;[5] it took away the daily sacrifice from him, and the place of his sanctuary was brought low.

{12} Because of rebellion, the host of the saints and the daily sacrifice were given over to it. It prospered in everything it did, and truth was thrown to the ground.

End of Sequence

{13} Then I heard a holy one speaking, and another holy one said to him, 'How long will it take for the vision to be fulfilled—the vision concerning the daily sacrifice, the

Interlaced thoughts

some of the teachings of each religious system on earth.

{11} The horn from the north then set itself up before the people on Earth to be as great as the Prince of hosts in heaven who is Jesus; the horn from the north then led the world to reject the great significance of Jesus' work on behalf of individuals in heaven's sanctuary by leading them to reject Christ's truth about His intercession for them, and then the horn from the north forced the people of earth to accept his authority rather than obey the teachings of Jesus. Thus, respect for the wonderful and exalted place of Christ's ministry in the heavenly sanctuary was made to appear foolish, even contrary to the truth of God.

{12} Because the world followed after this horn of rebellion, many saints of Jesus perished and the daily intercession of Jesus on behalf of sinners came to an end because the world chose to accept this horn power rather than receive Christ as its Savior. The horn from the north prospered in everything he did, and truth about salvation was thrown to the ground and interest in Christ's ministry in heaven was greatly despised by the people of earth.

{13} Then, I heard an angel speaking. By his Hebrew name, Palmoni, I recognized he was a holy numberer. Another angel asked him five questions:

Interlaced thoughts

1. 'How long will it take for the vision to be fulfilled?
2. When will the daily services of Jesus be taken away?
3. How long will be the rebellion that causes desolation?
4. How long will the purpose of the sanctuary be surrendered?
5. How long will the host of saints be trampled underfoot?'

{14} Palmoni turned and spoke to me saying, 'I can't answer all these questions right now, but regarding question four, it will take 2,300 evenings and mornings of Jubilee time; then, the concluding sanctuary services in heaven will begin so that the plan of salvation can be completed. Daniel, you saw scenes of this service in your previous vision. Remember the courtroom scene? That service in heaven's sanctuary involves the final works of Jesus before the Second Coming. That work is the judgment of human beings. This prophecy of 2,300 Jubilee day/years will commence when Artaxerxes gives the decree to restore and rebuild Jerusalem in 457 B.C.'

More answers:

The other questions were answered later but the answers are included here for the reader's sake:

Q. How long will it take for the vision to be fulfilled?

NIV

rebellion that causes desolation, and the surrender of the sanctuary and of the host that will be trampled underfoot?'

{14} He said to me, 'It will take 2,300 evenings[6] and mornings; then the sanctuary[7] will be reconsecrated.'

NIV

Interlaced thoughts

A. Daniel 12:7 "...When the power of the holy people has been finally broken, all these things will be completed."

Q. When will the daily ministry of Jesus be taken away?

A. Daniel 12:7 "It will be for a time, times and half a time (then the horn will have succeeded in the contest for souls.)

Q. How long will be the rebellion that causes desolation?

A. Daniel 12:11 "From the time that the daily service of Jesus on behalf of the world is abolished and the abomination that causes desolation is set up, there will be 1,290 days.

Q. How long will the host of saints be trampled underfoot?

A. Daniel 12:12 "Blessed is the one who waits for and reaches the end of the 1,335 days."

NIV:

{15} While I, Daniel, was watching the vision and trying to understand it, there before me stood one who looked like a Man. {16} And I heard a man's voice from the Ulai calling, 'Gabriel, tell this man the meaning of the vision.'

{17} As he came near the place where I was standing, I was terrified and fell prostrate. 'Son of man,' he said to me, 'understand that the

Interlaced thoughts:

{15} "While I, Daniel, was watching the vision and trying to understand it, there before me stood one who looked like the Son of Man. {16} And I heard Him call from the Ulai, 'Gabriel, tell Daniel the meaning of the vision.

{17} As he came near the place where I was standing, I was terrified by his size and his brilliance and fell prostrate. 'son of man,' he said to me, 'understand that most of this

Interlaced thoughts

vision concerns the distant future, the time of the end.'

{18} While he was speaking to me, it seemed as though my life evaporated and I was in a deep sleep with my face to the ground. Then he touched me and raised me to my feet.

{19} He said again: 'I am going to tell you what will happen at the end of the world. There will be a period of time during which God's wrath will be poured out upon earth. This vision is given to you so that those who shall live at that time can know that they are the final generation. God has decreed an appointed time for the end. Before I can speak about the appointed time of the end, I must first tell you about the Ram and Goat because this portion of the vision establishes a historical footing so that God's people can know when the courtroom scene in your first vision begins. Daniel, understand that the courtroom scene, the cleansing of heaven's temple, begins 2,300 years after the decree of Artaxerxes. That date will be A.D. 1844.

{20} Here's the sequence of the prophecy. The two-horned ram that you saw represents the kings of Media and Persia. The horn that came up last and reached farther than the other represents the Persian side of the kingdom.
{21} The shaggy goat is the king of Greece, and the large horn between

NIV

vision concerns the time of the end.'[8]

{18} While he was speaking to me, I was in a deep sleep, with my face to the ground. Then he touched me and raised me to my feet.

{19} He said: 'I am going to tell you what will happen later in the time of wrath, because the vision concerns the appointed time of the end.[9]

{20} The two-horned ram that you saw represents the kings of Media and Persia.

{21} The shaggy goat is the king of Greece, and the large horn between

NIV

his eyes is the first king.
{22} The four horns that replaced the one that was broken off represent four kingdoms that will emerge from his nation but will not have the same power.

{23} 'In the latter part of their reign, when rebels have become completely wicked, a stern-faced king, a master of intrigue, will arise.

{24} He will become very strong, but not by his own power. He will cause astounding devastation and will succeed in whatever he does. He will destroy the mighty men and the holy people.

{25} He will cause deceit to prosper, and he will consider himself superior. When they feel secure, he will destroy many and take his stand against the Prince of princes. Yet he will be destroyed, but not by human power.

Interlaced thoughts

his eyes is the first king, Alexander the Great. {22} The four horns that replace Alexander will be his four generals. They will divide the kingdom of Grecia into four states, but none of them will have the same global powers as Alexander did.

{23} Now about the horn from the north, many years will pass after Grecia falls. Many kingdoms will rise and fall, but in the very last days of the reign of earthly kings, when rebels against God have become completely wicked, a demanding king, a master of manipulation, deceit and intrigue, will arise out of nowhere. He is this horn from the north. {24} He will become very strong, but not by his own power. The Most High God will grant him a season of power and authority. Billions of people will follow after him and they will give him glory and great authority over them. The horn from the north will cause astounding devastation and will succeed in whatever he does. He will destroy some of the 144,000 and many of the saints. They will be powerless against him for a time.

{25} That horn is the devil himself. He will cause deceit to prosper, and he will consider himself superior over all mankind. When many feel secure that the horn from the north is actually God, the devil will lead the world into a great war and destroy many. Just before the Second Coming the devil will take

Interlaced thoughts

his stand against Jesus Christ, the Prince of princes and King of kings. Even though the devil will be thought to be invincible, he will be destroyed, not by human power, but by the sword that comes out of the mouth of Jesus at the Second Coming.

{26} Daniel, the vision of the 2,300 evenings and mornings that has been given you is true, but seal up the vision because no one will be able to understand it until the appointed time in the distant future arrives.'

{27} I, Daniel, was exhausted and lay ill for several days. I couldn't explain what I had seen, but I knew it was horrible. Then I got up and went about the king's business. I was appalled by the vision; it was beyond understanding.

NIV

{26} 'The vision of the evenings and mornings that has been given you is true, but seal up the vision, for it concerns the distant future.'

{27} I, Daniel, was exhausted and lay ill for several days. Then I got up and went about the king's business. I was appalled by the vision; it was beyond understanding.

References

1. "Them" in this verse refers to winds because "winds" is feminine. The gender of the pronoun agrees with the antecedent "winds" because the word "horns" is masculine. The point of this verse is that in the distant future, a horn just appears out of nowhere instead of appearing out of some historical beast as in Daniel 7. See Prophecy 6.
2. Unlike Daniel 7, the context of this chapter requires that this horn represents a single

References

man at the end of time. Compare with verses 8 and 21. Also see Luke 1:69, Ezekiel 29:21, 1 Samuel 2:1,10 and Psalm 89:24.

3. Ezekiel 20:6
4. 2 Chronicles 33:3-5; 2 Kings 21:5, 23:4,5; Zephaniah 1:5
5. 1 Kings 22:19; 2 Chronicles 18:18; Nehemiah 9:6
6. A morning and an evening constitute one complete day. See Genesis 1:3,8,13. Because these days occur during the operation of the Jubilee calendar, each day represents one year. See Appendix D. The commencement of this time period is revealed in Prophecy 4.
7. Hebrews 8:1,2,5, 9:12,23
8. Habakkuk 2:3, Luke 21:24
9. Psalms 75:2, 102:13; Daniel 11:27,35; Matthew 8:29

Prophecy 4

Daniel 9:24-27

Beginning point in time: 457 B.C.
Ending point in time: Second Coming of Jesus
Synopsis: This prophecy adds important detail to the prophetic matrix, especially Prophecy 3. Historical data is provided so that we can identify the beginning of the 70 week and 2,300 year prophecies. The 2,300 day prophecy dates the courtroom scene in Daniel 7. Also, the ministry and death of Jesus confirms two things. First, the decree of Artaxerxes in 457 B.C. (Ezra 7) fully harmonizes with the time given in this prophecy. Secondly, the presence and synchronism of the Jubilee calendar is fully confirmed by the fulfillment of predicted events.

NIV

{1} In the first year of Darius son of Xerxes (a Mede by descent), who was made ruler over the Babylonian kingdom— {2} in the first year of his reign, I, Daniel, understood from the Scriptures, according to the word of the Lord given to Jeremiah the prophet, that the desolation of Jerusalem would last seventy years.

{3} So I turned to the Lord God and pleaded with him in prayer and petition, in fasting, and in sackcloth and ashes.

{20} While I was speaking and praying, confessing my sin and the sin of my people Israel and making my request to the Lord my God for his holy hill— {21} while I was still in prayer, Gabriel, the man I had seen in the earlier vision, came to me in swift flight about the time of the evening sacrifice.

Interlaced thoughts

{1} In the first year of Darius son of Xerxes (a Mede by descent), who was made ruler over the Babylonian province— {2} In the first year of his reign, I, Daniel, understood from the Scriptures, according to the word of the Lord given to Jeremiah the prophet, that the desolation of Jerusalem would last 70 years because our nation had violated 70 Sabbatical years.[1] I also knew that since the beginning of our captivity, almost 70 years had passed. {3} So I turned to the Lord God and pleaded with him in prayer and petition, in fasting, and in sackcloth and ashes asking the Lord to keep His promise and set my people free. {20} While I was speaking and praying, confessing my sin and the sin of my people, Israel, and making my request to the Lord my God for his holy mount— {21} while I was still in prayer, Gabriel, the man I had seen in my second vision concerning the 2,300 days, came to me in swift flight about the time of the evening sacrifice.

Interlaced thoughts

{22} He instructed me and said to me, "Daniel, I have now come to give you insight and understanding. {23} As soon as you began to pray, an answer was given, which I have come to tell you, for you are highly esteemed. Therefore, consider the message and understand more about the vision concerning the 2,300 days:

{24} Seventy Jubilee weeks (see Appendix D) are cut off of the 2,300-day prophecy. In other words Daniel, your people have been granted 490 Jubilee day/years of mercy. This final grace period is allotted to your people and your holy city for four reasons. First, your people must stop worshiping false gods. Secondly, they must put an end to their immorality. Thirdly, they must atone for their wickedness by humbling themselves so that they can bring in everlasting righteousness. If they will do these things, God's original plan for Israel can still be fulfilled. Lastly and most importantly, *if* your people will love the Lord their God and be His representatives, this vision will be forever sealed up and its terrible predictions shall never come to pass. In fact, *if* your people fully cooperate, they shall have the greatest honor of anointing the Most Holy One of Israel. He will establish the throne of David for ever and ever.

NIV

{22} He instructed me and said to me, "Daniel, I have now come to give you insight and understanding. {23} As soon as you began to pray, an answer was given, which I have come to tell you, for you are highly esteemed. Therefore, consider the message and understand the vision:

Sequence begins

{24} Seventy 'sevens' are decreed for your people and your holy city to finish transgression, to put an end to sin, to atone for wickedness, to bring in everlasting righteousness, to seal up vision and prophecy and to anoint the most holy.

NIV

{25} "Know and understand this: From the issuing of the decree to restore and rebuild Jerusalem until the Anointed One.[2] the ruler, comes, there will be seven 'sevens,' and sixty-two 'sevens.' It will be rebuilt with streets and a trench, but in times of trouble.

{26} After the sixty-two 'sevens,' the Anointed One will be cut off and will have nothing. The people of the ruler[3] who will come will destroy the city and the sanctuary. The end will come like a flood: War will continue until the end, and desolations have been decreed.

Interlaced thoughts

{25} Daniel, know and understand this: From the issuing of the decree by Artaxerxes in the Jubilee year of 457 B.C. to restore and rebuild Jerusalem until the Anointed One – the Ruler of Heaven and Earth – comes, there will be seven Jubilee weeks until the temple and the wall is rebuilt and then 62 more Jubilee weeks will pass. Jerusalem will be rebuilt with streets and a trench, but in troublous times because her neighbors will be jealous.

{26} Unfortunately Daniel, your people Israel will not meet the conditions granted them. After the 62 Jubilee weeks have passed, the Anointed One of the Most High God will appear and begin His ministry on earth. He will be rejected by His own people and then He will be cut off from Israel just as a common criminal is cut off from any inheritance. In rejecting Messiah, the nation will forfeit its protection from the great destroyer, the devil. The devil will stir up hostilities against Jerusalem and he will bring Rome against Jerusalem and the city and the sanctuary will be totally destroyed. The devastation coming upon Jerusalem will come like a great flood. But this is not the end of the world, Daniel. Wars and rumors of war will continue until the end of time, and desolations all over the world have been decreed upon many nations just like Israel.

Interlaced thoughts

{27} Oh yes, Daniel, the Anointed One of God will confirm God's greatest gift to man: the everlasting covenant of salvation. He will do this during the 70th Jubilee week of seven years. In the middle of that week, 30 A.D., the Lamb of God will put an end to sacrifices and offerings. His timely death will confirm the accuracy of this prophecy and the decree of Artaxerxes in 457 B.C. restoring Jerusalem. This is important because the 2,300 day prophecy also begins at the same time as this prophecy. Lastly, this prophecy of 70 Jubilee weeks also confirms the timing and operations of the Jubilee calendar which end in 1994.

One final note, Daniel. The devil will continue to attack the people of God long after the destruction of Jerusalem. His evil deeds will bring much death and desolation around the world, but his end is decreed and at the appointed time, the justice of God will be poured out on him and he shall not escape total destruction."

NIV

{27} He will confirm a covenant[4] with many for one 'seven.' In the middle of the 'seven' he will put an end to sacrifice and offering. And [on a wing of the temple]* he will set up an abomination that causes desolation, until the end that is decreed is poured out on him. "

*some early manuscripts say [on wings of abominations]

References

1 II Chronicles 36:21
2. Matthew 12:18; Mark 12:35,26
3. John 16:11, 14:30; Luke 11:15
4. Matthew 26:28

Prophecy 5

Daniel 11:2-35

Beginning point in time: 538 B.C.
Ending point in time: Primarily A.D. 70
Synopsis: This prophecy was given for the sake of early Christians who would be able to compare contemporary history with the approaching end of Jerusalem. The story in this prophecy is told in such a way that the student can see how God's people came to be caught between two great rivals. Like the story of the image in Daniel 3, there is an important parallel in this story for Christians living in the last days. They shall likewise be caught in the middle a great struggle over world dominion just before Jesus comes.

NIV

An introduction to Prophecy 6 is given in Daniel 10 and is included:

{1} In the third year of Cyrus king of Persia, a revelation was given to Daniel (who was called Belteshazzar). Its message was true and it concerned a great war. The understanding of the message came to him in a vision. {2} At that time I, Daniel, mourned for three weeks. {3} I ate no choice food; no meat or wine touched my lips; and I used no lotions at all until the three weeks were over. {4} On the twenty-fourth day of the first month, as I was standing on the bank of the great river, the Tigris, {5} I looked up and there before me was a man dressed in linen, with a belt of the finest gold around his waist. {6} His body was like chrysolite, his face like lightning, his eyes like flaming torches, his arms and legs like the gleam of burnished bronze, and his voice like the sound of a multitude. {7} I, Daniel, was the only one who saw the vision; the men with me did not see it, but

Interlaced thoughts

Interlaced thoughts

{13}But the prince of this world, the devil, thwarted my efforts for twenty-one days. Then Michael, the archangel, came to my aide because the devil was determined to keep the Jews in captivity even though the 70 years were expired. Now, with the release of your people decreed by Cyrus, {14} I have come to explain what will happen to your people in the future, for the vision reaches down to a time in the distant future.

NIV

such terror overwhelmed them that they fled and hid themselves. {8} So I was left alone, gazing at this great vision; I had no strength left, my face turned deathly pale and I was helpless. {9} Then I heard him speaking, and as I listened to him, I fell into a deep sleep, my face to the ground. {10} A hand touched me and set me trembling on my hands and knees. {11} He said, "Daniel, you who are highly esteemed, consider carefully the words I am about to speak to you, and stand up, for I have now been sent to you." And when he said this to me, I stood up trembling. {12} Then he continued, "Do not be afraid, Daniel. Since the first day that you set your mind to gain understanding and to humble yourself before your God, your words were heard, and I have come in response to them. {13} But the prince of the Persian kingdom resisted me twenty-one days. Then Michael, one of the chief princes, came to help me, because I was detained there with the king of Persia.

{14} Now I have come to explain to you what will happen to your people in the future, for the vision concerns a time yet to come." {15} While he was saying this to me, I bowed with my face toward the ground and was speechless. {16}Then one who looked like a man touched my lips, and I opened my mouth and began

NIV

to speak. I said to the one standing before me, "I am overcome with anguish because of the vision, my lord, and I am helpless. {17} How can I, your servant, talk with you, my lord? My strength is gone and I can hardly breathe." {18} Again the one who looked like a man touched me and gave me strength. {19} 'Do not be afraid, O man highly esteemed,' he said. 'Peace! Be strong now; be strong.' When he spoke to me, I was strengthened and said, 'Speak, my lord, since you have given me strength.' {20} So he said, 'Do you know why I have come to you? Soon I will return to fight against the prince of Persia, and when I go, the prince of Greece will come;

{21} but first I will tell you what is written in the Book of Truth. (No one supports me against them except Michael, your prince.

{1} And in the first year of Darius the Mede, I took my stand to support and protect him.)

The sequence begins

{2} Now then, I tell you the truth: Three more kings will appear in Persia, and then a fourth, who will be far richer than all the others. When he has gained power by his

Interlaced thoughts

{20} So the angel said to me, "Do you know why I have come to you, Daniel? I have come to bring you understanding for generations to come. Soon I will return to earth to remove the kingdom of Persia, and when I have finished my work, the kingdom of Greece will arise;

{21} but first I will tell you some secrets that are written in the Book of Truth which is sealed with seven seals in heaven. (No one else knows about my orders of managing earthly kingdoms except Michael, the Prince of heaven and earth.

{1} And in the first year of Darius the Mede, I began to bless his activities and protect him according to the plans of the Most High.)

{2} Now then Daniel, I tell you the truth about the kingdom of the Persians and the Grecians that will follow: Three more kings will rule over Persia: Cambyses, False

Interlaced thoughts

Smerdis and Darius I, and then a fourth will rise who will be called Xerxes, and he will be far richer than the other three. And when he has gained much power by his wealth, he will stir up his kingdom of the Medes and Persians against the rising kingdom of Greece.

{3} Later, a mighty king will appear in Grecia, who will gain control of the world and rule with great power and do as he pleases. {4} After he has ruled for a very short time, he—Alexander the Great—will die an untimely death and his empire will be broken up and parceled out toward the North, South, East and West. Alexander's empire will not go to his descendants, nor will his successors have the compelling power he exercised. In time, his empire will be uprooted and shall be given to the Romans.

Daniel, keep in mind that the Most High chose the geographic site for His holy hill—Jerusalem. He set Jerusalem in the center of nations. His purpose is that all nations should learn of the tiny nation of Israel and thereby hear of His greatness and His everlasting covenant with mankind."

Note: After Alexander's death, the Grecian empire was eventually divided into four kingdoms and four generals from Alexander's empire ruled over them. Ptolemy ruled in the South, Cassander in the West, Lysimachus in the North and

NIV

wealth, he will stir up everyone against the kingdom of Greece.

{3} Then a mighty king will appear, who will rule with great power and do as he pleases.

{4} After he has appeared, his empire will be broken up and parceled out toward the four winds of heaven. It will not go to his descendants, nor will it have the power he exercised, because his empire will be uprooted and given to others.

NIV

Interlaced thoughts

Seleucus in the East. Although many changes in power and geography took place in the world after the break-up of Greece, many changes did not directly affect the tiny nation of Israel. By 331 B.C., the regeneration of Israel as a nation was well under way and their greatest concern about international matters was the occasional army that passed through their land enroute to some great conquest.

Israel knew they lived between two very large and powerful kingdoms. One resided to their north—the other, to their south. Thus the terms, the king of the North and the king of the South must be understood from Israel's perspective on geography. Simply said, the Jews lived between two great rivals.

This prophecy was given to Israel in terms of kings coming from the *direction* of the north or the south because as generations passed, the names of conquerors would change but the *direction* would not change. God wisely used this method so that His people living at the end of Israel's probation could align the progression of this prophecy with contemporary history. Jesus warned His disciples of the coming destruction of Jerusalem and He referred them to this prophecy (Matthew 24:15) for information about coming events upon Jerusalem. As a result, all Christians fled Jerusalem before it was

Interlaced thoughts

destroyed in A.D. 70. Not one perished in the siege that had been foretold.

{5} "The angel begins: One of Alexander's generals, Ptolemy I Soter, will become king of Egypt. As king of the South, he will become strong, but one of the other three generals, Seleucus I Nicator, will become even greater than Ptolemy and Selecus will extend his domain so that he will rule over the entire North with great power.

{6} After some years, these two kings will die. Then, their offspring will become allies through marriage. Bernice, the daughter of Ptolemy II, the king of the South, will go to Antiochus II, the king of the North, to make an alliance. Antiochus will divorce his wife, Laodice, for Bernice and they will produce an heir. But, this won't last long. Eventually, Bernice will be divorced by the vacillating Antiochus because Laodice and Antiochus will be reconciled. Antiochus II will not live long after returning to his first wife. In those days Bernice, her royal escort and her son by Antiochus will be killed by Laodice. The king himself, Antiochus II, will also be killed by his wicked wife, Laodice.

{7} Later, Bernice's brother in Egypt, Ptolemy III, will rise to the throne in the South and take her place. In revenge for Bernice's death, he will attack the army of the new king of the North, Seleucus

NIV

{5} The king of the South will become strong, but one of his commanders will become even stronger than he and will rule his own kingdom with great power.

{6} After some years, they will become allies. The daughter of the king of the South will go to the king of the North to make an alliance, but she will not retain her power, and he and his power will not last. In those days she will be handed over, together with her royal escort and her father and the one who supported her.

{7} One from her family line will arise to take her place. He will attack the forces of the king of the North and enter his fortress; he will fight against them and be victorious.

NIV

{8} He will also seize their gods, their metal images and their valuable articles of silver and gold and carry them off to Egypt. For some years he will leave the king of the North alone. {9} Then the king of the North will invade the realm of the king of the South but will retreat to his own country.

{10} His sons will prepare for war and assemble a great army, which will sweep on like an irresistible flood and carry the battle as far as his fortress.

{11} "Then the king of the South will march out in a rage and fight against the king of the North, who will raise a large army, but it will be defeated.
{12} When the army is carried off, the king of the South will be filled with pride and will slaughter many thousands, yet he will not remain triumphant.

Interlaced thoughts

II. He will enter his fortress; he will fight against them and be victorious.
{8} He will seize their gods, their metal images and their valuable articles of silver and gold and carry them off to Egypt. For some years Ptolemy III will leave the king of the North alone. {9} After several years pass, Seleucus II will invade the realm of the king of the South to retrieve the gold and silver that was taken from him, but Selecus II will be defeated and return to his own country empty-handed.
{10} With hearts set on revenge, Seleucus III and Antiochus III, the two sons of Seleucus II, will prepare for war and assemble a great army, which will sweep on like an irresistible flood of devastation and carry the battle as far as the area of Transjordan which will be ruled by the next king of the South, Ptolemy IV.

{11} Then Ptolemy IV will march out in a rage and fight against Antiochus III, the king of the North, at Raphia, but the large army of Antiochus III will be defeated. {12} When the army from the North is shamed with defeat, Ptolemy IV, the king of the South, will be filled with much arrogance and will continue his mighty conquests, slaughtering thousands as far as the border of India, yet he will not remain triumphant. He and his wife will die mysteriously and in their place, Ptolemy V Epiphanes,

Interlaced thoughts

their five-year-old son, will ascend the throne of the South.
{13} Meanwhile, Antiochus III, the king of the North, will muster another army, larger than the first; and after several years, he will advance toward Egypt with a huge army fully equipped.

{14} Daniel, understand that during the reign of Ptolemy IV, many will rise up against the arrogant king of the South. Even some of the zealots and violent men among your own people will rebel against him in fulfillment of the vision, but without success.

{15} But, Antiochus III, the king of the North, will come and build up siege ramps and will capture the fortified city of Sidon. The forces of the South will be powerless to resist; even their best troops will not have the strength to stand.

{16} Many years later, a new group of invaders from the North will appear and they will do as they please for a long time; no one will be able to stand against them. They will eventually establish themselves as a military force all over the world, including the Beautiful Land of Israel and they will have the power to destroy anyone rebelling against him. {17} At that time, the invaders from the North will be called Rome. It's ruler, Julius Caesar, will come with the might of

NIV

{13} For the king of the North will muster another army, larger than the first; and after several years, he will advance with a huge army fully equipped.

{14} In those times many will rise against the king of the South. The violent men among your own people will rebel in fulfillment of the vision, but without success.

{15} Then the king of the North will come and build up siege ramps and will capture a fortified city. The forces of the South will be powerless to resist; even their best troops will not have the strength to stand.

{16} The invader will do as he pleases; no one will be able to stand against him. He will establish himself in the Beautiful Land and will have the power to destroy it.

{17} He will determine to come with the might of his entire kingdom and will make an alliance with the king of the South. And he will give him a daughter in marriage

NIV

in order to overthrow the kingdom, but his plans will not succeed or help him.

{18} Then he will turn his attention to the coastlands and will take many of them, but a commander will put an end to his insolence and will turn his insolence back upon him.

{19} After this, he will turn back toward the fortresses of his own country but will stumble and fall, to be seen no more.
{20} His successor will send out a tax collector to maintain the royal splendor. In a few years, however, he will be destroyed, yet not in anger or in battle.

Interlaced thoughts

many legions and will make an alliance with Ptolemy XI, the king of the South during those days. In effect, the two children of Ptolemy XI, Cleopatra and Ptolemy XII, will be put under the guardianship of Rome. In years to come, Cleopatra and Ptolemy XII, the heirs to the throne in the South, will try to overthrow Roman control of Egypt. Cleopatra will conduct illicit love affairs with Julius Caesar and Mark Antony in order to gain power. But later, Julius Caesar will be assassinated and Mark Antony will be killed in battle. So, her plans will not succeed or help Egypt.

{18} After making the alliance with Ptolemy XI, Julius Caesar will turn his attention to the people living on the islands of the coastlands of Africa and he will subdue them, thus, Julius Caesar will put an end to the rebellion of Scipio and will turn his rebellion into defeat.

{19} After this, Julius Caesar will return home and receive many honors and titles but he is mortal. He will die at the hand of an assassin and will be seen no more.
{20} Caesar's successor, Octavius – later named Augustus – will send out tax collectors all over the kingdom to maintain royal splendor. After a reign of 40 years, he too will die, not in anger or in battle. He will die of natural causes.

Interlaced thoughts

{21} Augustus will be succeeded by Tiberius, a contemptible person who will not come through the royal line. Tiberius will be adopted by Augustus and thus become heir to the throne. Tiberius will take the throne of the kingdom without conflict, in fact, he will seize it through intrigue and the help of his manipulating mother, Livia.

{22} Tiberius Caesar will prove to be a brilliant general. He will be eminently successful against powerful armies that oppose him in Germany, Armenia and Parthia. During his reign, the Holy One of Israel shall be born and the great Prince of God's everlasting covenant will be murdered.

{23} Now Daniel, let me review a few things about the rise of Rome and how this will affect Israel in the future. During its rise to power, Rome will offer mutual assistance pacts with various kingdoms throughout the world. After these kingdoms reach a friendly agreement with Rome, Rome will act deceitfully, and with only a few people manipulating its great army, it will rise to great power so that no one can argue with it.

{24} When the richest provinces feel secure, Rome will invade them and will achieve complete dominion over them. Rome's authority will go beyond anything that other kingdoms ever achieved. Rome will finance its conquests by freely distributing plunder, loot and wealth among its

NIV

{21} He will be succeeded by a contemptible person who has not been given the honor of royalty. He will invade the kingdom when its people feel secure, and he will seize it through intrigue.

{22} Then an overwhelming army will be swept away before him; both it and a prince of the covenant will be destroyed.

{23} After coming to an agreement with him, he will act deceitfully, and with only a few people he will rise to power.

{24} When the richest provinces feel secure, he will invade them and will achieve what neither his fathers nor his forefathers did. He will distribute plunder, loot and wealth among his followers. He will plot the overthrow of fortresses—but only for a time.

NIV

{25} With a large army he will stir up his strength and courage against the king of the South. The king of the South will wage war with a large and very powerful army, but he will not be able to stand because of the plots devised against him.

{26} Those who eat from the king's provisions will try to destroy him; his army will be swept away, and many will fall in battle.

{27} The two kings, with their hearts bent on evil, will sit at the same table and lie to each other, but to no avail, because an end will still come at the appointed time.

Interlaced thoughts

mercenary soldiers. Consequently, its armies will become large, numerous and very powerful. Rome will plot the overthrow of kingdoms everywhere – but only for a time. As with all nations, Rome will come to an end, too.

{25} Now, let me tell you more about Augustus. With a large army, Augustus will stir up strength and courage against Antony, the king of the South. At the Battle of Actium (31 B.C.), the king of the South will wage war with a large and very powerful army, but Antony will not be able to stand because of the plots devised against him.

{26} Some who are very close to Antony, even those who eat at his table, will try to destroy him; and, Antony's army will be swept away, and many will fall in battle. However, Antony will remain for a little longer. {27} Augustus and Antony, with their hearts bent on evil, will sit at the same table and lie to each other, but to no avail. Both want control of the world and that is not possible for either of them.

Daniel, also understand that the Most High God has a great purpose for Jerusalem that can be fulfilled at the appointed time if Israel will cooperate. Empires and kings come and go but God's purposes happen right on time.

Interlaced thoughts

{28} Augustus, the king of the North, will return to his own country after the Battle of Actium with great wealth from Egypt. Years later (A.D. 66), Vespasian, the ruler of Rome at that time, will be angered by the behavior of the Jews, who are trustees of God's holy covenant. Vespasian will take action against a number of cities and he will specifically war against Jerusalem, but news from his homeland about the death of Tiberius will cause him to return to his own country without defeating Jerusalem.

{29} At the appointed time, Titus, the son of Vespasian, will invade the South again, but this time the outcome will be different from what it was before. {30} Many ships from the western coastlands of Africa and Egypt will oppose him, and he will lose the will to fight them. However, he will change his course and vent his fury against the rebellious city of Jerusalem because the Romans will hold special hatred for the stiff-necked Jews. Understand that Titus will resume the siege of Jerusalem which his father began and Titus will spare the lives of those who forsake their religious convictions. {31} His armed forces will plunder the city and they will completely destroy the temple complex believed to be impregnable so that daily religious services cannot be conducted there. Then Rome will have carried out the

NIV

{28} The king of the North will return to his own country with great wealth, but his heart will be set against the holy covenant. He will take action against it and then return to his own country.

{29} At the appointed time he will invade the South again, but this time the outcome will be different from what it was before.
{30} Ships of the western coastlands will oppose him, and he will lose heart. Then he will turn back and vent his fury against the holy covenant. He will return and show favor to those who forsake the holy covenant.

{31} His armed forces will rise up to desecrate the temple fortress and will abolish the daily sacrifice. Then they will set up the abomination that causes desolation.

NIV

{32} With flattery he will corrupt those who have violated the covenant, but the people who know their God will firmly resist him.

{33} Those who are wise will instruct many, though for a time they will fall by the sword or be burned or captured or plundered.

{34} When they fall, they will receive a little help, and many who are not sincere will join them.

{35} Some of the wise will stumble, so that they may be refined, purified and made spotless until the time of the end, for it will still come at the appointed time.

Interlaced thoughts

decree of God. This awful decree is that Israel is to be destroyed and left desolate because your people will violate the grace of 70 Jubilee weeks granted to them.

{32} With flattery and false ideas, the Romans will further corrupt those who have violated the covenant of God. But, there will be a remnant, a small number of people who know their God, and they will firmly resist the infiltration of errors introduced by Rome.
{33} As years pass, the truth about the Most High God will be kept alive by those who are wise and are filled with the Holy Spirit. They will instruct the scattered people of God, though for a predestined period of time of 1,260 years they will fall by the sword or be burned or captured or plundered.
{34} Even though they fall, they will not entirely perish, for they will receive a enough help to keep the torch of truth burning, and as Christianity becomes popular, many who are not sincere will join them. It too will become corrupt.
{35} Some of the remnant of God will stumble for lack of faith, so that they may be refined, purified and made spotless until the time of the end. But be patient Daniel, for the end does not come until earth shall reach the appointed time set by the Most High God.

Note: Sources for these conclusions come from a variety of

Interlaced thoughts

commentaries. Because none have endeavored to align the historical details with the rules as stated on page 4, no one source brings all the details together as presented here.

But, perhaps the strongest evidence that this prophecy unfolds as presented here, is that not one Christian perished in the siege of Jerusalem in A.D. 70. Could this be the passage in Daniel that Jesus referred to in Matthew 24:15?

NIV

Prophecy 6

Daniel 11:36-12:3

Beginning point in time: The physical appearing of the devil
Ending point in time: Second Coming
Synopsis: This prophecy expands upon Prophecy 3. In this prophecy, the horn power of Daniel 8 becomes the *king of the North*. By having dual identities, we learn significantly more about the physical appearing of the devil which happens during the fifth trumpet (Revelation 9:1-11). In Prophecy 3, the horn is identified as a mighty king. In Prophecy 6, he is the undisputed king of the North, the direction of destruction.[1] This mighty king will make war and persecute the saints just like the little horn of Daniel 7 in ages past.

NIV

{36} "The king will do as he pleases. He will exalt and magnify himself above every god and will say unheard-of things against the God of gods. He will be successful until the time of wrath is completed, for what has been determined must take place.

Interlaced thoughts

{36} "When the devil shall physically appear upon the earth, he will claim to be God.[2] As God, he will want the honor of king over all religions of the world. In this prophecy, the devil king bears the title, king of the North, for two reasons. First, as a point on the compass, the north symbolizes the dwelling place of God. (See Job 37:22.) Secondly, in the previous prophecy, Israel was caught between two great rivals – the kings of the north and south. In this prophecy, the people of God in the last days will again be caught between two great rivals – those who receive the devil as God and those who refuse to obey either the devil or the God of heaven. However, the devil will do as he pleases for no man can stop him. He will exalt and magnify himself above every god known to man and will say unheard-of things against the Most High God. He will be successful until the time of God's wrath upon the world is completed,[3] for what has been

Interlaced thoughts

determined by the Most High God will take place.

{37} Daniel, just as Israel rebelled against the God of their fathers, the devil will show no respect for the gods which religious people of the world worship.[4] Neither will he have any regard for the coming Holy One which many women of Israel hope to give birth to, nor will the devil regard any god at all. He will exalt himself above them all. Be warned. This king is a man subject to no law or authority. He will also be known as the man of lawlessness.[5] {38} Instead of respecting the gods that people trust, he will eventually require the whole world to honor a new religion. He will use force as necessary to unite the world. He will demand that all people obey the laws of his new world religion. Such a religious system has not been seen before and is therefore, unknown to any on earth at this time. But, be warned. At the appointed time the devil will consolidate the world's seven religious systems into one organization and he will honor himself by receiving gold and silver, precious stones and costly gifts.[6]

{39} When he has enough followers believing that he really is God, he will attack the brave people of the Most High, but the 144,000 and their supporters will resist the schemes of the devil even though

NIV

{37} He will show no regard for the gods of his fathers or for the one desired by women, nor will he regard any god, but will exalt himself above them all.

{38} Instead of them, he will honor a god of fortresses; a god unknown to his fathers he will honor with gold and silver, with precious stones and costly gifts.

{39} He will attack the mightiest fortresses with the help of a foreign god and will greatly honor those who acknowledge him. He will make them rulers over many people and will distribute the land at a price.

NIV	Interlaced thoughts
	many in the world will join in with the devil in rebellion against the clearest evidences of truth. The world has never seen anything comparable to what the devil is going to do and he will greatly honor those who acknowledge him. After the great war of the sixth trumpet,[7] he will establish ten rulers over the people of the world[8] and he will distribute the land at a price.
{40} At the time of the end the king of the South will engage him in battle, and the king of the North will storm out against him with chariots and cavalry and a great fleet of ships. He will invade many countries and sweep through them like a flood.	{40} At the time of the sixth trumpet, there will be many in the world who are opposed to the devil's powerful advances, and they will engage the forces of the devil in battle just like the see-saw battles between the kings of the North and South in the previous prophecy. The devil will storm out against his adversaries with chariots and cavalry and a great fleet of ships, for he will have millions of followers. He will invade many countries and sweep through them with enormous destruction just like a flood.[9]
{41} He will also invade the Beautiful Land. Many countries will fall, but Edom, Moab and the leaders of Ammon will be delivered from his hand.	{41} He will also invade the homeland of Israel. Many countries will fall, but there will be some survivors who will remain faithful just as some of your people escaped the destruction of Nebuchadnezzar by fleeing to the remote areas of Edom, Moab. Those like the leaders of Ammon who protected your people will also be delivered from his hand.[10] {42} As ruler of earth, the devil will extend his power over many countries; Egypt will not

Interlaced thoughts

escape. {43} He will gain control of the treasures of gold and silver and all the riches of the world, and even those who hate him and those who hate the Most High God will have to submit for fear of want, for no one can buy or sell unless they obey his laws.[11]

{44} But reports of violent activity in the eastern sky, and the voice of Jesus who rules upon the throne located on the sides of the north will be heard from heaven pronouncing the devil's destruction. This, of course, will greatly alarm him, and the devil will set out in a torrent of rage to destroy and annihilate all of God's people by demanding a universal death decree.

{45} Daniel, you know from previous visions that God intends to make Jerusalem the great city of the world, but it shall not happen. In a similar fashion, the devil will make Babylon the great city of the world. For a short time, he will consolidate the world into one unwieldy empire. He will establish his throne in Babylon and will rule over the whole world. Yet he will come to his end, and no human will be able to prevent it.

{12:1} Just when the devil takes his seat upon his earthly throne at the time of the seventh trumpet, to rule a conquered world, Michael, the great Prince of heaven and earth, who protects His people, will arise from his intercession at the right

NIV

{42} He will extend his power over many countries; Egypt will not escape.

{43} He will gain control of the treasures of gold and silver and all the riches of Egypt, with the Libyans and Nubians in submission.

{44} But reports from the east and the north will alarm him, and he will set out in a great rage to destroy and annihilate many.

{45} He will pitch his royal tents between the seas at the beautiful holy mountain. Yet he will come to his end, and no one will help him.

{12:1} At that time Michael, the great prince who protects your people, will arise. There will be a time of distress such as has not happened from the beginning of nations until then. But at that time your people – everyone whose name

NIV

is found written in the book—will be delivered.

{2} Multitudes who sleep in the dust of the earth will awake: some to everlasting life, others to shame and everlasting contempt.

{3} Those who are wise will shine like the brightness of the heavens, and those who lead many to righteousness, like the stars for ever and ever.

End of Sequence

{4} But you, Daniel, close up and seal the words of the scroll until the time of the end. Many will go here and there to increase knowledge."

Interlaced thoughts

hand of God's throne. The mediatorial work of Jesus will be ended and He will send the seven last plagues. There will be a time of distress such as has not happened from the beginning of nations until then. But at that time your people—everyone whose name is found written in the Book of Life—will be delivered from the experience of death. {2} A few days before the Second Coming, multitudes of martyrs who died during the fifth seal will awake during this special resurrection to everlasting life, also, those who participated in the crucifixion of Jesus will be resurrected so that they might see Jesus coming in clouds of glory. Their shame and contempt will stay with them until they are destroyed at the Second Coming.

{3} But, the 144,000 will be victorious. They will shine like the brightness of the heavens, and they will lead many to righteousness, and they will shine like the stars for ever and ever.

{4} But you, Daniel, close up and seal the words of this vision until the time of the end. Many will try to understand your book, they will go here and there to increase knowledge, but the Most High God has sealed this book until the final generation arrives. {5} Then I, Daniel, looked, and there before me

Interlaced thoughts

stood two beings, one on this bank of the river and one on the opposite bank. {6} One of them said to Jesus, who was clothed in linen and was standing above the waters of the river, 'How long will it be before these astonishing things are fulfilled?'

{7} Jesus lifted his right hand and his left hand toward heaven, and I heard him swear by the Most High God who lives forever, saying, 'It will be for a time, times and half a time.[12] When the power of my holy people has been finally broken, all these things will be finally completed.'[13]

{8} I heard the words, but I did not understand their relationship to this vision. So I asked, 'Lord, what will the outcome of all this be?'

{9} He replied, 'Go your way, Daniel, because the words of this prophecy are closed up and sealed until the time just before the end.

{10} My people will be purified, made spotless and refined, and the wicked will continue to be wicked. None of the wicked will understand these things, but at the appointed time of the end, those who are wise in spiritual matters will understand these things.

{11} Daniel, write this down because my people who shall make up the last generation need to know

NIV

{5} Then I, Daniel, looked, and there before me stood two others, one on this bank of the river and one on the opposite bank. {6} One of them said to the man clothed in linen, who was above the waters of the river, "How long will it be before these astonishing things are fulfilled?"

{7} The man clothed in linen, who was above the waters of the river, lifted his right hand and his left hand toward heaven, and I heard him swear by him who lives forever, saying, 'It will be for a time, times and half a time. When the power of the holy people has been finally broken, all these things will be completed.' {8} I heard, but I did not understand. So I asked, 'My lord, what will the outcome of all this be?'

{9} He replied, 'Go your way, Daniel, because the words are closed up and sealed until the time of the end.

{10} Many will be purified, made spotless and refined, but the wicked will continue to be wicked. None of the wicked will understand, but those who are wise will understand.

{11} From the time that the daily sacrifice is abolished and the

NIV

abomination that causes desolation is set up, there will be 1,290 days.

{12} Blessed is the one who waits for and reaches the end of the 1,335 days.

{13} 'As for you, go your way till the end. You will rest, and then at the end of the days you will rise to receive your allotted inheritance.'

Interlaced thoughts

this: 'A time is coming in heaven when my corporate intercession on behalf of the world will come to an end. Yes, at that time I will cease from my daily work of standing between the wrath of God and a guilty world. This end of my corporate ministry in the heavenly sanctuary will be marked by a great world-wide earthquake.[14] From that time, count the days. From the end of my daily ministry in heaven until the devil is able to set up a universal death decree for my people, there will be 1,290 days. {12} But, blessed is the one who patiently waits for and reaches the end of the 1,335 days, for he shall hear my voice saying, 'My grace is sufficient for you!'[15]

{13} As for you Daniel, go on with your business until the end of your life. You will rest in sleep, and then at the end of earth's days you will rise to receive your allotted inheritance. And you will be well rewarded for your faithfulness.

References

1. Jeremiah 4:6, 6:1, 47:2, 50:9,41; Job 37:22
2. 2 Thessalonians 2:3-12, Revelation 17:11, Daniel 11:45
3. Revelation 15:1
4. Hebrews 3:10,11
5. Ezekiel 28:2,12-19; Isaiah 14:15-20

References

6. Revelation 13:14, 17:13,14
7. Revelation 9:13-21
8. Daniel 2:44
9. Jeremiah 47:2, Hosea 5:10, Isaiah 8:6-8
10. Jeremiah 40:11
11. Revelation 13:16
12. Revelation 10:5,6, Revelation 11:3
13. Revelation 11:7
14. Revelation 8:2-5, Revelation 6:7,8, 2 Thessalonians 2:7,8
15. Matthew 25:31-46, 2 Corinthians 12:9

Prophecy 7

Revelation 4:1-6:17

Beginning point in time: 1798
Ending point in time: Second coming
Synopsis: This prophecy complements events described in Daniel 7, 8 and 9. The story begins with John being taken up into heaven to observe things that begin in 1798. For more information on the timing of this scene, see appendix E. The reader should keep in mind that the centerpiece of this prophecy is the book with seven seals and the Lamb who is found worthy to open it.

NIV	Interlaced thoughts
{1} After this I looked, and there before me was a door standing open in heaven. And the voice I had first heard speaking to me like a trumpet said, "Come up here, and I will show you what must take place after this."	{1} After beholding Jesus and hearing His admonition to His seven churches, I looked up into heaven, and there before me was a great temple, much greater than the one I attended in Jerusalem it was destroyed. However, the door to the inner sanctuary, the Most Holy Place, was standing wide open. This was most unusual since no one could go through that door except the High Priest, and only then, on the annual Day of Atonement. Then, Jesus said, "Come up here John, and I will show you what must take place after the door to this part of the temple is opened."[1]
{2} At once I was in the Spirit, and there before me was a throne in heaven with someone sitting on it.	{2} At once I was in another state of being,[2] I was zoomed up to heaven and forward in time to 1798. I soon surmised that I was about to behold scenes dealing with the end of the world and the revelation of all that Jesus really is. After passing through the open door, there before me was an enormous room. In the center stood a great throne, high and lifted up, and the Father was

Interlaced thoughts

sitting on it. I realized that a most important meeting was about to begin. {3} The one who sat on the throne had an appearance like sparkling crystal quartz mixed with bright red colors of fire. A rainbow of colors completely encircled the throne in many arcs just like rainbows dancing upon a pile of emeralds.

{4} Surrounding the exalted throne of the Father were twenty-four other thrones[3], and seated on them were twenty-four elders. The elders are twenty-four people who Jesus resurrected and called to heaven as representatives of the human race so that they might serve as observers of the human race.[4] They were dressed in white and had been given golden crowns of victory which they wore on their heads. I learned that the Father had especially honored these twenty-four people because they were people of great integrity during their lives on earth. {5} Around the Father's throne came flashes of lightning, rumblings and peals of thunder. His glory was indescribable and the atmosphere was filled with tremendous energy. I saw seven lampstands blazing like torches before the Father. These seven lampstands represent the seven churches which I saw Jesus walk among in the first chapter of Revelation.[5] These are God's selected agencies, empowered by the Holy Spirit, through which

NIV

{3} And the one who sat there had the appearance of jasper and carnelian. A rainbow, resembling an emerald, encircled the throne.

{4} Surrounding the throne were twenty-four other thrones, and seated on them were twenty-four elders. They were dressed in white and had crowns of gold on their heads.

{5} From the throne came flashes of lightning, rumblings and peals of thunder. Before the throne, seven lamps were blazing. These are the seven spirits of God.

NIV

{6} Also before the throne there was what looked like a sea of glass, clear as crystal. In the center, around the throne, were four living creatures, and they were covered with eyes, in front and in back.

{7} The first living creature was like a lion, the second was like an ox, the third had a face like a man, the fourth was like a flying eagle.

{8} Each of the four living creatures had six wings and was covered with eyes all around, even under his wings. Day and night they

Interlaced thoughts

knowledge of His saving truth is transmitted throughout the earth.

{6} The glorious throne of the Father sat upon a large expanse that looked like a giant expanse of glass because the platform was clear as crystal and in the center, surrounding the Father, were four highly exalted beings.[6] These appeared similar to angels, but were greater than angels. These four living creatures have highest authority and power. I wondered if these beings were a representation of the of the Holy Spirit for these were integral to the throne and they have omnivision: the ability to see everything taking place throughout the universe.

{7} Each creature had four faces: the face of a lion, an ox, a man and an eagle. So that I could understand something about the character of their work, God represented the beings to me in this manner because these beings possess powers beyond human comprehension. I learned that each face is related to a special work. Even though each creature had four faces, I could only see one face at a time. The first living creature had a face like a lion, the second was like an ox, the third had a face like a man, the fourth was like that of a flying eagle. {8} Each of the four living creatures had six wings. Their flight from point to point seemed instantaneous. They were covered

Interlaced thoughts	NIV
with eyes all over, even under their wings. This, I understood, represents their ability to see everything taking place in God's vast universe. Because they can see all the works of God day and night, they never stop saying: "Holy, holy, holy is the Lord God Almighty, who was present before anything existed, and is present throughout His universe, and who will exist through all ages to come."	never stop saying: "Holy, holy, holy is the Lord God Almighty, who was, and is, and is to come."
{9} Because the four living creatures can see the works of the Father taking place all over the universe, they give wonderful reports about the Father and they ascribe glory, honor and thanks to Him who sits on the throne and who lives for ever and ever,	{9} Whenever the living creatures give glory, honor and thanks to him who sits on the throne and who lives for ever and ever,
{10} and whenever they reveal the marvelous and wonderful acts of God, the twenty-four elders fall down before the Father who sits on the throne, and they worship him who lives for ever and ever. When the elders hear the thrilling reports of the Father's goodness and kindness toward His subjects, they remove their golden crowns and fall upon their faces before Him, saying:	{10} the twenty-four elders fall down before him who sits on the throne, and worship him who lives for ever and ever. They lay their crowns before the throne and say:
{11} "You are worthy, our Lord and God, to receive glory and honor and power, for you created all things, and by your will they were created and have their being."	{11} "You are worthy, our Lord and God, to receive glory and honor and power, for you created all things, and by your will they were created and have their being."
{5:1} As I watched, a herald called the meeting to order and billions of angels were seated around the throne. Then I saw in the right	{5:1} Then I saw in the right hand of him who sat on the throne a scroll with writing on both sides and sealed with seven seals.

NIV

{2} And I saw a mighty angel proclaiming in a loud voice, "Who is worthy to break the seals and open the scroll?"

Interlaced thoughts

hand of him who sat on the throne, a book containing highly sensitive information. The writing on the outside of the book identified the usual things found on scrolls: the name of the book, the date it was written, and the name of the author. I saw that the name of the scroll was the Book of Life. The author was the Father and I saw that this book was written before the creation of Lucifer and the angels. It was perfectly clear that the Father wanted no one to see what He had written in this book until the right time. This is why the book was sealed up with seven seals. Ever since angels had been created, this book has been guarded. I suspected this book had something to do with the Father's foreknowledge and what He knew before He created angels and human beings. I could tell by the reaction of the angels that the existence of this book was well known throughout heaven. I also discovered that a few people on earth knew of this book,[7] but no one other than the Father knew what was written inside.

{2} And I saw a mighty angel proclaiming in a loud voice, "Who is worthy to break the seals and open the Book of Life?" I found this invitation most interesting. There before me sat the Father, the Most High God of the Universe, and now, the Father was willing to allow anyone the right to open this book and expose the contents if

Interlaced thoughts

they were qualified to expose His secrets! I wondered about the connection between *being qualified* and exposing the secrets within the Book of Life, but said nothing.

{3} At the words of the mighty angel, an consternation fell upon the faces of that vast assembly because this was no casual offer. I didn't understand what all the concern was about until I heard angels discussing the matter. As it turned out, no one in heaven or earth, dead or alive, was found worthy to open the Book of Life or even look inside it.

{4} Time passed. I began to comprehend what was going on. The Father was on trial! If no one could be found worthy to open the Book of Life and reveal its contents, then the Father could not be vindicated from false allegations that Lucifer had brought against Him a long time ago. As I studied the situation, I realized that the glorious and kind Father was vulnerable to ruinous allegations and my heart broke to think that someone would actually misrepresent the Father from whom all blessings flow. Like a knife, this realization brought pain. Here's the problem: The Father is infinite in every way and He does so many things simultaneously that His creatures cannot immediately understand all that He is doing. Therefore, if someone brought a false charge against Him, the charge *could be made to appear as true for*

NIV

{3} But no one in heaven or on earth or under the earth could open the scroll or even look inside it.

{4} I wept and wept because no one was found who was worthy to open the scroll or look inside.

NIV

{5} Then one of the elders said to me, "Do not weep! See, the Lion of the tribe of Judah, the Root of David, has triumphed. He is able to open the scroll and its seven seals."

Interlaced thoughts

awhile. If the accusations were skillfully done, they could be very convincing because it takes time to understand what the Father is doing. In fact, in some cases it may take thousands of years to understand His infinite purposes.

So, this was it! The very thing that makes Him God and sets Him apart from the rest of His creation is the very thing that makes Him vulnerable to suspicion. Now, the angel's invitation made sense. Who was in a position to truly and convincingly demonstrate that the Father was above reproach? As much as the four living creatures and the twenty-four elders loved and adored the Father, I realized that they couldn't save Him. I wept and wept because I too was unworthy to open the scroll and reveal the contents. I couldn't help my wonderful Father. I would gladly die for Him for I loved Him with all my heart, but I couldn't exonerate Him. This was more than I could bear.

{5} After while, one of the twenty-four elders noticed my grief. He came over to me and said, "John, do not weep! Look, the Lion of the tribe of Judah, the Root of David, has triumphed. He alone has been found credible and worthy by the angels. He is able to open the scroll and its seven seals."

Interlaced thoughts

{6} I had been so lost in my grief that I did not see Jesus come forward in response to the invitation.

Apparently, the qualifications of Jesus had been carefully reviewed and He was found worthy to vindicate the Most Excellent Name of the Father. Through my tears I saw a Lamb, looking as if it had been slain, standing in the center of the throne which was encircled by the four living creatures and the elders. But this was no ordinary Lamb. This Lamb had willingly set aside His divinity and became subject to the plan of salvation which required His death. But now, on the basis of His worthiness, He was given omnipotence and the seven horns represent that power. The Lamb was given omniscience and the seven eyes represent that power.[8] The Lamb was also given authority over the eternal Spirit which is sent throughout the realms of heaven and earth.[9] {7} Then, after receiving all authority, the Lamb came before the Father and took the Book of Life from the right hand of him who sat on the throne. With this accomplished, the Father retired to watch the actions of the Lamb as He began to open the seven seals on the "Lamb's Book of Life."

{8} And when the Lamb had taken the book, the four living creatures and the twenty-four elders fell down before Jesus. As representatives of

NIV

{6} Then I saw a Lamb, looking as if it had been slain, standing in the center of the throne, encircled by the four living creatures and the elders. He had seven horns and seven eyes, which are the seven spirits of God sent out into all the earth.

{7} He came and took the scroll from the right hand of him who sat on the throne.

{8} And when he had taken it, the four living creatures and the twenty-four elders fell down before the Lamb. Each one had a harp

NIV

and they were holding golden bowls full of incense, which are the prayers of the saints.

{9} And they sang a new song: "You are worthy to take the scroll and to open its seals, because you were slain, and with your blood you purchased men for God from every tribe and language and people and nation.

{10} You have made them to be a kingdom and priests to serve our God, and they will reign on the earth."

Interlaced thoughts

the human race, each elder had a harp and a golden bowl full of incense. This scene was similar to temple scenes I had witnessed in Jerusalem. The golden bowls served as censers and when special incense was placed upon the coals in the censers, a most wonderful fragrance filled the courtroom. The elders put incense in their censers when Jesus was promoted because millions of faithful people across the centuries are looking to Jesus for salvation. Now that He is about to enter a special phase of work as man's High Priest, the sweet fragrance of the incense reminds Jesus of man's total dependency upon Him.

{9} And then the elders and the four living creatures sang a new song. New songs occur in heaven when some experience happens that has not happened before. They sang to the Lamb: "You are worthy to take the scroll and to open its seals, because you were slain, and with your blood you have redeemed men for God from every tribe and language and people and nation. You have proven that you loved man more than you loved your own life. {10} Even more, You have exalted human beings to be a new order within the universe and you have ordained them as priests to serve our God, and they will serve you when You set up your kingdom."

Interlaced thoughts

{11} Then I looked around and heard the voices of many angels, numbering thousands upon thousands, and ten thousand times ten thousand. They encircled the throne and the living creatures and the elders. {12} In a loud voice they joined in and sang: "Worthy is the Lamb, who was slain. We are satisfied to see Him exalted. We are convinced that He alone should receive the seven elements of divine sovereignty: power, wealth, wisdom, strength, honor, glory and praise!" {13} Then I heard Heaven ring with sounds louder than anything I've ever heard. It sounded as though every creature in heaven and on earth and under the earth and on the sea, and all that is in them, was singing. This great choir sang: "To him who sits on the throne and to the Lamb be praise and honor and glory and power, for ever and ever! We have considered the works of the Lamb and we find Him credible and worthy, and we find You, O Father, more than fair in conducting this invitation." {14} The four living creatures ended the new song by saying, "Amen," and again, the elders fell down and worshiped.

{6:1} After the praise ended, the crowd was seated. Jesus took an exalted position at the right hand of the Father.[10] Having been invested with all authority and power, I closely watched as the Lamb broke the first of the seven seals. Then, Jesus spoke quietly to the first living

NIV

{11} Then I looked and heard the voice of many angels, numbering thousands upon thousands, and ten thousand times ten thousand. They encircled the throne and the living creatures and the elders. {12} In a loud voice they sang: "Worthy is the Lamb, who was slain, to receive power and wealth and wisdom and strength and honor and glory and praise!"

{13} Then I heard every creature in heaven and on earth and under the earth and on the sea, and all that is in them, singing: "To him who sits on the throne and to the Lamb be praise and honor and glory and power, for ever and ever!"

{14} The four living creatures said, "Amen," and the elders fell down and worshiped.

{6:1} I watched as the Lamb opened the first of the seven seals. Then I heard one of the four living creatures say in a voice like thunder, "Come!"

NIV

{2} I looked, and there before me was a white horse! Its rider held a bow, and he was given a crown, and he rode out as a conqueror bent on conquest.

Interlaced thoughts

creature. Then, the first living creature spoke in a loud voice like thunder. The one who spoke had the face of a lion. He said, "Come and behold the responsibility given me by the Lamb!" {2} As I watched, the first living creature transformed himself into a white horse. I remembered that Zechariah saw the work of the Holy Spirit in different forms, including the form of four colored horses.[11] I heard some angels say that Jesus was sending the four living creatures throughout the earth to accomplish four special missions. The riders on the horses represent the mission that Jesus wants accomplished. Just as a rider directs the efforts of a horse, so Jesus directs the work done under each seal.

The first living creature was given a very large task. His assignment was to go throughout Europe and the new world and open the minds of people to their great need of salvation through Jesus. For centuries men had been taught that salvation came through the Roman Church and now the world needed to know that salvation was only available through a direct connection with Jesus. I saw that this work would lay a solid foundation for the consummation of the gospel which would be delivered to the whole earth in the *last days.* The bow in the rider's hand indicates warfare. Every time God's truth is proclaimed with clarity and power,

Interlaced thoughts

there will be division and suffering. For this reason, I am a prisoner on the isle of Patmos. But, the rider was given a *stephanos*, a golden crown of victory. This represents the reward that will be given to all who receive Christ's salvation. So, the first living creature left the throne and went down to earth searching for souls hungering for truth as a lion looks for prey. And, I saw a great revival of interest in salvation begin in the United States and in Europe.

{3} Time passed. Then, the Lamb broke open the second seal. He spoke quietly to the second living creature, the one who had the face like the ox. Then, I heard the second living creature loudly say, "Come and behold the responsibility given me by the Lamb!" {4} With this, the second living creature transformed himself into a red horse. He went out of the throne room to accomplish his mission. His work closely complemented the work begun by the first living creature. This living creature was given the great sword of Truth, the Word of God.[12] Just as an ox faithfully completes its chores, this living creature was given the responsibility of prompting people to translate and distribute the Bible all over the earth. I quickly saw a harmony between the first two creatures. As the first living creature caused men to hunger for the salvation of Jesus, the need for Bibles grew

NIV

{3} When the Lamb opened the second seal, I heard the second living creature say, "Come!"

{4} Then another horse came out, a fiery red one. Its rider was given power to take peace from the earth and to make men slay each other. To him was given a large sword.

NIV

Interlaced thoughts

proportionately. Soon, I saw millions of Bibles carefully translated and distributed throughout the earth.

Bible truth separates people. The more powerful the presentation of truth, the more opposed are those who love evil. Therefore, this activity will surely bring deadly conflict in the end. During the great tribulation which is to come, God's truth, clearly written in the Bible, will be brought to the forefront of every mind. Then, evil men will kill those who love God's Word so that their testimony cannot be heard. But for now, we watched from heaven as the first two living creatures went throughout the earth on their missions. Then, Jesus broke the third seal.

He spoke quietly to the third living creature who had the face of a man. I could tell by the face of this creature that this mission was going to be quite different than the others.

{5} When the Lamb opened the third seal, I heard the third living creature say, "Come!" I looked, and there before me was a black horse! Its rider was holding a pair of scales in his hand.

{5} When 1844 arrived, the Lamb opened the third seal, the third living creature, having the face of a man, said, "Come and behold the responsibility given me by the Lamb!" We watched as the third living creature transformed himself into a black horse! He left heaven with a pair of scales in his hand and he carried a very important message for the people of earth. His work was to raise up a special group of people out of those who

Interlaced thoughts

had responded to the works of the first two living creatures. This special group of people were to be given an understanding of a new work begun by Jesus in the heavenly sanctuary. In return, these people were to tell the world that Jesus had started the final phase of salvation's plan. When this seal opened, I saw Jesus begin to investigate the lives of men and women according to their deeds. I saw that the activity of this seal began right on time in 1844. As I looked down upon the earth, I marveled at the opportunity given to men and women. The judgment-hour message was so wonderful, but they were so few and the world so large.

{6} Then I heard the third living creature say to those of us observing these scenes in heaven, "Even though the judgment hour message is not in its final form, a quart of wheat will be paid for a day's wages, and three quarts of barley will be paid for a day's wages, and the laborers shall also receive the best oil and the wine!" I thought about this matter for some time before the meaning came to me. Then I understood. These words of promise specifically applied to those who would carry the judgment-hour message around the world. In other words, those who labor to teach the 1844 sanctuary message will be fully rewarded for their services just as Solomon rewarded the builders of God's

NIV

{6} Then I heard what sounded like a voice among the four living creatures, saying, "A quart of wheat for a day's wages, and three quarts of barley for a day's wages, and do not damage the oil and the wine!"

NIV	Interlaced thoughts
	temple with wheat, barley, oil and wine! But, the reward of this message is not the honor of seeing the Second Coming.
	These scenes were most interesting to watch. Two things intrigued me about the first three seals. First, I was impressed how the activity of each seal was additive, that is, each activity built upon the previous accomplishments of other seals. Secondly, I was impressed how the first three seals combine to reveal the final activities of Jesus in the administration of the plan of salvation.
	Then we waited for 150 years.[13] Jesus allowed this span of time to expire so that a world-wide network of people could be established. I saw that Jesus wanted people all over the world to know about the judgment hour message. This was very important because at a later time, He would hand pick 144,000 people from all nations and tongues who understood the judgment hour message. These would be empowered by the Holy Spirit to proclaim the great doctrines found in the Bibles that had been distributed all over the world – especially, the truth about the activities that would take place when the fourth seal was opened.
{7} When the Lamb opened the fourth seal, I heard the voice of the fourth living creature say, "Come!"	{7} After the Lamb broke the fourth seal, He spoke quietly to the fourth living creature. Then, the fourth living creature who had the

Interlaced thoughts

face of a flying eagle said, "Come and behold the responsibility given me by the Lamb!" {8} I watched as the fourth living creature transformed himself into a dapple-gray horse. I saw in his face the deadly mission of a flying eagle looking for prey. His mission was death and he caused hundreds of millions of people to die, and the grave followed close behind him, swallowing up the dead. In a period of time reaching down to the Second Coming of Jesus, the fourth living creature killed one fourth of the people upon earth with God's judgments of sword, famine and plague, and wild beasts.[14] The sight of this was more than I could behold. But, in fairness to Jesus I must say that violence, hatred, dishonesty and sexual immorality had almost swallowed up the people of earth. With the opening of this seal, I saw Jesus step directly into the affairs of man with terrible judgments so that He might gain the attention of the world. With the opening of this seal, the authority of Jesus was suddenly and powerfully revealed to all mankind. Jesus carefully directed the activities of this seal so that He could gather in all who would receive His precious truths which were being presented by the 144,000.[15]

The response of men to the fourth seal was terrible. They did all sorts of vile things under the guise of appeasing God. I will explain this

NIV

{8} I looked, and there before me was a pale horse! Its rider was named Death, and Hades was following close behind him. They were given power over a fourth of the earth to kill by sword, famine and plague, and by the wild beasts of the earth.

NIV

{9} When he opened the fifth seal, I saw under the altar the souls of those who had been slain because of the word of God and the testimony they had maintained.

{10} They called out in a loud voice, "How long, Sovereign Lord, holy and true, until you judge the inhabitants of the earth and avenge our blood?"

{11} Then each of them was given a white robe, and they were told to wait a little longer, until the number of their fellow servants and brothers who were to be killed as they had been was completed.

Interlaced thoughts

latter, for now, I wondered what the next seal would bring. And then the Lamb broke open the fifth seal.

{9} When he opened the fifth seal, I saw something that reminded me of the sanctuary service in Jerusalem. There, it was customary for the priests to pour the blood of slain sacrifices into a large container at the base of the altar of burnt offering.[16] Now, in heaven, I saw what looked like the altar of burnt offering and beneath the altar, I saw the blood of those who had been slain because of the word of God and the testimony they had maintained. {10} They called out in a loud voice, "How long, Sovereign Lord, holy and true, must this martyrdom go on? How long O God, until you finish judging the inhabitants of the earth and avenge our innocent blood?" {11} Then each of them was promised a white robe, and they were told to be patient. They were told that Jesus had determined that the martyrdom of saints would be allowed until a determined number was reached.[17]

So this was the killing that occurs as a result of the second seal! I saw that Jesus permitted a specific number of His faithful people to be slain by evil men for two reasons. First, there is no greater or more convincing testimony than a faith-full and intelligent testimony unto death. Secondly, the Lamb only has to speak—and millions who now sleep

Interlaced thoughts

in the dust will come forth from the grave to life immortal![18] The point is that God permits some of His saints to be put to death so that they might sleep through the final days of earth which will be even more horrific. Even though the cries of the martyrs were great, the assurance and grace which Jesus sent to each martyr was greater. Each martyr seemed satisfied that Jesus intimately knew about his suffering and that He would remember him when He returned to earth.

I then noticed that the Lamb's Book of Life had two seals remaining on it. I wondered when we would get to see the contents of the book. These thoughts were interrupted, for Jesus then broke open the sixth seal. {12} I watched as the Lamb opened the sixth seal. There was a great earthquake on earth. Earth's sun turned black like sackcloth made of goat hair, the whole moon turned blood red, {13} and many meteors impacted the earth, as late figs drop from a fig tree when shaken by a strong wind. {14} Then, the sky receded like a scroll, rolling up, and every mountain and island was removed from its place. {15} Then the kings of the earth, the princes, the generals, the rich, the mighty, and every slave and every free man hid in caves and among the rocks of the mountains. {16} They called to the falling hailstones and rocks,

NIV

{12} I watched as he opened the sixth seal. There was a great earthquake. The sun turned black like sackcloth made of goat hair, the whole moon turned blood red,

{13} and the stars in the sky fell to earth, as late figs drop from a fig tree when shaken by a strong wind. {14} The sky receded like a scroll, rolling up, and every mountain and island was removed from its place. {15} Then the kings of the earth, the princes, the generals, the rich, the mighty, and every slave and every free man hid in caves and among the rocks of the mountains. {16} They called to the mountains and the rocks, "Fall on us and hide

NIV

us from the face of him who sits on the throne and from the wrath of the Lamb!

{17} For the great day of their wrath has come, and who can stand?"

Interlaced thoughts

some as big as mountains, saying, "Fall on us and hide us from the face of the Father who sits on His throne and from the wrath of the Lamb who sits at His right hand! {17} For the great day of their wrath has come, and who can stand?" This seal describes the horror of the wicked at the Second Coming of Jesus.

As I thought about these scenes, three things impressed me. First, even at the Second Coming, the Book of Life is not opened so that the Father is not yet vindicated. I learned that the seventh seal is not opened until the millennium is finished.[19] Secondly, I was impressed with the fact that the seals are progressive and additive in nature. Each broken seal reveals a brighter and clearer understanding of who Jesus really is and the powers that He has. For example, the first seal reveals the salvation of Jesus, the second seal reveals the supremacy of His Word, the third seal reveals His ministry in heaven, the fourth seal reveals His authority over men, the fifth seal reveals the faith of Jesus in His martyrs and the sixth seal physically reveals the true King of Kings.

Lastly, the first six seals relate to each other in a special way. The first three seals are *causes,* and the next three seals are their *effects*. For example, the first seal describes the work of the first living creature

Interlaced thoughts

impressing upon man the need of salvation through Jesus and the sixth seal is the full realization of that salvation. The second seal describes the distribution of the teachings of Jesus (Bible) all over the world and the fifth seal culminates with martyrdom over Bible truth. Finally, the judgment-hour message begun during the third seal is consummated during the horrific destruction of the fourth seal. During the third seal, the dead of ages past are judged while under the fourth seal, the living upon earth are judged. Thus, the fourth seal affirms the validity of the message begun during the third seal.

NIV

References

1. Revelation 3:7-8; 2 Chronicles 4:22; Isaiah 22:22
2. 2 Corinthians 12:2
3. Daniel 7:9
4. Psalm 68:17,18; Matthew 27:52
5. Revelation 1:20
6. Ezekiel 1 & 10
7. Exodus 32:32; Psalms 139:13-17; Luke 10:20
8. Zechariah 4:10
9. Daniel 7:13,14; Luke 1:32; Hebrews 2:8
10. Hebrews 8:1, 9:12
11. Zechariah 1:8-11; 4:6
12. Hebrews 4:12, Ephesians 6:17
13. Appendix D
14. Ezekiel 14:12-23
15. Appendix C
16. Exodus 29:12
17. Revelation 14:13
18. 1 Thessalonians 4:16,17; John 6:38-40
19. Revelation 20:12

Prophecy 8

Revelation 7:1-8:1

Beginning point in time: Selection of 144,000 around 1994?
Ending point in time: End of the millennium
Synopsis: This prophecy begins with Jesus selecting 144,000 servants from among the spiritual heirs of Abraham. These servants will faithfully tell the world about the terms of salvation during the tribulation that God is going to send upon the world. A large, numberless multitude will receive salvation during the great tribulation as a result of the 144,000. Then, John briefly mentions the opening of the seventh seal. This final event reveals what God knew before He began to create anything.

NIV	Interlaced thoughts
{1} After this I saw four angels standing at the four corners of the earth, holding back the four winds of the earth to prevent any wind from blowing on the land or on the sea or on any tree.	{1} I, John, seemed to return to earth after the scenes in heaven's throne room. I learned that before Jesus returned to earth with great glory, He was going to send seven redemptive judgments upon mankind. I also saw that before these judgments should fall, He would select 144,000 people to tell the world about the meaning of the judgments. I saw the earth laid out like a great compass. I saw four angels standing at the four corners, holding back the wrath of God. The four winds are God's judgments. Sword, famine, plague and wild beasts will fall upon the land, sea and trees when 144,000 servants of Jesus are ready.[1]
{2} Then I saw another angel coming up from the east, having the seal of the living God. He called out in a loud voice to the four angels who had been given power to harm the land and the sea:	{2} Then I saw Jesus approaching the earth from the east. This was not the Second Coming, but His coming like a thief.[2] He had the seal of the living God in His hand[3], which He was going to place upon those people who had been found worthy to serve as prophets of the

Interlaced thoughts

Most High God. He called out in a loud voice to the four angels who had been given authority and power to harm the land and the sea: {3} "Do not harm the land or the sea or the trees until I put a seal on the foreheads of the servants of our God." I understood this seal to be the approval of God. The people who received the name of God in their foreheads were reckoned by God as worthy of suffering on behalf of the gospel. They were about to enter into experience that Jesus went through when He was upon earth – the experience of hateful rejection. {4} Then I heard the number of those who were sealed: 144,000 believers from all the nations on earth.[4] These are the firstfruits of those who have become heirs of the promise given to Abraham, because like Abraham, they know how to live by faith. This is why they are identified as the offspring of Israel:

{5} From the tribe of Judah 12,000 were sealed, Reuben 12,000, Gad 12,000, {6} Asher 12,000, Naphtali 12,000, Manasseh 12,000, {7} Simeon 12,000, Levi 12,000, Issachar 12,000, {8} Zebulun 12,000, Joseph 12,000, and from the tribe of Benjamin 12,000.

Note: The tribe of Dan is not mentioned here for that tribe probably disappeared during the apostasy of ancient Israel. See Deuteronomy 4:26,27. Because they

NIV

{3} "Do not harm the land or the sea or the trees until we put a seal on the foreheads of the servants of our God."

{4} Then I heard the number of those who were sealed: 144,000 from all the tribes of Israel.

{5} From the tribe of Judah 12,000 were sealed, from the tribe of Reuben 12,000, from the tribe of Gad 12,000, {6} from the tribe of Asher 12,000, from the tribe of Naphtali 12,000, from the tribe of Manasseh 12,000, {7} from the tribe of Simeon 12,000, from the tribe of Levi 12,000, from the tribe of Issachar 12,000, {8} from the tribe of Zebulun 12,000, from the tribe of Joseph 12,000, from the tribe of Benjamin 12,000.

NIV	Interlaced thoughts
	occupied the northern frontier, they likely perished at the hands of invaders from the North. However, the tribe of Levi, which was not counted in the inheritance of the twelve, takes the place of Dan in this list. Also, the tribe of Joseph is another name for the tribe of Ephraim. Lastly, the reader should notice that only 12,000 *from* each tribe shall be chosen as servants of the gospel of Christ during end times.
{9} After this I looked and there before me was a great multitude that no one could count, from every nation, tribe, people and language, standing before the throne and in front of the Lamb. They were wearing white robes and were holding palm branches in their hands.	{9} After I saw the selection and sealing of the 144,000 servants, I saw the great harvest of their labors shortly after the activities of the Second Coming were completed. When we arrived in heaven, I looked and there before me was a great multitude that no one could count, from every nation, tribe, people and language, standing before the throne and in front of the Lamb. They were wearing white robes and were holding palm branches in their hands.
{10} And they cried out in a loud voice: "Salvation belongs to our God, who sits on the throne, and to the Lamb."	{10} And they cried out in a loud voice: "Salvation belongs to our God, who sits on the throne, and to the Lamb." The redeemed sang this song because they had received God's free gift of righteousness. It was theirs because they were willing to grasp it by faith.
{11} All the angels were standing around the throne and around the elders and the four living creatures.	{11} All the angels were standing around the throne and around the elders and the four living creatures. Heaven had assembled to welcome

Interlaced thoughts

home these earthly pilgrims. At the song of the redeemed, the angels, living creatures and elders fell down on their faces before the throne and worshiped God,

{12} saying: "Amen! Praise and glory and wisdom and thanks and honor and power and strength be to our God for ever and ever. Amen!"

{13} Then one of the elders came over to me and asked, "These in white robes – who are they, and where did they come from?" {14} I answered, "Sir, you know." And he said, "John, your readers need to know that these are they who have endured the great tribulation. These are the harvest which the 144,000 gathered in; these chose to place their faith in Jesus by obeying His Word; they have washed their robes and made them white by putting their faith in the blood of the Lamb. {15} Therefore, they serve closest to the throne of God. They serve Him as priests and kings, day and night in His temple; and He who sits on the throne will spread His tent over them. {16} Never again will they hunger like they did during the great tribulation; never again will they thirst as they did during the days of God's wrath. The sun will not beat upon them, nor any scorching heat as in the days of tribulation." {17} For the Lamb at the center of the throne will be their shepherd; He will lead them to springs of living water. And God

NIV

They fell down on their faces before the throne and worshiped God,

{12} saying: "Amen! Praise and glory and wisdom and thanks and honor and power and strength be to our God for ever and ever. Amen!"

{13} Then one of the elders asked me, "These in white robes – who are they, and where did they come from?" {14} I answered, "Sir, you know." And he said, "These are they who have come out of the great tribulation; they have washed their robes and made them white in the blood of the Lamb.

{15} Therefore, they are before the throne of God and serve him day and night in his temple; and he who sits on the throne will spread his tent over them.

{16} Never again will they hunger; never again will they thirst. The sun will not beat upon them, nor any scorching heat.

{17} For the Lamb at the center of the throne will be their shepherd; he will lead them to springs of living

NIV

water. And God will wipe away every tear from their eyes."

{8:1} When he opened the seventh seal, there was silence in heaven for about half an hour.

Interlaced thoughts

will wipe away every tear from their eyes. He will grant them joy and happiness beyond understanding."

As I watched this glorious scene, I wondered why anyone would choose to miss heaven. I wondered how Jesus would reveal these things to the billions of earth.

{8:1} Then, my view was directed to the end of the millennium. I saw the Book of Life which had one remaining seal upon it. Immediately, I remembered the story surrounding the book. Now, the book would be opened!

I saw Jesus standing before all inhabitants of Heaven and Earth. Only at this time in earth's existence will everyone be alive who has ever lived upon earth. The righteous were in the Holy City. The wicked had been resurrected and were standing outside the city. Then, everyone looked up into heaven to watch a panorama of their life. They saw their life pass in full review. They saw their life's record which had been faithfully recorded by angels. In addition, to their life's record, everyone beheld Christ's shame at Calvary—then everyone saw and understood the seriousness of the plan of salvation. Then, every person saw *why* he was either inside or outside the Holy City, the New Jerusalem. The panorama lasted for some time. After it ended, people stood in awe. The wicked could not argue with the fairness of their

Interlaced thoughts

sentence. The saints could not fathom the mercy of God. And then, Jesus broke open the seventh seal. Again, a panoramic revelation was given to everyone. As we watched, there was silence—this time, for about a half-hour. What we saw made every knee bow! Then I understood the seventh seal.

With the first panorama, everyone had recognized and admitted the justice or mercy of Jesus as it pertained to their eternal destiny. Every person had admitted before the great white throne that Jesus' judgment was righteous and true altogether. But, when Jesus broke open the last seal on the Book of Life, the effect was overwhelming, for the Father had written down everything that had happened in advance. The Father knew who would choose salvation and who wouldn't even before the angels were created. But, everyone saw at the same time that He did not use His foreknowledge to predestine the outcome. Everyone had exercised their own choices. The books of record were identical with the Book of Life with one exception. Those who had rejected the Holy Spirit were not found in the Book of Life. They could not live for eternity—their names had been blotted out of the Book of Life. See Prophecy 17.

NIV

References

1. Revelation 6:7,8
2. Matthew 24:36-25:13
3. Revelation 3:12
4. Before ancient Israel entered the Promised Land, they were required to send one man, a leader, from each tribe to spy out the land and then give a report to the people. (Numbers 13:1) Further, a census was required. The purpose for the census was to determine how the land should be distributed. It was to be divided according to the size of the tribes. (Numbers 1 & 26; Joshua 11:23) In a similar way, before entering heaven, Jesus will select 144,000 servants. He will reveal to them the imminent establishment of the kingdom of heaven. Then, these are to tell the world of the return of Jesus so that all the world might prepare to meet its Maker. When the roll is called in heaven after the Second Coming, the 144,000 will be identified as those faith-full servants who fearlessly proclaimed the final message of mercy. These will be the sons of Jacob (Israel) in the earth made new. (Romans 9:7,8, 11:17-26; James 1:1; Revelation 21:12)

Prophecy 9

Revelation 8:2-9:21

Beginning point in time: 1994?
Ending point in time: About the time of the close of probation
Synopsis: This prophecy explains how the judgments of the fourth seal will be implemented upon the world. Be warned that 25% of earth will perish before the Second Coming of Jesus. The purpose of these six trumpets is redemptive; that is, God wants people to wake up and hear the final call of mercy. The story is horrible. But, what does it say of the human race when Jesus is left with no other means of getting our attention than by sending horrific judgments?

NIV

{2} And I saw the seven angels who stand before God, and to them were given seven trumpets.

{3} Another angel, who had a golden censer, came and stood at the altar. He was given much incense to offer, with the prayers of all the saints, on the golden altar before the throne.

Interlaced thoughts

{2} I looked up into heaven and I saw the seven angels of the seven churches who stand before God. Each one of them was given a trumpet. I saw that the first four trumpets were horrific warnings from Jesus that He was angry with the sins of man. I saw that the last three trumpets were horrible events that will lead the people of the world to complete ruin. {3} Then, I saw a highly exalted angel holding a golden censer. This instrument of atonement had been in use for a long time. It is used each day in heaven in a service of atonement for the sins of the whole world. Christ's intercession for man began the day He stepped between the wrath of God and Adam and Eve. Ever since, Jesus has spared the *world* from immediate destruction through corporate intercession. Now that Jesus had been given all power and was seated on the throne, the care of this censer had been entrusted to an exalted angel which stood before the altar of incense.

Interlaced thoughts

The angel was given much incense to offer on the altar because many saints on earth were earnestly praying to God for strength to face the judgments that were about to fall upon the earth. {4} The smoke of the incense, together with the petitions of the saints, went up before God from the angel's hand. Then Jesus commanded the Holy Spirit to empower the praying saints. The Latter Rain fell, first upon the 144,000 and then upon those who believed their prophetic messages. The 144,000 warned all who would listen that the corporate intercession of Jesus on behalf of the world was about to end. The nations were due to receive God's wrath. But, the seven trumpets would be mixed with mercy so that individuals who did not yet know God's truth about salvation could be awakened and saved.

{5} To signify the end of Jesus' corporate intercession for the nations, the angel took the censer, filled it with fire from the altar, and hurled it down to the earth.[1] And immediately there came peals of thunder from heaven. The 144,000 heard the thunder and recognized the voice of Jesus as He spoke to them.[2] There were rumblings deep inside the earth as though demons were terrified by these events. The people of earth were awed by great flashes of lightning that filled the whole sky. The lightning was brighter than the sun at noon. And

NIV

{4} The smoke of the incense, together with the prayers of the saints, went up before God from the angel's hand.

{5} Then the angel took the censer, filled it with fire from the altar, and hurled it on the earth; and there came peals of thunder, rumblings, flashes of lightning and an earthquake.

NIV

Interlaced thoughts

then, a great earthquake shook the whole world.[3] Even the most avowed agnostic was shaken. Every person on earth knew something had happened, but only a few understood what was going on. The praying saints understood that Christ's ministry on behalf of the world was finished, and now time for the judgments of God had come. The saints had anticipated these signs. They had waited and watched for this hour, and now filled with the Holy Spirit, they went forward proclaiming the gospel and the terms of salvation with even greater boldness.

{6} Then the seven angels who had the seven trumpets prepared to sound them.

{6} Then, the seven angels who had the seven trumpets prepared to sound them so that the people of earth could know that Jesus was closing His intercession in heaven on behalf of individuals. The angels waited to sound their trumpets until Jesus told them to sound.

{7} The first angel sounded his trumpet, and there came hail and fire mixed with blood, and it was hurled down upon the earth. A third of the earth was burned up, a third of the trees were burned up, and all the green grass was burned up.

{7} The first angel sounded his trumpet, and there came a fiery hailstorm that mixed with the blood of many people. The hail came in the form of a meteoric shower of burning rocks that affected every continent of earth. From my view, a third of the land was burned up, a third of the trees were burned up, and all the green grass was burned up in the affected areas. The four angels I saw holding back the four winds of God's wrath in Prophecy 8 are the same angels of the first four

Interlaced thoughts

trumpets. These had been told to hold back their destruction until the 144,000 were sealed. Now that God's servants were ready, Jesus dispatched the first angel of the seven trumpets. The widespread destruction of crops, trees and land by the fires from the first trumpet reverberated throughout the whole earth. All nations quickly concluded that God was angry. Then, some of the people of earth listened more carefully to the 144,000. A large number of sincere people gave their lives to Jesus as a result of this trumpet.

{8} With Jesus' approval, the second angel sounded his trumpet, and a blazing half-mile wide asteroid flew through the earth's atmosphere at a terrific rate of speed. It impacted the sea and immediately, a third of the ships upon the sea were destroyed by the enormous tidal wave that followed.[4] Many wicked sea ports were also buried in a wall of water that was very great in height. Because the asteroid was so hot, it boiled the oxygen out of the water {9} and a third of the living creatures of this sea died. Later, red algae took over the area and the sea looked like blood. Red algae thrives in anoxic water. The effects of this judgment were felt by the whole world until the end of time.

The people of earth were filled with fear. The 144,000 spoke of more

NIV

{8} The second angel sounded his trumpet, and something like a huge mountain, all ablaze, was thrown into the sea. A third of the sea turned into blood,

{9} a third of the living creatures in the sea died, and a third of the ships were destroyed.

NIV	Interlaced thoughts
	judgments to come. And, people openly lamented the sinful conditions of the world, but many refused to submit to the terms of God's salvation.
{10} The third angel sounded his trumpet, and a great star, blazing like a torch, fell from the sky on a third of the rivers and on the springs of water–	{10} With Jesus' approval, the third angel sounded his trumpet, and a great star, having a long tail like a blazing torch, fell from the sky on a third of the rivers and on the springs of water. This second and even larger asteroid fell upon a nation known for its wickedness. It collided with the earth at a high rate of speed and it released the energy of millions of atomic bombs. It seemed as though the earth itself would break into pieces. Indeed, the great tectonic plates of earth were broken and everyone felt a great shock. Ground waves travelled from the impact zone at hundreds of miles per hour. The event happened so fast that people didn't know what happened at first. The ground waves sheered water-wells and septic systems everywhere. Great aquifers beneath cities became contaminated with sewage and the water became contaminated. As a result, tens of thousands died from drinking the water.
{11} the name of the star is Wormwood. A third of the waters turned bitter, and many people died from the waters that had become bitter.	{11} People called the star, the star of death. In my day, they would have called it "Wormwood" which means a taste of death.
{12} The fourth angel sounded his trumpet, and a third of the sun was struck, a third of the moon, and a	{12} With Jesus' approval, the fourth angel sounded his trumpet, and the Pacific ring of fire erupted. Many great volcanoes spewed

Interlaced thoughts

billions of tons of ejecta into the atmosphere. It seemed as though Mother Earth was vomiting up all the evil that was buried in her soil. So great were the convulsions that darkness fell upon the earth. Sunlight could not penetrate the clouds of ash and debris. At first, the pall of night covered the face of earth. Then, weather patterns organized the darkness. The jet stream carried large quantities of ash around the world in a large band. A third of earth did not receive the light of the sun, moon and stars. Wherever the band of darkness was carried, one third of the world turned very dark. So, a third of the planet was without light from heaven night and day. {13} As I watched these horrific scenes, I heard the fourth living creature, the one who had the face of the eagle. He was flying in midair, and he called out in a loud voice: "Woe! Woe! Woe to the inhabitants of the earth, because of the trumpet blasts about to be sounded by the other three angels!"

I soon understood the meaning of this cry. In Prophecy 7, the fourth living creature had transformed himself into a pale horse and he had come to earth to kill 25% of the people with sword, famine, plague and wild beasts after Jesus opened the fourth seal. I saw that the judgments of the trumpets explained how sword, famine, plagues and wild beasts are

NIV

third of the stars, so that a third of them turned dark. A third of the day was without light, and also a third of the night.

{13} As I watched, I heard an eagle that was flying in midair call out in a loud voice: "Woe! Woe! Woe to the inhabitants of the earth, because of the trumpet blasts about to be sounded by the other three angels!"

NIV

Interlaced thoughts

implemented. So, the fourth living creature spoke because *he* was overseeing the destructive works of the seven angels with the seven trumpets.

But, this warning message by the fourth living creature is especially directed at those in the world who have not submitted to the terms of the gospel. This message warns that Jesus is about to send three curses upon mankind. In other words, the effects of the trumpets are going to get much worse and more specific! Before this vision had finished, I understood what he meant.

{9:1} The fifth angel sounded his trumpet, and I saw a star that had fallen from the sky to the earth. The star was given the key to the shaft of the Abyss.

{9:1} With Jesus' approval, the fifth angel sounded his trumpet and the first of three curses fell upon mankind. I saw a star that had fallen from the sky to the earth with his followers.[5] This fallen star was once the highest of all angels. His name was Lucifer, which means son of the dawn, the first of creation, and he was next in rank to the archangel, Michael. (Michael, incidently, is the name Jesus had before He was born of woman.) After Lucifer was expelled from heaven, Gabriel was appointed to serve in his place. Now on earth, Lucifer's name was changed. He is known as the devil, the adversary of mankind. I saw him fall like a star when He was kicked out of heaven. There will more information about the devil in Prophecy 12.

Interlaced thoughts

The devil was given the key to his prison in the Abyss where he and his demons had been placed. Actually, the Abyss is an expression meaning the spirit world, the place where demons live. When the devil was finally cast out of heaven, he was required to stay on earth and required to stay in the spirit world. In other words, God restricted the devil from certain physical manifestations. But, upon receiving the key to the Abyss, the devil and his demonic followers are free to physically appear before the people of earth.[6]

{2} So the devil quickly opened his prison. I saw a cloud rising from the Abyss like smoke from a gigantic furnace. The sun and sky were darkened by the cloud from the Abyss. The physical appearing of the devil and his angels in the heavens was so great that they darkened the sky. Such was the demonstration of their demonic powers. {3} Down from the sky, thousands of evil angels came like a swarm of locusts and they were granted authority by Jesus to harm people with their scorpion-like venom. {4} They were forbidden to harm the physical elements of earth such as crops, plants or trees, for these had already suffered great destruction. But, they could not harm the 144,000.

NIV

{2} When he opened the Abyss, smoke rose from it like the smoke from a gigantic furnace. The sun and sky were darkened by the smoke from the Abyss.

{3} And out of the smoke locusts came down upon the earth and were given power like that of scorpions of the earth.

{4} They were told not to harm the grass of the earth or any plant or tree, but only those people who did not have the seal of God on their foreheads.

NIV

{5} They were not given power to kill them, but only to torture them for five months. And the agony they suffered was like that of the sting of a scorpion when it strikes a man.

{6} During those days men will seek death, but will not find it; they will long to die, but death will elude them.

Interlaced thoughts

{5} They were also told that they could not kill their victims, but only to torture them for five months. I saw the agony the people suffered and it was like the agony of the sting of a scorpion when it strikes a man. {6} The pain was unbearable. During those days men will seek death, but will not find it; they will long to die, but death will elude them. I wondered why Jesus would allow the devil to torment the people to such extreme. Then the answer came.

The purpose of the trumpets is three-fold. First, Jesus wants to awaken every person on earth to the realization that He is returning to earth. Secondly, Jesus wants every person to know that He is King and Lord over the peoples of earth. But, if we choose to reject our Creator as Lord and King, then we are left with the devil as our lord and king. Human beings *are* lower in rank than angels and are thus subject to them. But, the issue is *whom* human beings will serve: The Lamb or the devil. Thirdly, the trumpets will propel every person on earth into a decision. All will have to take a stand. While the 144,000 are faithfully telling the world about the salvation of God, the devil is working through the religious systems of the world to subvert their message and destroy those who worship the Most High God. So, the crux of the matter comes down to this: one group will

Interlaced thoughts

obey the Lamb, the other will obey the devil.

For these reasons, the Lord allows the devil to physically appear on earth. The people of earth are entitled to see whom they are really following. The devil will appear and claim that he is God Almighty. The devil and his demons will use their tormenting powers of unbearable agony. They will torment those rebelling against the devil and his great blasphemies. Those who speak out will be "struck" by the demons with unbearable pain. Fear of painful punishment will subdue most. But, Jesus only grants the devil five months of time to appear on earth and arrange his forces to take control of the world.

{7} I watched as the locust-like swarm of Satan's angels came closer to earth. From a distance they looked like riders on horses prepared for battle. It was clear they were on a mission of destruction. On their heads they wore something that looked like crowns of gold, perhaps identifying their rank in the devil's army and their faces resembled human faces. They were beautiful, but fearful in appearance. {8} Their hair was long and flowing like women's hair, and their teeth were strong like lions' teeth. {9} They had breastplates like breastplates of iron, and the sound of their wings was like the thundering of many horses and

NIV

{7} The locusts looked like horses prepared for battle. On their heads they wore something like crowns of gold, and their faces resembled human faces.

{8} Their hair was like women's hair, and their teeth were like lions' teeth.

{9} They had breastplates like breastplates of iron, and the sound of their wings was like the

NIV

thundering of many horses and chariots rushing into battle.

{10} They had tails and stings like scorpions, and in their tails they had power to torment people for five months.

{11} They had as king over them the angel of the Abyss, whose name in Hebrew is Abaddon, and in Greek, Apollyon.

Interlaced thoughts

chariots rushing into battle. From these characteristics, I realized the angels of the devil were far superior to any man of war. Men were powerless against them. Bullets could not kill them. Bombs could not stop them. The angels of the devil had powers greater than any man. The wicked felt helpless and vulnerable. The saints knew their only hope was in Jesus.

{10} The Lord showed me something about the angels of the devil. He represented their method of hurting people with tails and stings like scorpions, for in their tails they had power to torment people for five months. Actually, the angels didn't have long ugly tails that scorpions have. But, they did inflict unbearable pain on the wicked whenever they touched them. Thus, through the penalty of pain, many people submitted to the devil. The devil's angels punished anyone who spoke out against their king, the devil. Only the 144,000 were free from the sting of sin.

{11} As I watched the devil, I realized three things about him. First, he claimed to be the God of heaven. It was obvious that he had great miracle-working powers and he used them to advance his evil plans. He could be nice when he wanted to appear that way and he could be a dragon whenever that suited his purposes. Secondly, in those days, there seemed to be no law or

Interlaced thoughts

reason. Terror ruled the day. People were killed for no reason. Any act could be construed as evil and punishment was swift and certain. The devil acted according to whim and none could stop him.

Many people rejected God's truth as presented by the 144,000 and they accepted the devil as their leader. To gain his favor, they would attack God's people and kill them as they could. This pleased the devil greatly for he and his angels could not harm God's people directly. I asked why Jesus would allow his people to perish like this. I was told that Jesus wants the universe to behold the extremity of sin and rebellion. This is an awesome fact: wicked men will destroy the innocent on a wholesale scale even when they know it is wrong. This has been done throughout history and it will be done again. (The reader may want to review the matter of martyrdom in Prophecy 7, Revelation 6:9.)

Lastly, I saw the devil's control of earth grow steadily. It was awful. The angel from the Abyss became king over the world. In Hebrew the name of the devil is Abaddon, and in Greek, Apollyon. Both names mean the same thing: the ultimate destroyer. {12} I heard a voice say, "The first woe is past; two other woes are yet to come." Given the severity of this woe, I could not stand to look upon the scenes that

NIV

{12} The first woe is past; two other woes are yet to come.

NIV

{13} The sixth angel sounded his trumpet, and I heard a voice coming from the horns of the golden altar that is before God.

{14} It said to the sixth angel who had the trumpet, "Release the four angels who are bound at the great river Euphrates."

{15} And the four angels who had been kept ready for this very hour and day and month and year were released to kill a third of mankind.

Interlaced thoughts

followed until I was strengthened by an angel from the Lord.

{13} With Jesus' permission, the sixth angel sounded his trumpet, and I heard the voice of the mighty angel who stood at the golden altar of incense that is before God. This great angel is responsible for presenting the prayers of the saints before Jesus. He also insures that each person's commitment to Jesus is noticed in heaven. Because he saw that a few people had not yet made a final decision for God's salvation, {14} He said to the sixth angel who had the trumpet, "Release the four angels who are bound at the great river Euphrates." This phrase means "Let the angels of God who stir the winds of war go throughout the earth."[7]

{15} And the four angels who had been kept ready for this very hour and day and month and year were released to kill a third of mankind.

The four angels holding back global war let go when the five months of the fifth trumpet ends. Now, a tide of war will sweep over the world. Immediately, the devil rallied his followers. He sent his demons all over the world to incite rebellion against the 144,000 and others who oppose him. The devil swiftly moved to take control of the world. Yes, the war may be between men, for the devil and his angels are not allowed to take the life of any man, but men will obey the devil.

Interlaced thoughts

This war will not be one country against another. Rather, it will be family against family, friend against friend, brother against brother. It will be a civil war where everyone fights his brother. The issue is control of the world. The devil demands that his followers take over the governments and religious systems of the world so that all might be welded into a new, one-world order with himself as king.

{16} Currently, the world has less than eight million troops in uniform. However, the number of mounted troops in those days was millions of millions. I heard the number and it was beyond calculation because everybody will be involved in this struggle.

{17} The horses and riders I saw in my vision looked different than the horses and riders of the fifth trumpet. These horses were not so powerful and invincible. These horses belonged to men. They looked like this: Their breastplates were made of cloth. Some were fiery red, dark blue, and yellow like sulfur. I noticed their weapons. The heads of their horses resembled the heads of lions, and out of their mouths came fire, smoke and sulfur. While this isn't a true description of their weapons, it represents the devices they used to kill one another. It appeared to me that they used explosives to shoot at one another and poisonous gas to kill

NIV

{16} The number of the mounted troops was two hundred million. I heard their number.

{17} The horses and riders I saw in my vision looked like this: Their breastplates were fiery red, dark blue, and yellow as sulfur. The heads of the horses resembled the heads of lions, and out of their mouths came fire, smoke and sulfur.

NIV

{18} A third of mankind was killed by the three plagues of fire, smoke and sulfur that came out of their mouths.

{19} The power of the horses was in their mouths and in their tails; for their tails were like snakes, having heads with which they inflict injury.

{20} The rest of mankind that were not killed by these plagues still did not repent of the work of their hands; they did not stop worshiping demons, and idols of gold, silver, bronze, stone and wood - idols that cannot see or hear or walk.

Interlaced thoughts

thousands. The carnage was great. {18} A third of mankind was killed by the three plagues of fire, smoke and sulfur that came out of their mouths.

{19} I also noticed horses from the sky. They could shoot from the front or from the tails of their horses.

The war was the bloodiest ever fought on earth. The cruelty between people was unbelievable. I asked, 'why did this awful war have to happen?' The answer that came back was, 'so that every person might be reached with the gospel and so that every person might finally decide for or against the truth.' Then I understood. When the war began, God's people scattered everywhere. Obviously, they carried the gospel with them. In this manner, the most remote places of earth heard the gospel so that everyone could decide what they were going to do. It was perfectly wonderful how Jesus accomplished His goals as the devil set out to accomplish his.

{20} By the end of the war, the devil accomplished four things. First, he had gained control of the world. Secondly, he had created a "one world look alike" religious system; that is, he had consolidate the world's religious systems into one world-wide religion. Thirdly, he had divided the world into ten sectors and placed powerful men as rulers

Interlaced thoughts

over the people of earth. And lastly, he set up an economic system designed to starve out any opposition. He required that if any person wanted to buy or sell, he had to wear a tatoo on his hand or forehead. This would show allegiance to his one-world order. By doing this, the devil planned to starve his opposition into submission.

The amazing thing about this war is that the rest of mankind that were not killed by these plagues still did not repent of the work of their hands; they did not stop worshiping demons, and idols of gold, silver, bronze, stone and wood - idols that cannot see or hear or walk.
{21} Nor did they repent of their murders, their magic arts, their sexual immorality or their thefts.

By the end of this great war, everyone had reached a decision about God. Everyone had submitted to either the laws of the devil or to the law of God. The first two woes had accomplished a great deal, awful as they were. Then I beheld the severity of the final woe which Jesus is going send upon the world. That woe will be poured out without mercy. It will be felt by all who worship the devil and receive his mark. It will be introduced in Prophecy 11.

NIV

{21} Nor did they repent of their murders, their magic arts, their sexual immorality or their thefts.

References

1. Daniel 12:11
2. Revelation 10:4
3. Hebrews 12:27
4. Luke 21:25,26
5. Revelation 12:4
6. Revelation 17:8
7. Isaiah 8:6-8; Hosea 5:10; Daniel 9:26, 11:10,40

For a parallel description of trumpet five, read Joel 2. Especially contrast the appearing of Satan with the appearing of the Lord.

Prophecy 10

Revelation 10:1-11:13

Beginning point in time: Late 1993?
Ending point in time: Just before the Second Coming
Synopsis: This prophecy explains to a great extent, the ministry and work of the 144,000. In addition, this story reveals an important secret. The 144,000 will be taken to heaven about 45 days before the Second Coming and they will return with Jesus at His Second Coming! Imagine the bewilderment of the wicked when they see martyrs resurrected in glorious bodies. Even more, what will they say when the hated 144,000 reappear with Jesus! What a day of vindication that will be.

NIV

{1} Then I saw another mighty angel coming down from heaven. He was robed in a cloud, with a rainbow above his head; his face was like the sun, and his legs were like fiery pillars.

{2} He was holding a little scroll, which lay open in his hand. He planted his right foot on the sea and his left foot on the land,

Interlaced thoughts

{1} My view of events on earth was taken back to a time before the 144,000 were sealed. I saw Jesus tell the four angels holding back the four winds to wait while He took care of some business. Jesus was robed in a cloud so that His glory might not be seen by the world. The rainbow above his head and the brilliance of His face was like the sun. His legs were like glowing fiery pillars. There was no question that this being was Jesus. {2} He was holding a small book, which lay open in his hand. This was a different book than the Book of Life which had seven seals on it. This book was much smaller and at this point in time, the Book of Life still had four more seals to be opened. I wondered what this book might represent. As I watched, Jesus planted his right foot on the sea and his left foot on the land. His stance was like that of a confident military general. I gathered from His posture that Jesus had taken a bold position against His adversary

Interlaced thoughts

{3} and he gave a loud shout like the roar of the king of beasts. This shout was heard and understood by the 144,000. They knew who they were and that they had been empowered to begin a special work. I understood the shout but the rest of the world only heard a thunder. When Jesus shouted, seven thunderous voices also spoke.

{4} And when the seven thunders spoke, I understood what they said and was about to write down their words; but someone spoke to me from heaven saying, "John, seal up what the seven thunders have said and do not write it down." At first, I thought this was strange until I understood that those who have ears to hear will hear and understand the different messages of the seven thunders when they are given. These messages will occur at selected moments as the saints go through the tribulation. They will receive these messages from God and be greatly encouraged in their struggle.

{5} Then Jesus raised his right hand toward heaven. {6} And he swore by the Name of the Father, the Maker of everything and said, "There will be no more waiting![1] The time has come for My wrath to be poured out.[2] Earth has filled its cup of iniquity. Seventy Jubilee cycles of time have fully expired and now, the earth must be visited in mercy with the judgments of the seven trumpets.[3] All who repent and call upon the Name of the Lord

NIV

{3} and he gave a loud shout like the roar of a lion. When he shouted, the voices of the seven thunders spoke.

{4} And when the seven thunders spoke, I was about to write; but I heard a voice from heaven say, "Seal up what the seven thunders have said and do not write it down."

{5} Then the angel I had seen standing on the sea and on the land raised his right hand to heaven. {6} And he swore by him who lives for ever and ever, who created the heavens and all that is in them, the earth and all that is in it, and the sea and all that is in it, and said, "There will be no more delay!

NIV

{7} But in the days when the seventh angel is about to sound his trumpet, the mystery of God will be accomplished, just as he announced to his servants the prophets."

{8} Then the voice that I had heard from heaven spoke to me once more: "Go, take the scroll that lies open in the hand of the angel who is standing on the sea and on the land."

{9} So I went to the angel and asked him to give me the little scroll. He said to me, "Take it and eat it. It will turn your stomach sour, but in your mouth it will be as sweet as honey."

Interlaced thoughts

will be saved. {7} But in the days when the seventh angel is about to sound his trumpet, the mystery of God will be accomplished. The mystery revealed is that God is going to bestow victory upon all who want power over sin.[4] This will be the time of the empowerment of the latter rain, and all who choose to live by the testimony of Jesus, and are willing to live by faith—these will be given power over sin. This gift has been revealed to My 144,000 servants, the prophets."

{8} Then a voice spoke to me from heaven. It invited me to go through the experience of the 144,000 so I could write down the plans of God. I eagerly agreed to cooperate, for serving King Jesus is always a joy. The voice said, "Go, take the little book that lies open in the hand of Jesus who is standing on the sea and on the land." {9} So I went over to Jesus and asked him to give me the little book. He said, "Take it and eat it. It will turn your stomach sour, but in your mouth it will be as sweet as honey."[5] I asked Jesus what the little book represented. He said it represented the prophecies of Daniel and Revelation which were now unsealed.[6] He said the 144,000 would understand these prophecies *before* the predicted events occur. He also said that the understanding would be a wonderful and sweet experience. He emphasized that it is important for the 144,000 to

Interlaced thoughts

understand the prophecies so that they could show all nations about God's plans and purposes from the written word: the Bible. During the tribulation, it will be very important to know and understand the Bible because men will eventually kill one another over what is truth. This is the bitter part and the 144,000 will be among the most rejected and persecuted people on earth.
{10} So, I took the little book from the hand of Jesus ate it. The understanding of the prophecies was sweet as honey, but when I began to experience the things predicted in the little book, the experience was very bitter. {11} I was then told, "You must prophesy again about many peoples, nations, languages and kings." I thought about these words for some time. I knew that under the operation of the third seal, a judgment-hour message had gone throughout the earth in a limited way. I also knew that few people correctly understood the works of Jesus in the heavenly sanctuary. I then realized that the judgment hour message given under the third seal was incomplete. This is why the 144,000 must preach *again* from the books of Daniel and Revelation. They would proclaim a complete message. Now it made sense. The seven trumpets would awaken the world to hear the gospel, and the 144,000 would proclaim the prophetic stories of Daniel and Revelation with great

NIV

{10} I took the little scroll from the angel's hand and ate it. It tasted as sweet as honey in my mouth, but when I had eaten it, my stomach turned sour.

{11} Then I was told, "You must prophesy again about many peoples, nations, languages and kings."

NIV	Interlaced thoughts
	clarity and power and many would be saved! I marvelled at the works of Jesus.
{11:1} I was given a reed like a measuring rod and was told, "Go and measure the temple of God and the altar, and count the worshipers there.	{11:1} My first experience, as one of the 144,000 was a difficult one. I was given a measuring-stick and was told, "Go and determine the true size of the temple of God. You will find many in the temple who profess to be followers of Jesus, but don't be deceived. Go into the temple and you will find the people of God at the altar of the inner court. I immediately understood the connection. In Jerusalem, there were two courts at the temple. The Gentile worshiped in the outer court and the inner court was reserved for the Jews. The idea is that the inner court represents those who were more favored by God than those who were loved, but farther from His truth. So, I was to go into the church and explain the messages in the little book. Then, I was to count those who received the testimony of Jesus. I recognized that God could not use those in the inner court who would not measure up to the message in the little book. I anticipated that many in the temple would not want to hear this message and they would become very angry with me. This was the beginning of bitterness.
{2} But exclude the outer court; do not measure it, because it has been given to the Gentiles. They will trample on the holy city for 42 months.	{2} I was told, "But exclude the outer court; do not measure it, because it has been given to the Gentiles. Their time will come. In addition, the Gentiles will trample on My people

Interlaced thoughts

for 42 literal months."[7] I understood this to mean that for the moment, the 144,000 were not to concentrate on the people of the world for they had not had an opportunity to understand what the full gospel is all about. They were not to be counted until the time period of the trumpets. It dawned upon me that the faithful Gentiles would be gathered in and numbered during the time period of the seven trumpets and I thrilled again to see the works of Jesus.

I also recognized that many in the inner court and a great number in the outer court would not receive the saving message of the 144,000. I saw that they would persecute the 144,000 and those who believe them for 42 months. I was most grateful that the time granted to those who oppose God's truth is limited.

{3} Jesus told me that He would give power to His two witnesses, and they will prophesy with great power and clarity for 1,260 days, in distressing circumstances. Of course, I wanted to know who the two witnesses were. I knew that in the days of Moses, two or more witnesses were always required by the Lord to condemn a person to death.[8] I came to understand that during the final days, Jesus will give great power to His two witnesses and whoever refuses their testimony will be condemned to death.

NIV

{3} And I will give power to my two witnesses, and they will prophesy for 1,260 days, clothed in sackcloth."

NIV

{4} These are the two olive trees and the two lampstands that stand before the Lord of the earth.

Interlaced thoughts

{4} An angel told me the two witnesses were the two olive trees and the two lampstands that stand before the Lord of the earth. Because I was acquainted with Zechariah's visions, I understood. The two olive trees represent the source of eternal power. The trees symbolize the origin of the oil that fuels the works of the 144,000. This is the work of the Holy Spirit. In heaven, Zechariah saw two olive trees that produce oil so that the truth of God is kept alive upon the earth.[9] The two lampstands puzzled me at first. In the first part of Revelation, I had observed seven lampstands before the throne of God, but now there were only two. Even worse, I remembered that Zechariah saw only one lampstand. What was going on? After a few moments, I learned the meaning. The lampstands represent His agencies on earth through which He reveals the gospel of salvation. In ancient times, His holy word was given to the nation of Israel. They were the single lampstand. After Israel failed to accomplish all that God wanted, God set up seven lampstands. These represented the seven churches to which I sent copies of this vision. But, the seven churches went the ways of ancient Israel. They apostatized too. So, the last agency to reveal the gospel of salvation is the Bible. One lampstand represents the Old Testament which contains the

Interlaced thoughts

prophecy of Daniel, the other lampstand represents the New Testament which contains the prophecy of Revelation. So this is why I ate the open book in Jesus' hand! When the truth found in the Old and New Testaments are united with the two phases of Holy Spirit power, (the two trees represent early and latter rains) the world will be enlightened with the full gospel of Jesus.

{5} I saw that if anyone tries to destroy the two witnesses, they will be cut down. God will give the 144,000 great miracle-working powers to confirm their message of truth. There is nothing more powerful than a message whose time has come. The enemies of God will not be able to withstand the truth, for just as a sword comes from the mouth of Jesus at the Second Coming and devours His enemies, so truth will come from the mouths of the 144,000 and their enemies will not be able to stand. All who reject the testimony of the Bible and Holy Spirit must die the second death. {6} The 144,000 will have power to shut up the sky so that it will not rain during the time they are prophesying; and they will have power to turn the waters into blood and to strike the earth with every kind of plague as often as they want. God will grant the 144,000 these powers so that people will listen to what they say and be saved. But, the devil will have

NIV

{5} If anyone tries to harm them, fire comes from their mouths and devours their enemies. This is how anyone who wants to harm them must die.

{6} These men have power to shut up the sky so that it will not rain during the time they are prophesying; and they have power to turn the waters into blood and to strike the earth with every kind of plague as often as they want.

NIV

Interlaced thoughts

thousands of false prophets who can perform miracles and many people will like their deceptions and reject the truth. Many will believe the lies of the false prophets and be damned. Watch out: the distinguishing difference between false prophets and God's prophets is Bible truth. False prophets can perform signs and miracles, but they cannot back up their deceitful messages from the Bible. Tell the people to require a "plain thus saith the Lord."

{7} Now when they have finished their testimony, the beast that comes up from the Abyss will attack them, and overpower and kill them.

{7} Now when the Bible and the Holy Spirit have completely finished their saving testimony of salvation to the world, the devil and his angels that were unlocked from the Abyss will attack them, and overpower and utterly kill their influence. By this time, the devil will have lead the rest of the world into great rebellion against the Holy Spirit and the truth of God as found in the Bible. So, the work and influence of the Bible and Holy Spirit will come to an end. They will be finished. Everyone will have made their decision about the truth of God. Everyone will be found in one of two categories. One group will be saved, the other will be destroyed.

{8} Their bodies will lie in the street of the great city, which is figuratively called Sodom and Egypt, where also their Lord was crucified.

{8} After the seventh trumpet sounds, the remaining 144,000 will be regarded as dead men. The great powers they once had will be gone, for they are no longer necessary. They faithfully accomplished the works given them to do, but the

Interlaced thoughts

door to salvation is now closed. At this time, the devil will have established his great empire, which is figuratively called Sodom and Egypt. Sodom represents unrestrained evil and Egypt represents hardness of heart. The attitude of the world toward God's truth and His people at that time will be just like the days when Jesus was crucified.

{9} During the seven last plagues, God will send terrible judgments upon the empire of the devil. In a rage, the devil will unite all the forces of the world into a global militia. Their purpose will be to kill and destroy the remaining saints of God, especially, the remaining 144,000. The leaders of the world will assemble and agree upon a universal death decree. Three and a half days after the agreement, the decree is to be enacted and every saint is to be killed. Men from every people, tribe, language and nation will look at the poor people of God. Many will be imprisoned, others are to be captured. The saints will be told that they are the same as dead men, but they cannot kill them until the appointed hour arrives. {10} The inhabitants of the earth will gloat over the impending destruction and they will celebrate by sending each other gifts, because the saints will not be able to escape from their hands. The wicked exult, thinking that now, these people can be destroyed.

NIV

{9} For three and a half days men from every people, tribe, language and nation will gaze on their bodies and refuse them burial.

{10} The inhabitants of the earth will gloat over them and will celebrate by sending each other gifts, because these two prophets had tormented those who live on the earth.

NIV

{11} But after the three and a half days a breath of life from God entered them, and they stood on their feet, and terror struck those who saw them.

{12} Then they heard a loud voice from heaven saying to them, "Come up here." And they went up to heaven in a cloud, while their enemies looked on.

{13} At that very hour there was a severe earthquake and a tenth of the city collapsed. Seven thousand people were killed in the earthquake, and the survivors were terrified and gave glory to the God of heaven.

Interlaced thoughts

{11} When the appointed time came, three and a half days after the agreement on a universal death decree, something unexpected happened. Great power from God came upon His suffering and tormented people, and they burst out of captivity. They stood on their feet, illuminated with glory from God as Moses when he came down from the mount. Terror struck those who saw them. The wicked were powerless to carry out their evil plan of universal destruction. But even more, the ground began to move, there was an enormous earthquake and the wicked beheld the resurrection of millions of martyrs. This was too much! There before them stood their enemies in strength and power. {12} Then, the saints heard a loud voice from heaven saying, "Come up here." And the 144,000 servants of God went up to heaven in a cloud, while their enemies looked on in greater amazement.[10] While the rest of the saints waited for the Second Coming, they beheld the complete disintegration of Babylon with their own eyes.[11]

{13} When the earthquake occurred, the throne of the devil collapsed. The devil's empire, ruled by ten kings, began to fall. The first to fall was the throne of Babylon. Seven thousand officials of Satan's empire were killed in the earthquake, and God's people, who just moments before were about to be destroyed,

Interlaced thoughts

were terrified at the collapse of the devil's empire, but they gave glory to the God of heaven for His wonderful deliverance.

NIV

References

1. Daniel 12:7
2. Daniel 8:17,19; 11:36
3. Appendix D
4. Ephesians 6:19, 3:6; Colossians 1:25-27; 1 John 3:2,3
5. Ezekiel 2 & 3
6. Daniel 12:9
7. Revelation 13:5
8. Deuteronomy 17:6
9. Zechariah 4
10. Revelation 14:1-5, 19:1-8; 1 Thessalonians 4:14
11. Psalm 91

Prophecy 11

Revelation 11:14-19

Beginning point in time: Close of mercy
Ending point in time: Close of mercy
Synopsis: This prophecy covers the developments in heaven and on earth that mark the beginning of the third woe. The third and greatest woe is the seven last plagues. These are poured out on those receiving the mark of the beast. The heart of this prophecy centers on the transition of Jesus. He moves from the position of Savior and High Priest, to Avenger of the saints and King of earth. At this point in time, the people of earth cannot escape the fact that they really are the property of a great and Almighty King.

NIV

{14} The second woe has passed; the third woe is coming soon.

{15} The seventh angel sounded his trumpet, and there were loud voices in heaven, which said: "The kingdom of the world has become the kingdom of our Lord and of his Christ, and he will reign for ever and ever."

Interlaced thoughts

{14} After watching the segment of the vision concerning the Two Witnesses, the fourth living creature directed my attention to the end of the sixth trumpet. He said, "The second woe has passed and soon, the third woe will begin. Before you observe the final woe, you must understand two things:

{15} First, the gospel will fully reach every nation, kindred, tongue and people just before the seventh trumpet sounds.[1] After the last person makes his decision for or against the gospel, the Father will give the order to sound the seventh trumpet. This is the all important moment that no one knows the day nor hour—not the angels, not even the Son.[2] This trumpet marks the end of His patience and mercy with the people of earth. At this point in time, everyone will have heard the gospel and made a decision to either obey the commandments of Jesus or obey the oppressive laws of the devil.[3]

Interlaced thoughts

Secondly, when the seventh angel sounds his trumpet, this signals an important transition in heaven. Jesus ends His mediatorial work and begins to reign as King of Heaven and Earth. There will be no more mercy for rebels on earth. In fact, the first work of King Jesus will be a revelation of His fury against the despisers of His grace.

These two points are important because of what He is about to do.

I heard loud voices in heaven affirming the authority of Jesus and His sovereign right to deal with the people of earth as He saw fit. The four living creatures and the elders had watched the entire process. They were satisfied that Jesus had been fair and faithful in each case. And they said: "The kingdom of the world has become the kingdom of our Lord Jesus Christ, and He will reign for ever and ever." {16} And the twenty-four elders, who were seated on their thrones before God, fell on their faces and worshiped God, {17} saying: "We give thanks to you, Lord God Almighty, the One who is and who was, because you have so carefully taken your great power and have *now begun* to reign.

One of the elders explained to me that this transition of Jesus from High Priest to King of kings was directly connected to the third woe. I learned that the third woe falls upon those who have received the

NIV

{16} And the twenty-four elders, who were seated on their thrones before God, fell on their faces and worshiped God,

{17} saying: "We give thanks to you, Lord God Almighty, the One who is and who was, because you have taken your great power and have begun to reign.

NIV

{18} The nations were angry; and your wrath has come. The time has come for judging the dead, and for rewarding your servants the prophets and your saints and those who reverence your name, both small and great - and for destroying those who destroy the earth."

Interlaced thoughts

mark of the beast. Jesus is going to expressly punish these rebels. His anger is great because they *willfully and intelligently* rejected His truth, His gracious salvation, and His invitation of mercy. Further, those who received the mark of the beast had nothing but contempt and hatred for those who received the gospel. Many saints had died for the cause of Jesus. And, to show His fury with the wicked, He will send seven last plagues upon them.

In God's sight, the guilt for conspiracy is no different than directly participating in the crime. So, Jesus, as King of kings, will stand up, He will put on His kingly robes and deal with the rebels on a little speck of dust in His vast universe called, "Earth."

{18} The elder continued saying, "At the time of the seventh trumpet, the nations of earth will be filled with anger and bitterness for the devil has forcibly taken control of the world. And, the conqueror is a demonic destroyer. He will require obedience from every person on earth upon pain of death. The people of the world in those days will suffer conditions worse than prisoners in concentration camps in World War II.

At this time, the full measure of God's wrath will begin.[4] God's vengeance will be poured out. There will be no mercy upon those who chose the mark of the beast. This

Interlaced thoughts

outpouring of wrath is the third and final woe. (See Prophecy 14.)

So, when the seventh trumpet sounds, Jesus will begin to avenge the blood of His martyrs, those who died for their testimony and faithfulness to Him. He will soon reward the hard work of the 144,000. He will reward the faithfulness of every saint. He will reward those who received His salvation, both small and great. And, Jesus will now bring a sequence of destruction upon the devil and the leaders of Babylon who have made the earth an awful place to live."

{19} Then, I looked up into heaven and saw a marvelous sign and I was not alone, everyone on earth saw this scene! God's temple in heaven was opened, and within his temple was seen the ark of his covenant. This greatly frightened all the people of earth. Wicked leaders of Babylon looked in awe at the holy law of God which they had willfully violated and forced others to reject. The Ten Commandments shown with great glory. Like Pharaoh, the wicked briefly saw their shame. They had compelled many to disobey the Creator's holy Sabbath as commanded in the decalogue. They had imposed heavy penalties upon those who were keeping His Sabbath holy. Like common thugs, they refused to consider their fate. They refused to believe that someday they would be held in

NIV

{19} Then God's temple in heaven was opened, and within his temple was seen the ark of his covenant. And there came flashes of lightning, rumblings, peals of thunder, an earthquake and a great hailstorm.

NIV	Interlaced thoughts

contempt and rebellion against the Great King. But, the dye had been cast. They had received the mark. They belonged to the one on earth claiming to be God and his mark was upon them.

The righteous also saw this scene in the heavens. They trembled at the standard of holiness required by God's law. They lost hope of salvation when they saw their lives contrasted with God's requirement of holiness. And, they would have been overwhelmed with discouragement except Jesus spoke words of encouragement to them.

And there came flashes of lightning, rumblings, peals of thunder, an earthquake and a great hailstorm of burning meteors. At this time Jesus poured out great judgments of fire upon particularly evil places and they were completely burned up like Sodom and Gomorrah. But the saints heard the voice of Jesus in the thunder. (This was one of the seven thunders.) He said, "Let him who does wrong continue to do wrong; let him who is vile continue to be vile; let him who does right continue to do right; and let him who is holy continue to be holy."[5] Then the saints realized their labors were finished. Their martyrdom had now ended and neither would Jesus allow one person who had refused the mark of the beast to be lost. And as they retreated to the solitary places of earth to wait for the third

Interlaced thoughts

woe to be completed, the saints wondered what it would be like to stand before the majesty of King Jesus.

NIV

References

1. Matthew 24:14
2. Revelation 14:14-16
3. Revelation 13:8
4. Revelation 15:1, Daniel 12:1
5. Revelation 22:11

Prophecy 12

Revelation 12:1-14:5

Beginning point in time: Birth of Jesus
Ending point in time: Just before the Second Coming
Synopsis: This prophecy reveals the calculated activities of the devil as he first attempted to destroy Jesus. John traces the efforts of the devil right down to the end of earth—even the victory of the 144,000 over the devil. John concludes chapter 12 with the devil preparing for war upon the remnant of God's people. When this prophecy is chronologically aligned with Prophecy 9, the rise of the dragonlike beast, Babylon, and appearing of the lamblike beast are rather easy to understand.

NIV

{1} A great and wondrous sign appeared in heaven: a woman clothed with the sun, with the moon under her feet and a crown of twelve stars on her head.

{2} She was pregnant and cried out in pain as she was about to give birth.

{3} Then another sign appeared in heaven: an enormous red dragon with seven heads and ten horns and seven crowns on his heads. {4} His tail swept a third of the stars out of the sky and flung them to the earth. The dragon stood in front of the woman who was about to give birth, so that he might devour her child the moment it was born. {5} She gave birth to a son, a male child, who will rule all the nations with an iron scepter. And her child was snatched up to God and to his throne. {6} The woman fled into the desert to a place prepared for her by God, where she might be taken care of for 1,260 days.

Interlaced thoughts

{1} A great and wondrous sign appeared in heaven: I saw a beautiful bride clothed with linen, bright as the sun. She was standing upon the moon and she wore a crown of victory containing twelve stars on her head. {2} She was pregnant and cried out in pain as she was about to give birth.
{3} Then another sign appeared in heaven: an enormous red dragon with seven heads and ten horns and he had seven crowns on his heads. {4} His tail had swept a third of the angels out of heaven. The dragon beast stood in front of the woman who was about to give birth, so that he might devour her child the moment it was born. {5} I watched as she gave birth to a special male child who will eventually rule all nations with an iron scepter.[1] Then, her child was snatched up to the right hand of God's throne.[2] {6} Afterwards, the woman fled into the desert to a place prepared for her by God,

Interlaced thoughts

where she might be taken care of for 1,260 years.[3]

I wanted to know the meaning of these scenes. Soon, an answer came. The bride represents faithful people who will someday be married to the Lamb.[4] Her bridal gown, which was as bright as the sun, represents the gift of Christ's righteousness that comes by faith.[5] The moon under her feet represents the marriage covenant which Christ has extended to her: *If you will be my people, I will be your husband.*[6] The crown of victory represents her final generation who will be victorious over the dragon. The twelve stars represent the elite of her twelve tribes, specifically, the 144,000.[7]

Then, I was shown the experience of the bride. I was transported to the time of the birth of Jesus. A virgin gave birth to a male child who will someday rule all nations with a scepter of iron. The iron scepter means that His rule shall never be broken. After living on earth for 33 years, He was taken up to heaven. At the appointed time, He sat down at the right hand of the Father.

The dragon tried to kill baby Jesus for the simple reason that Jesus would expose his evil deeds. The incarnation of Jesus exposed the five existing religious systems of that day as false. Upon failing to destroy Jesus, the devil then persecuted His people so that he might destroy

NIV

NIV

{7} And there was war in heaven. Michael and his angels fought against the dragon, and the dragon and his angels fought back.
{8} But he was not strong enough, and they lost their place in heaven.

Interlaced thoughts

them. God allowed the devil to chase His bride for 1,260 Jubilee days which is 1,260 literal years (A.D. 538 - 1798).[8] But, Jesus sustained those willing to live by faith. This lengthy period of persecution served to keep the faith of the bride pure until the appointed time of the end arrived.

After I was shown these things, I was taken back to Resurrection Sunday—a most glorious morning. Jesus arose early from the tomb and just as He was leaving to go to heaven, Mary found Jesus at the tomb. She wanted to visit with Him, but He told her He had to hurry to heaven right then.[9] Then I saw why:

{7} There was war in heaven that morning. Michael, (the name angels use when referring to the Son of God) and his angels fought against the devil and his angels. {8} But the devil's forces were not strong enough, and they lost their opportunity to ever enter heaven again. I knew from the book of Job that the devil could attend meetings in heaven.[10] However, when Jesus got to heaven on resurrection morning, He immediately sought a permanent restraining order against the devil. The Father granted the petition of Jesus, but the devil and his angels refused to go. So, the enmity between Christ and Satan that began before the creation of the world was brought to another contest.[11] There was war, Jesus and

Interlaced thoughts

his angels threw the devil out of heaven that morning and the Father exiled the devil and his angels to earth. The Father also required that the devil and his angels remain in the spirit world which is invisible to humans.[12] This spirit world is called the Abyss.

{9} This is why the great dragon was hurled down – that ancient serpent called the devil, or Satan, who leads the whole world astray. He was hurled to the earth, and his angels with him.

{10} I was so happy to see the victory of Jesus that day. Then I heard a loud voice in heaven commending Jesus. It said: "*Now* have come the salvation and the power and the kingdom of our God, and the authority of his Christ. For the accuser of our brothers, who accuses them before our God day and night, has been hurled down.

I saw the expulsion of the devil from heaven that day, and then, all heaven rejoiced over Jesus' great victory. He had not only defeated the devil, He had overcome sin for the salvation of man. The commendation of Jesus I heard made sense. *Now* have come the salvation and authority of Jesus! Now the accuser of mankind has been exposed for what he really is: the adversary of God. The angels were very pleased that the devil could no longer appear in heavenly

NIV

{9} The great dragon was hurled down – that ancient serpent called the devil, or Satan, who leads the whole world astray. He was hurled to the earth, and his angels with him.

{10} Then I heard a loud voice in heaven say: "Now have come the salvation and the power and the kingdom of our God, and the authority of his Christ. For the accuser of our brothers, who accuses them before our God day and night, has been hurled down."

NIV	Interlaced thoughts
	meetings and accuse God or mankind.
{11} They overcame him by the blood of the Lamb and by the word of their testimony; they did not love their lives so much as to shrink from death.	{11} Seeing that the devil was furious with his expulsion, I expected he would vent his rage on the people of God. Then I heard a voice granting the woman courage and faith. The voice said, "The people of Jesus will overcome the devil by the blood of the Lamb and by the word of their testimony. They will be given power and courage so that they will not shrink from death.
{12} Therefore rejoice, you heavens and you who dwell in them! But woe to the earth and the sea, because the devil has gone down to you! He is filled with fury, because he knows that his time is short."	{12} Therefore rejoice, you angels of heaven because the marriage of the Lamb will happen! But, woe the multitudes who live on earth, because the devil has focused his wrath on you! He is filled with fury, because he now knows that his days are limited."
{13} When the dragon saw that he had been hurled to the earth, he pursued the woman who had given birth to the male child.	{13} When the dragon saw that he had been locked out of heaven forever, when he saw that he could no longer accuse men before God, he focused his wrath on the bride who had *already given birth* to Jesus.
{14} The woman was given the two wings of a great eagle, so that she might fly to the place prepared for her in the desert, where she would be taken care of for a time, times and half a time, out of the serpent's reach.	{14} The woman was given the two wings of a great eagle, so that she might quickly flee to places prepared for her in the desert. There, she would be taken care of for a time, times and half a time, out of the serpent's reach. Again, as mentioned above, this time period in Jubilee days, is 1,260 literal years.
{15} Then from his mouth the serpent spewed water like a river,	{15} As the 1,260 years came to an end, the devil attempted to destroy the woman by spewing a flood out

Interlaced thoughts

of his mouth. He tried to overtake the woman and sweep her away with the torrent of war.[13] This was fulfilled by the French Revolution (1793-1798). The Revolution reveals the hatred of the devil against the bride. {16} But the earth helped the woman. Just before the French Revolution occurred, God had prepared a new continent that would help the bride. A new world offering religious liberty and freedom of conscience was opened up. So, the earth *physically* came to the rescue of the woman. Now the poor, the tired, the homeless and the persecuted could flee from the ravages of the devil.

{17} Then the devil was even more enraged at the woman and he disappeared for awhile. He went underground with his evil plans. His next activity will be to make war against the remnant of the bride. And, if he has to destroy the whole world to destroy them, he will do it. The devil is planning to destroy those who obey God's ten commandments and hold to the testimony of Jesus which is revealed by the Holy Spirit through 144,000 prophets.

{13:1} Then I found myself standing on the shore of a sea. And I saw a beast coming up out of the sea. I saw this beast rise to power in *response* to the devastation caused by the first four trumpets discussed in Prophecy 9. The form of this

NIV

to overtake the woman and sweep her away with the torrent.

{16} But the earth helped the woman by opening its mouth and swallowing the river that the dragon had spewed out of his mouth.

{17} Then the dragon was enraged at the woman and went off to make war against the rest of her offspring– those who obey God's commandments and hold to the testimony of Jesus.

{13:1} And the dragon* stood on the shore of the sea. And I saw a beast coming out of the sea. He had ten horns and seven heads, with ten crowns on his horns, and on each head a blasphemous name.

NIV

*because of the use of Greek pronouns, this verse is also translated, "And I stood on the shore of the sea."

Interlaced thoughts

beast's body was identical to the great red dragon described in Chapter 12. This beast had the *same* heads and horns, but there was an important difference. This beast is "a puppet" on the hand of the dragon. Those who are wise will see right through the puppet, this is why this beast is also red.[14] Just like the great red dragon, in Chapter 12, this beast had ten horns and seven heads.

In this scene, the crowns were on the horns. I wondered about the change, for when I first saw the dragon, he had crowns on his heads. Then I understood. These crowns are diadems which means they are crowns of authority. I saw that when the crowns were on the seven heads, the devil used the authority of religious systems to persecute the bride. However, when this beast appears, the crowns are placed on the horns because the devil will persecute the bride with civil authorities. More will be said about the identity of the heads and horns in Revelation 17.

I looked, and on each head there was a blasphemous name. This immediately led me to see that each head is anti-Christ. Each head claims the prerogatives of God, but their claims were false. In fact, all seven heads claim to represent God, but they don't. They also hate the bride of Jesus. I wanted to know the meaning of the seven heads but

Interlaced thoughts

was told to wait. I was also told that this beast's name is "Babylon" and that more information would be given about it in Revelation 17.

{2} *Unlike* the great red dragon in Chapter 12, this beast resembled a leopard, but it had feet like those of a bear and a mouth like that of a lion. The dragon gave Babylon his power and his throne and great authority.

This beast represents a coalition of the world's religious and political leaders. This coalition of confusion will occur after Jesus opens the fourth seal and sends His wrath upon earth. Then, the world will realize that God is angry with *all nations* and men will respond by forming a global coalition to appease God. This composite beast will rise to power at the appointed time and will persecute the bride. I knew from Daniel 7:11,12 that the leopard, bear and lion and terrible beast were allowed to live until the very end because they represent the remnant of all world empires. Therefore, this composite beast is a combination of all world empires; it was cunning and swift like a leopard, it had crushing strength like the jaws of a lion, and its claws allowed it to tear everything apart. Nothing could stand against it.

{3} As I watched, my attention was drawn to one head that was greater than the others. This head, the sixth of seven, had received a fatal

NIV

{2} The beast I saw resembled a leopard, but had feet like those of a bear and a mouth like that of a lion. The dragon gave the beast his power and his throne and great authority.

{3} One of the heads of the beast seemed to have had a fatal wound, but the fatal wound had been

NIV

healed. The whole world was astonished and followed the beast.

{4} Men worshiped the dragon because he had given authority to the beast, and they also worshiped the beast and asked, "Who is like the beast? Who can make war against him?"

{5} The beast was given a mouth to utter proud words and blasphemies and to exercise his authority for forty-two months.

Interlaced thoughts

wound,[15] but when the beast rose to power, the fatal wound had been healed. To say whole world was astonished at the speedy rise of Babylon is an understatement. It happened so fast that no one could believe it. Because the people of the world were greatly frightened by the judgments of God, most thought it perfectly reasonable to support the organization represented by this beast. This is because they were frightened at the awful devastations of the trumpets. {4} But, Babylon cannot solve the problem. Those who are wise can see right through this beast. They know that in obeying the laws which this beast will make, they are actually obeying the devil because he is the hand inside the glove. He is the authority within the beast. But, most people are blind to the schemes of the devil. So, most will obey the laws of the beast and in fear they will say, "Why should anyone resist the laws of this beast? Given the mighty manifestations of God's wrath, who can rebel against this global attempt to appease God without dire consequences?"

{5} The leaders of Babylon spoke out against the truths of God as revealed in the Bible, especially the fourth commandment.[16] They made claims about God that were entirely false and they claimed that their laws of worship were superior and necessary to appease Him. Their blasphemy against the God of

Interlaced thoughts

Heaven was limited to 42 literal months. I was glad to know that the authority of this beast was limited, because it was horrible.

{6} After some time went by, the devil himself and his angels physically appeared on earth and everyone was amazed at their glory.[17] Babylon, the coalition of the world's religious and political systems, received the devil as though he were the God of Heaven. The 144,000 loudly exposed the glorious being as nothing more than the devil masquerading as an angel of light. They were greatly persecuted for their proclamations.[18] The leaders of Babylon denounced those who refused to recognize the devil as the God of Heaven. They slandered God's name, His dwelling place and the angels of Heaven. The leaders claimed that God and his angels were now on earth and that all should obey the devil.

{7} With the devil's support, Babylon will make war against the saints and keep defeating them.[19] And, Babylon shall also gain control over everyone—everywhere. The point is that Jesus will allow Babylon to rule for a short time. Millions of saints died for their faith. (This is the martyrdom of the fifth seal.) {8} Anticipate the global reach of Babylon. All inhabitants of the earth will obey her laws – all whose names have not been written in the Lamb's Book of Life which

NIV

{6} He opened his mouth to blaspheme God, and to slander his name and his dwelling place and those who live in heaven.

{7} He was given power to make war against the saints and to conquer them. And he was given authority over every tribe, people, language and nation.

{8} All inhabitants of the earth will worship the beast – all whose names have not been written in the book of life belonging to the Lamb

NIV

that was slain from the creation of the world.

{9} He who has an ear, let him hear.

{10} If anyone is to go into captivity, into captivity he will go. If anyone is to be killed with the sword, with the sword he will be killed. This calls for patient endurance and faithfulness on the part of the saints.

{11} Then I saw another beast, coming out of the earth. He had two horns like a lamb, but he spoke like a dragon.

{12} He exercised all the authority of the first beast on his behalf, and made the earth and its inhabitants worship the first beast, whose fatal wound had been healed.

Interlaced thoughts

was written before the creation of the world.[20] (Remember, this is the book that was sealed with seven seals.)

{9} He who has an ear to understand the things of God, let him hear and understand this point.
{10} If anyone is to go into captivity, into captivity he will go. So, don't worry about your fate. Stand firm for God's truth and God will take care of you. If anyone is to be killed with the sword, with the sword he will be killed. Again, if God shall ask you to die for His cause, He will grant you the courage. So, be strong. A great reward awaits those who endure to the end. Therefore, this war calls for patient endurance and faithfulness on the part of the saints.

{11} As these scenes passed before me, I saw another beast, coming up out of the Abyss. This book looked identical to "the Lamb that was slain" except this lamb had two horns instead of seven,[21] and he eventually spoke like the dragon. I immediately saw that this beast was an imposter. He appeared to be "lamb-like". He wanted the people of earth to think he was God when in reality, he was the devil.
{12} Now the lamblike beast had greater authority than Babylon and everything he did at first, he did on behalf of the dragonlike beast whose name was Babylon. To gain religious

Interlaced thoughts

followers, the lamblike beast aligned himself with the seven blasphemous heads and as he travelled about, he commanded the people obey the religious laws of Babylon.

{13} The devil performed great and miraculous signs, even calling fire down from heaven in full view of men. This ability was a most compelling deception. Millions of people believed that God Himself had come to dwell among men. But this deception only served the evil schemes of the devil.

{14} Because of the signs he did on behalf of Babylon, the lamblike beast deceived billions of people on earth. Then, after gaining the allegiance of much of the world, He commanded his followers to set up a new "look-alike" religion in *honor* of Babylon since his presence among men necessitated that Babylon's great diversity pass away.

"With god among men," the devil said, "time has come for the world to unite into one religious body." The new body *borrowed* elements from each religious system so that the new system was patterned after the old. The devil especially honored the sixth head who was wounded by the sword and yet lived because it had established a spurious day of worship which most of the world accepted as the Lord's day.[22] {15} To prevent anyone from worshiping the God of Heaven, the lamblike beast gave authority to

NIV

{13} And he performed great and miraculous signs, even causing fire to come down from heaven to earth in full view of men.

{14} Because of the signs he was given power to do on behalf of the first beast, he deceived the inhabitants of the earth. He ordered them to set up an image in honor of the beast who was wounded by the sword and yet lived.

{15} He was given power to give breath to the image of the first beast, so that it could speak and

NIV

cause all who refused to worship the image to be killed.

{16} He also forced everyone, small and great, rich and poor, free and slave, to receive a mark on his right hand or on his forehead, {17} so that no one could buy or sell unless he had the mark, which is the name of the beast or the number of his name. {18} This calls for wisdom. If anyone has insight, let him calculate the number of the beast, for it is man's number. His number is 666.

{14:1} Then I looked, and there before me was the Lamb, standing on Mount Zion, and with him 144,000 who had his name and his Father's name written on their foreheads.

Interlaced thoughts

Babylon so that it could make laws regarding the worship of the devil and cause all who refused to obey those laws to be killed. {16} Then, the devil forced everyone, small and great, rich and poor, free and slave, to receive a tatoo on his right hand or on his forehead,[23] {17} so that no one could buy or sell unless he had the mark, which can either be his name or his number. {18} This calls for wisdom. If anyone has intelligence, he can easily calculate the number of the lamblike beast in those days, for it is the number of a man claiming to be God. (Just as Jesus became a man to save the world, the devil becomes a man to destroy the world.) However, he is not a god, he is mortal like man. He is the man of sin and his number is 666. Soon, when his name is known, his number will be easily understood. I wondered how the people of God could live through this terrible time. Without the tatoo, they couldn't buy or sell. Then I heard a voice saying, "The just shall live by faith in God."

{14:1} After this, my view was directed to the ascension of the 144,000.[24] I looked up and there before me was the Lamb, standing on Mount Zion, and with him were His 144,000 servants who had received His seal:[25] His name and His Father's name written on their foreheads. This was so different from the mark of the devil which was written on the foreheads of the

Interlaced thoughts

wicked. The mark of the devil was ugly and defacing whereas the name of the Father and the name of the Lamb was beautiful and glorious like a rainbow of light encircling the forehead.

{2} And I heard a sound from heaven like the roar of rushing waters and like a loud peal of thunder. Then I listened and the sound I heard was like that of harpists playing their harps.
{3} And the 144,000 sang a new song before the throne and before the four living creatures and the elders. This was a special event. I looked around and no one in heaven could learn the song except the 144,000 who had been redeemed from the earth. I wondered why no one else could sing their song. Then I realized that they had been through an ordeal that no one else had endured. {4} These are God's priests, totally dedicated to Him for ages to come. These are pure in heart. Hereafter, they shall follow the Lamb wherever he goes for they were purchased from among men and offered as firstfruits to God and the Lamb.[26] They are His special property! What honor has been bestowed upon them. {5} No lie was found in their mouths; they are blameless. These stood firmly for God's truth and they proclaimed it with forceful words. When you understand how much courage this took, when you understand how much abuse they suffered, when you

NIV

{2} And I heard a sound from heaven like the roar of rushing waters and like a loud peal of thunder. The sound I heard was like that of harpists playing their harps.

{3} And they sang a new song before the throne and before the four living creatures and the elders. No one could learn the song except the 144,000 who had been redeemed from the earth.

{4} These are those who did not defile themselves with women, for they kept themselves pure. They follow the Lamb wherever he goes. They were purchased from among men and offered as firstfruits to God and the Lamb.

{5} No lie was found in their mouths; they are blameless.

NIV

References

1. Revelation 19:15
2. Hebrews 8:1
3. Daniel 7:25
4. Revelation 19:7,8
5. Isaiah 61:10
6. Psalm 89:34-37; Hebrews 8:10,11; Revelation 21:7
7. Daniel 12:3; Philippians 2:14-16
8. Appendix D
9. John 20:17
10. Job 1:7
11. John 12:27-31, 14:30, 16:11
12. Luke 8:31
13. Isaiah 8:6-8, Hosea 5:10, Daniel 9:26, 11:10,40
14. Revelation 17:3
15. Daniel 7:21,22
16. Exodus 20:8-11
17. Revelation 9:1-12, Revelation 17:8, Revelation 11:7, 2 Thessalonians 2:3-11
18. Revelation 18:24
19. Daniel 12:7
20. Greek text also allows this translation - compare with Revelation 17:8
21. Revelation 5:6
22. Daniel 7:25
23. Exodus 13:9, 16
24. Revelation 11:12, 19:1-8
25. Revelation 7:1-4
26. Numbers 18:8-13

Interlaced thoughts

behold their rejection, you too will appreciate their faithful and determined efforts to carry the gospel to every nation.

NOTES

Prophecy 13

Revelation 14:6-15:4

Beginning point in time: The first trumpet
Ending point in time: Shortly after the Second Coming
Synopsis: This prophecy covers the mission and message of the 144,000. These three messages are best understood in the context of what they oppose. These messages stand in direct opposition to the legislation of Babylon and ultimately, the laws which the devil himself shall implement. This story calls for great patience and endurance on the part of the saints. Many will become martyrs in their bold stand for Christ.

NIV

{6} Then I saw another angel flying in midair, and he had the eternal gospel to proclaim to those who live on the earth – to every nation, tribe, language and people.

{7} He said in a loud voice, "Fear God and give him glory, because the hour of his judgment has come. Worship him who made the heavens, the earth, the sea and the springs of water."

Interlaced thoughts

{6} Then I saw three angels flying above the earth, and each carried a component of the everlasting gospel. I saw that the terms of salvation had not changed with time. Then, the first angel commanded that all who live on the earth, every nation, tribe, language and people, must exalt the God of Heaven. The gospel requires true worship, which is joyful obedience to God's Word. [1]

I learned that these three messages will be forcibly delivered by the 144,000 and their supporters. The whole world will hear and see these marvelous servants of Jesus and they will proclaim the good news of salvation to all who live on earth.

{7} The first angel said in a loud voice, "Respect Almighty God and give Him due homage, because the hour has come for Him to pass judgment upon the living. Worship Jesus who made the heavens that have been darkened by the fourth trumpet, the earth which has been burned by the first trumpet, the sea

Interlaced thoughts

which was impacted by the second trumpet and the springs of water which were contaminated by the third trumpet." I saw that when the seven trumpets begin, the judgment of the living commences. This means that Jesus is concluding His intercession in the heavenly sanctuary and His last work is to test the people of earth and allow them to choose their eternal destiny.[2] This first message to the world will be a clarion call to honor God and give Him due recognition as our Creator. This message insists that all observe the holy day of Almighty God. His holy day is Saturday. His Ten Commandments stand above all the laws of men and the fourth commandment clearly reveals that God's holy Sabbath, the seventh-day of the week, is the day that our Creator commands worship.

This message brought consternation to the people of the world because it came at a time when the religious systems of the world were making laws to appease the wrath of God. Laws regarding the sacredness of Friday, Saturday and Sunday were being enacted in nations according to the prevailing religious population. For example, Friday laws will be enacted in Moslem countries. Saturday laws will be enacted in Israel and Sunday laws will be enacted throughout Catholic and Protestant countries. Thus, the people of the world will be faced with a serious dilemma. Whose laws

NIV

NIV

{8} A second angel followed and said, “Fallen! Fallen is Babylon the Great, which made all the nations drink the maddening wine of her adulteries.”

Interlaced thoughts

shall we obey so that God will be pleased?

{8} A second message followed the first which said, “False! False is Babylon the Great. It does not speak for God even though it caused all nations to accept the maddening delusions of her schemes.[3] I quickly understood the thrust of this message. Babylon is the name of the dragonlike beast.[4] This beast represents a confused world-wide organization composed of seven false religious systems. Babylon is anti-Christ and those who cooperate with Babylon and those who obey the laws of Babylon, will be held in contempt by the Most High God. This message reveals a struggle for supremacy. Which is greater: the laws of Babylon or the laws of God? This is the great test of the tribulation. God wants to see who will put Him first—who will obey Him when the penalty for civil disobedience is great?

As a result of God’s wrath for violating His laws, Babylon’s leaders will see to it that all nations will drink in false religious ideas about pleasing God so that His judgments will cease. False religion always exhibits two unmistakable characteristics: first, it teaches that men can please God with external forms of worship. Secondly, the last resort of false religion is force. The truth is that God loves a humble

Interlaced thoughts

and contrite spirit. We please God when we trust and obey Him. But, external piety is no ticket to salvation. The voluntary surrender of the will to God; to go, to be and to do as He commands, this what God asks. In return, He grants salvation to anyone willing to live by faith.

Religious leaders will commit adultery by entering into an unholy union with the state. Religious laws regarding the sacredness of Sunday will be quickly implemented in America. Civil penalties for disobedience will be great. Those who keep God's Ten Commandments will be greatly persecuted. Especially when they proclaim the truth about the seventh-day Sabbath, God's holy day. Because the devil is the power inside Babylon, he will stir up the arrogance and pride of men. He will lead mere mortal men to think that they have the authority to void the law of Almighty God and tell others how and when they should worship. What blasphemy! This will be a most distressing time for *all* the nations of earth.

{9} When the devil physically appears before the people of earth claiming to be God, then a third message will sound around the world. This message will be heard everywhere: "If anyone worships the lamblike beast (the devil) or submits to his image (the new world order) and receives his mark on the forehead or on the hand, (tatoo)

NIV

{9} A third angel followed them and said in a loud voice: "If anyone worships the beast and his image and receives his mark on the forehead or on the hand,

NIV

{10} he, too, will drink of the wine of God's fury, which has been poured full strength into the cup of his wrath. He will be tormented with burning sulfur in the presence of the holy angels and of the Lamb.

{11} And the smoke of their torment rises for ever and ever. There is no rest day or night for those who worship the beast and his image, or for anyone who receives the mark of his name."

{12} This calls for patient endurance on the part of the saints who obey God's commandments and remain faithful to Jesus.

{13} Then I heard a voice from heaven say, "Write: Blessed are the dead who die in the Lord from now on." "Yes," says the Spirit, "they will rest from their labor, for their deeds will follow them."

Interlaced thoughts

{10} he, then, will drink of the wine of God's wrath, which has not yet been seen. But, His wrath will be poured *full* strength upon those receiving the mark of the beast. The wicked will be tormented with burning sulfur in the presence of the holy angels and of the Lamb when he shall appear."

{11} I, John, saw this to be true. I saw the destruction of the wicked and the smoke of their destruction will rise for ever and ever. Once God ignites the lake of fire, nothing can extinguish the fire until it has consumed wicked. I also saw that there is no peace of mind, day or night for those who obey the laws of Babylon or the new world order, or for anyone who receives the mark of his name. How can there be any peace when serving the devil?

{12} After the third message begins, the people of God will greatly suffer. There will be wholesale martyrdom of those refusing to obey the glorious being, the one who claims to be God. This calls for patient endurance on the part of the saints who obey God's ten commandments and remain faithful to Jesus. {13} Then I heard a voice from heaven say, "Write: Blessed are the dead who die in the Lord from *now on.*" "Yes," says the Spirit, "they will rest from their labor, for their deeds will follow them." I saw that those who died during the third angel's message will

Interlaced thoughts

be resurrected during the special resurrection described in Prophecy 11. That will be a glorious moment when wicked murderers behold the resurrection of those they killed.

{14} After the third message had be fully proclaimed to the world, I looked into heaven, and there before me was a white cloud, and Jesus was seated on the cloud with a crown of gold on his head and a sharp sickle in his hand. {15} I saw an angel come out of the temple bearing a message from the Father. He called in a loud voice to Jesus who was sitting on the cloud, "Put your sickle to the harvest, because the time to reap has come, all the earth is ready." Everyone has made their decision. {16} So he who was seated on the cloud swung his sickle over the earth, and the earth was harvested.

This symbolic gesture of waving a sickle over the earth reveals two important things. First, Jesus is told by the Father when to close the door to mercy. This is why Jesus said long ago, "No one knows that day nor hour, not even the angels nor the Son."[5] The Father has reserved that decision for Himself. Secondly, after the third message has gone throughout the world, everyone will have made their decision, thus, the door of mercy closes *because there are no more decisions to be made.*

NIV

{14} I looked, and there before me was a white cloud, and seated on the cloud was one "like a son of man" with a crown of gold on his head and a sharp sickle in his hand.

{15} Then another angel came out of the temple and called in a loud voice to him who was sitting on the cloud, "Take your sickle and reap, because the time to reap has come, for the harvest of the earth is ripe."

{16} So he who was seated on the cloud swung his sickle over the earth, and the earth was harvested.

NIV

{17} Another angel came out of the temple in heaven, and he too had a sharp sickle.

{18} Still another angel, who had charge of the fire, came from the altar and called in a loud voice to him who had the sharp sickle, "Take your sharp sickle and gather the clusters of grapes from the earth's vine, because its grapes are ripe."

{19} The angel swung his sickle on the earth, gathered its grapes and threw them into the great winepress of God's wrath.

{20} They were trampled in the winepress outside the city, and blood flowed out of the press, rising as high as the horses' bridles for a distance of 1,600 stadia.

{15:1} I saw in heaven another great and marvelous sign: seven angels with the seven last plagues—last, because with them God's wrath is completed.

{2} And I saw what looked like a sea of glass mixed with fire and, standing beside the sea, those who had been victorious over the beast

Interlaced thoughts

{17} Then, I saw a mighty angel came out of the temple in heaven, and he too had a sharp sickle. He is the angel of death. {18} Then, the angel who had charge of the fire at the altar of incense, came from the altar and called in a loud voice to him who had the sharp sickle, "Take your sharp sickle and gather the clusters of grapes from the earth's vine, because its grapes are ready for the winepress."
{19} The angel of death swung his sickle over the earth and in so doing, he gathered the grapes and threw them into the great winepress of God's wrath.

{20} I saw the wicked trampled in the winepress outside the city, which means the wicked were cut off from their inheritance.[6] So great was the number of wicked in the winepress that wine flowed out of the press as high as the horses' bridles for a distance as great as the width of the Mediterranean.

{15:1} Then I looked up into heaven and I saw another marvelous scene: seven angels having the seven last plagues – these are called "last", because through them, Jesus' wrath will be satisfied. The seven last plagues contain the punishment of the wicked that are trampled in the winepress of God's wrath.
{2} Then, I saw another scene. Inside the throne room. I saw a great expanse upholding the throne of God. It looked like a sea of

Interlaced thoughts

glass mixed with sparkling fires.[7] Standing beside the sea of glass, I saw those who had been victorious over the beast and his image and over the number of his name. This group of people was translated without seeing death. They had faithfully endured the great tribulation. They held harps given them by God {3} and they sang the song of Moses the servant of God and the song of the Lamb: "Great and marvelous are your deeds, Lord God Almighty. Just and true are your ways, King of the ages."

{4} These, who witnessed the outpouring of God's wrath during the seven last plagues justified the wrath of Jesus by singing, "Who will not fear you, O Lord, and bring glory to your name? For you alone are holy. All nations will come and worship before you, for your righteous acts have been revealed."

NIV

and his image and over the number of his name. They held harps given them by God

{3} and sang the song of Moses the servant of God and the song of the Lamb: "Great and marvelous are your deeds, Lord God Almighty. Just and true are your ways, King of the ages.

{4} Who will not fear you, O Lord, and bring glory to your name? For you alone are holy. All nations will come and worship before you, for your righteous acts have been revealed."

References

1. John 4:23, 14:15, 1 John 5:3
2. Revelation 3:10, Luke 21:34,35
3. Jeremiah 25:15-18
4. Revelation 13:2
5. Matthew 24:36
6. Leviticus 24:14; Numbers 15:35
7. Ezekiel 1

Prophecy 14

Revelation 15:5-16:21

Beginning point in time: Close of mercy
Ending point in time: The Second Coming
Synopsis: This prophecy covers the outpouring of God's wrath upon those who have resisted the greatest evidences of His truth. At first, the reader may wonder about the balance between God's justice and mercy. Keep in mind, the full malignity of sin will have been seen before these events occur. God will not only avenge the undeserved suffering of His people, He will vindicate His faithful people. One thing stands out above all others in this compelling story: God is Sovereign. His authority is above all others. There is none like Him.

NIV	Interlaced thoughts
{5} After this I looked and in heaven the temple, that is, the tabernacle of the Testimony, was opened.	{5} Then I saw a scene that began just after the seventh trumpet sounded. I looked up into heaven and I saw the temple and the throne of God. Then I saw something full of awe. I saw the temple opened up which contains the holy Law of God, that is, His Ten Commandments. I recognized the opening of the temple meant that God's authority would now be seen. Sentence would be executed upon all who had received the mark of the beast.[1]
{6} Out of the temple came the seven angels with the seven plagues. They were dressed in clean, shining linen and wore golden sashes around their chests.	{6} Out of the temple came the seven angels who had sounded the seven trumpets. With that work done, they were now given a new task of executing the wrath of God: the seven *last* plagues. Unlike the trumpet plagues, these plagues reveal God's wrath on those people who had willfully rejected His truth and joined the devil's forces. These seven angels were mighty angels, highly exalted angels. They were dressed in clean, shining linen and they wore golden sashes around their chests.

Interlaced thoughts

{7} One of the four living creatures gave to the seven angels seven golden bowls filled with the potent wrath of God Almighty, who lives for ever and ever. All heaven watched with solemn interest, for such a manifestation of God's wrath had never been seen before. {8} At this point in time, Jesus concluded His mediatorial work in heaven's temple and to mark the end of mercy for individuals, He threw down another censer filled with live coals and incense. As a result, the temple was filled with smoke from the glory of God and from his righteous power. It was as though the glory of God had been unveiled and no one could enter the temple until the seven plagues of the seven angels were completed. I wondered about this brilliant manifestation of God's glory. Then I remembered the incident at Mt. Sinai when Moses asked to see God's glory. He was told that no one could look upon God's face and live. But Moses was placed in a cleft of a rock where he was protected from the consuming glory of His splendor. This made sense. I was beholding the *revealed* glory of God. Even the billions of angels who were attending this convocation could not remain in His presence. And this manifestation of God's glory in heaven was observed by the people of earth. So that the saints would not be harmed by His glory, Jesus directed that angels shield His

NIV

{7} Then one of the four living creatures gave to the seven angels seven golden bowls filled with the wrath of God, who lives for ever and ever.

{8} And the temple was filled with smoke from the glory of God and from his power, and no one could enter the temple until the seven plagues of the seven angels were completed.

NIV	Interlaced thoughts
	followers. Only those who had received the mark of the beast should feel His wrath.
{16:1} Then I heard a loud voice from the temple saying to the seven angels, "Go, pour out the seven bowls of God's wrath on the earth."	{16:1} Then I heard Jesus say to the seven angels, "Go, pour out the seven bowls of God's wrath on the earth." To the first angel, Jesus said, "The devil has caused everyone to receive his mark except those who are faithful to me. He has shut off all food supplies to my people. So go and curse the ground, poison the soil and then let those with the mark of Satan eat food that is cursed."
{2} The first angel went and poured out his bowl on the land, and ugly and painful sores broke out on the people who had the mark of the beast and worshiped his image.	{2} The first angel went and poured out his bowl of poison on the land, and ugly and painful sores broke out on the people who had the mark of the beast and worshiped his image. I saw that after the food was poisoned, those who ate the food developed horrible boils. But, the saints were not affected. But, when people saw the land was cursed, they turned to the sea for food. Then Jesus said, "Neither shall the sea provide food."
{3} The second angel poured out his bowl on the sea, and it turned into blood like that of a dead man, and every living thing in the sea died.	{3} The second angel poured out his bowl on the sea, and it turned into a thick blood-like fluid, like that of a dead man, and every living thing in the sea died. The poison in the second angel's bowl killed everything in the ocean and millions of tons of dead fish floated upon the shores. The stench covered the whole world and it made the wicked

Interlaced thoughts

violently sick. But, the saints were not affected.

The devil pacified the world by saying that these plagues came upon the world as a result of a curse placed upon them by the remaining 144,000 prophets. At a great rally, the devil demanded that all who had refused his mark should be killed. He cried out, "Let their blood fill the oceans." Jesus who was watching from heaven heard the approving cheers of the wicked. He said, "They have called for the blood of my people, then let them have blood to drink."

{4} The third angel poured out his bowl of poison on the rivers and springs of water, and they became like the sea, deadly and bloody looking. There was no clean drinking water anywhere. I saw the great agony of millions and millions without water. Their suffering was unbearable to watch. These plagues were so horrible I could hardly watch the scenes. But, I was greatly astonished at the response of those who had received the mark of the beast. They refused to repent. In fact, they became even more determined in their rebellion than before.

{5} Then I heard the third angel who poisoned the drinking water say to Jesus: "You are just and fair in these judgments, you who are and who were, the Holy One, because you have so judged;

NIV

{4} The third angel poured out his bowl on the rivers and springs of water, and they became blood.

{5} Then I heard the angel in charge of the waters say: "You are just in these judgments, you who are and who were, the Holy One, because you have so judged;

NIV

{6} for they have shed the blood of your saints and prophets, and you have given them blood to drink as they deserve." {7} And I heard the altar respond: "Yes, Lord God Almighty, true and just are your judgments."

{8} The fourth angel poured out his bowl on the sun, and the sun was given power to scorch people with fire.

{9} They were seared by the intense heat and they cursed the name of God, who had control over

Interlaced thoughts

{6} for they have shed the blood of your saints and *prophets*, and you have given them blood to drink as they deserve." {7} And I heard the mighty angel who served at the altar of incense respond: "Yes, Lord God Almighty, your assessment of the wicked is true, and your punishments are justifiable."

These statements impressed me, for these angels are impartial observers of human conduct and yet they declare the actions of Jesus are fully justified. I saw that the saints were not affected by the poisoned drinking water. In fact, angels were commissioned to provide water and food to God's waiting people.

As I looked about, the wicked were in great distress. I saw that the darkness of the fourth trumpet still lingered over large parts of earth and scientists had asked the devil to make the sun shine upon earth again. The devil, masquerading as God, promised to clear up the sky so that crops might flourish. At that time, Jesus commissioned the fourth angel.

{8} The fourth angel poured out his bowl on the sun, and the darkness went away. The people were pleased at first thinking that the devil had blessed them, but then the sun scorched the earth with unbearable heat. {9} Objects became so hot that people were burned by touching them and they cursed the 144,000 and their God who had

Interlaced thoughts

control over these plagues. But, they absolutely refused to repent and give homage to the God of heaven.

After the fourth plague had been poured out, the people of earth earnestly begged their exalted leader, the devil, to do something about their unbearable suffering. They said to the devil, "if you are God, put a stop to these things. Ever since you ascended the throne, our condition has become worse and worse. Use your great miracle working powers and end our suffering!" This put the devil in predicament for he openly claimed to be Almighty God.

Of course, the devil did not want to the world to know that he was powerless to stop the plagues of Almighty God. So, the devil called for a meeting of his advisors. Together, they prepared a plan to stop the plagues. The *final solution*, the devil suggested, was a universal death decree for the people of God. This, he proposed, would forever rid earth of those who had put *satanic* curses upon them. Then, they could begin to restore the world into a garden like Eden. Word of the plan was passed around. As world leaders prepared to meet and vote on the matter, Jesus commissioned the next angel to immediately deliver the fifth plague.

{10} The fifth angel poured out his bowl on the throne of the devil, and the administrators of Babylon were

NIV

these plagues, but they refused to repent and glorify him.

{10} The fifth angel poured out his bowl on the throne of the beast, and his kingdom was plunged into

NIV

darkness. Men gnawed their tongues in agony

{11} and cursed the God of heaven because of their pains and their sores, but they refused to repent of what they had done.

{12} The sixth angel poured out his bowl on the great river Euphrates, and its water was dried up to prepare the way for the kings from the East.

Interlaced thoughts

plunged into darkness by a plague causing painful blindness. These had chosen blindness to God's truth—these wanted the people of God out of their sight, so God sentenced them to darkness as great as He sent upon ancient Egypt. Men gnawed their tongues in agony {11} and they cursed the God of heaven because of their pains and their sores, but they refused to repent of what they had done.

This plague stunned the whole world. Everyone begin to question the one that claimed to be God. Why would the devil send a curse of painful blindness upon his own administration? Why would he treat his followers with such contempt unless he really was the devil? With this plague, the truth about the identity of the devil was revealed. Now, the wicked saw the devil for who he was. The 144,000 had been right. Oh, what unspeakable guilt!

{12} Next, Jesus sent the sixth angel to earth. He poured out his bowl on the great river Euphrates, and its water was dried up to prepare the way for the appearing of the Father and the Son, the great kings of Heaven and Earth that come from the east. The drying up of the Euphrates means that the devil will lose the authority over men which was gained during the sixth trumpet war.[2] During the sixth trumpet, the great river Euphrates had been let loose and the world was flooded

Interlaced thoughts

with war. Now, after revealing the true identity of the devil, Jesus takes away the devil's controlling authority so that all the universe can see that sin is nothing more than total rebellion against God's authority. The drying up of the river Euphrates means that the devil will lose control of the world by the very means he used to gain control. Thus, in a desperate and final attempt, Satan sets out to rally the world in his plan to destroy the saints of God before Jesus arrives to rescue them. At this time, the devil puts forth his greatest and most impressive efforts.

{13} Then I saw a great wonder. I saw the devil announce the soon appearing of Almighty God. The devil explained that Jesus was coming to rescue His followers and the only hope for mankind was to destroy all of God's people before Jesus should arrive. Even more, men must be prepared to destroy the Father and Son when they appear in the sky. To bolster his argument, the devil admitted that the plagues were the works of God and that now, men must fight against God or they would be destroyed.

The reader should remember that the devil has used this argument before. He actually convinced angels to fight against Michael and His angels! And, at this time, he convinces wicked men, mere mortals, to do the same.

NIV

{13} Then I saw three evil spirits that looked like frogs; they came out of the mouth of the dragon, out of the mouth of the beast and out of the mouth of the false prophet.

NIV

{14} They are spirits of demons performing miraculous signs, and they go out to the kings of the whole world, to gather them for the battle on the great day of God Almighty.

Interlaced thoughts

The devil has mighty angels who serve him just like the God of Heaven has angels that serve Him. I saw the devil send his demons throughout the whole world. And just like the millions of frogs that covered all of Egypt in the days of Pharaoh, these evil ambassadors covered the whole world with the news that men must prepare to war against the soon coming Son of God. To give men false hope of winning the battle, the demons worked many mighty miracles. One of their most powerful miracles was their ability to make dead people appear to be alive even though they really aren't. Just as the 144,000 had invoked the name of the Father, Son and Holy Spirit to perform miracles, these would invoke the name of the dragon, the empire of Babylon, and the name which the devil used in his disguise as God, and dead people would literally appear as living people. What a masterful delusion. {14} But, I clearly saw that these are nothing more than demons performing miraculous signs, and they go out to the ten kings of the world, to unite them in destroying the saints of God with a universal death decree.

I was amazed at the stupidity of wicked people. Now, they followed the devil knowing full well that he was the devil. The devil's mighty angels united the world in a two-part plan. First, the world would kill all the saints of God.

Interlaced thoughts

Then, the wicked would prepare atomic warheads to destroy Jesus who was soon to appear. However, in all of these plans, the wicked only accomplished the will of Almighty God.

I then realized what Jesus had accomplished. His purpose with the sixth plague was to gather together all who are opposed to Him. By gathering them together at one time, He would then come and confront His enemies. But, what is man? What is an angel compared to God? Woe to those who quarrel with their Maker. Even though the saints learned of their death decree, there was nothing they could do but wait upon deliverance from the Lord.

{15} Then Jesus spoke to His anxious saints. He said, "Behold, I am coming soon! Don't be discouraged by the death decree. It will not stand. Trust in God. Blessed is he who stands firm in faith and remains alert. Do not worry, for my enemies will be stripped of their useless armor so that their nakedness and shame will be exposed."

{16} Then the demons of Satan gathered the kings of earth together to the place that in Hebrew is called Armageddon. This place is not a geographical place. It is a situation or predicament. In Hebrew, the word Armageddon is a combination of two words meaning "the mountain of Megiddo." There

NIV

{15} "Behold, I come like a thief! Blessed is he who stays awake and keeps his clothes with him, so that he may not go naked and be shamefully exposed."

{16} Then they gathered the kings together to the place that in Hebrew is called Armageddon.

NIV	Interlaced thoughts
	is no literal mountain bearing this name. However, there is a plain called Megiddo where king Josiah was foolishly killed when he went out to fight the king Neco of Egypt against God's orders.[3]
	The figurative meaning of Armageddon is twofold. First, a mountain symbolizes the place of God and on this summit, the God of gods will be revealed just like in the days of Elijah at Mt. Carmel.[4] Secondly, Megiddo symbolizes death to those who fight against God. So, the people of earth will see a great revelation at Armageddon. They shall see the One who is King of kings and Lord of lords.
	The kings of earth unite to kill the remnant of God and destroy Jesus when He appears. Their vote will be cast with the devil and his demons. As a result, they will quickly move to kill all the people of God and just as they attempt to execute the death decree, they will be arrested by Jesus. The leaders of the world will be caught *red-handed* with intent to murder the innocent of Almighty God. The arrest will be a powerful manifestation of God. The shame of the wicked will be fully seen.
	Once powerful but now powerless, once strong but now broken, once believing in the devil but now stubborn in their stupidity, now seeing the world as completely uninhabitable, now bearing the ugly

Interlaced thoughts

tatoo of their leader on their foreheads and hands, the wicked continue to stand in opposition to the Eternal God. They have fought in vain. First they refused to receive salvation, now they refuse to comprehend the results of sin and rebellion against Jesus.

During the next 45[5] days, the wicked will behold the collapse of their authority and rule over earth as Jesus takes each element within Babylon apart. It will be a pathetic picture. The saints will stand in awe as they behold the world reduced to ruins right before their eyes. Then Jesus will commission the seventh angel.

{17} The seventh angel poured out his bowl into the air, and out of the temple came a loud voice from the throne, saying, "It is finished!" The angels and the universe were more than satisfied with the consummation of the plan of salvation. The consequences of evil had been fully revealed. None shall ever again question the holiness, authority or love of God. {18} Then, around the earth came flashes of lightning, rumblings, peals of thunder and a severe earthquake. No earthquake like it has ever occurred since man lived on earth, so tremendous was the quake. {19} The great city of Babylon, the throne of the devil, was split into three parts, and the cities of all nations also collapsed. God remembered every deed of

NIV

{17} The seventh angel poured out his bowl into the air, and out of the temple came a loud voice from the throne, saying, "It is done!"

{18} Then there came flashes of lightning, rumblings, peals of thunder and a severe earthquake. No earthquake like it has ever occurred since man has been on earth, so tremendous was the quake.

{19} The great city split into three parts, and the cities of the nations collapsed. God remembered Babylon the Great and gave her the cup

NIV

filled with the wine of the fury of his wrath.

{20} Every island fled away and the mountains could not be found.

{21} From the sky huge hailstones of about a hundred pounds each fell upon men. And they cursed God on account of the plague of hail, because the plague was so terrible.

Interlaced thoughts

Babylon the Great and she drank the fury of His wrath just as she had made His saints drink from her cup. {20} Then, the Father and Son, and all their glorious angels appeared in the sky. Every island fled away and the mountains could not be found so great was the earthquake. {21} From the heavens, huge rocks fell upon men. As Jesus appeared in the clouds, men cried "fall on us and hide us from them that sit on the throne." And they cursed God on account of the plague of the hailstones, because the plague was so terrible.

References

1. Revelation 11:19
2. Revelation 9:13-21
3. 2 Kings 23:29
4. 1 Kings 18:24
5. Time between 1290 and 1335 days of Daniel 12:11,12

Commentary

Revelation 17:1-18

Synopsis: The chronology of the apocalyptic prophecies pauses momentarily with this chapter. Here, several explanations are given so that we might clearly identify certain elements. Remember, the specifications for each element have to be carefully incorporated in our interpretation. This chapter is often regarded as one of the most difficult to understand in all of Revelation. However, once the contents of this chapter are understood, they make perfect sense *just as they read.* The reader is encouraged to read this chapter several times and then Prophecies 10-18 will make much more sense.

NIV	Interlaced thoughts
{1} One of the seven angels who had the seven bowls came and said to me, "Come, I will show you the punishment of the great prostitute, who sits on many waters.	{1} One of the seven angels who had the seven bowls of God's wrath came to me and said, "Come with me John, and I will show you the punishment of the great prostitute who will sit upon many nations, languages and peoples. This is very important John, for she will be great throughout the earth. Only the saints will refuse her evil demands.
{2} With her the kings of the earth committed adultery and the inhabitants of the earth were intoxicated with the wine of her adulteries."	{2} The kings of the earth will greatly offend the God of Heaven by committing adultery with her and the inhabitants of the earth will be intoxicated with her wicked ideas. Her doctrine will be evil just as the union of church and state is evil."
{3} Then the angel carried me away in the Spirit into a desert. There I saw a woman sitting on a scarlet beast that was covered with blasphemous names and had seven heads and ten horns.	{3} Then the angel carried me away in the Spirit to see the world during the sixth trumpet. For the most part, it was barren like a great desert–destruction everywhere. There I saw a great prostitute sitting on the dragonlike beast that I had seen in Revelation 13. Again, I saw seven heads and ten horns and the heads had names of blasphemy written on them. The beast was red

Interlaced thoughts

because inside this beast, like a red hand in a latex glove, I saw the great red dragon. {4} The whore was dressed in royal purple, the color of kings; she was also adorned with scarlet, the color of clergy and to make herself outwardly beautiful, she was glittering with gold, precious stones and pearls. She held a golden cup in her hand, filled with horrible things and the filth of her adulteries. I wondered about the cup. I was told it was her cup of iniquity. This was an astonishing thing to behold. God grants people, nations and even this great prostitute an opportunity to reveal their attitude toward His authority and when they fill up their cup of iniquity, God responds.

I asked what the great prostitute represented. The angel said, "This whore represents the global union of church and state which the devil shall achieve during the sixth trumpet war. Remember in Prophecy 12 that the lamblike beast created an image of Babylon? That image and this whore are the *same* item represented in two different ways. In Prophecy 12, she is called an image because she is a "look-alike" clone of the false religious systems of the world. In this commentary, the consolidated religious system of the world is a great whore because she is totally detestable to God.

NIV

{4} The woman was dressed in purple and scarlet, and was glittering with gold, precious stones and pearls. She held a golden cup in her hand, filled with abominable things and the filth of her adulteries.

NIV

Interlaced thoughts

Compare the whole with the bride of Jesus. The beautiful woman in Prophecy 12 is the bride of Jesus. This harlot is the slave of Satan. The bride of Jesus is pure and the harlot of the devil is filthy. The bride of Jesus represents those who place explicit faith in Him and the harlot represents those who join with the devil in rebellion against God. The point is that when God sends the seven trumpets, everyone will have to either place faith in Jesus or align themselves with the devil. This is the great test of the human race. I looked again at the whore as she sat upon the religious and political systems of the world. She was greater than anything on earth. All people were required to obey her and to receive a mark on their forehead or on their right hand.

{5} This title was written on her forehead: **MYSTERY BABYLON THE GREAT THE MOTHER OF PROSTITUTES AND OF THE ABOMINATIONS OF THE EARTH.**

{5} She had a tatoo on her forehead. These names were written on her forehead: **MYSTERY, BABYLON THE GREAT, THE MOTHER OF PROSTITUTES AND OF THE ABOMINATIONS OF THE EARTH.** I thought about these names. The title, "Mystery," surely belongs to sin. There is no justification for it. The name, "Babylon the Great," reveals that the harlot is well respected among men because of her world-wide representation. The name, "The Mother of Prostitutes and of the Abominations of the earth," explains that she is the final product of all that is evil. She is the greatest

Interlaced thoughts

embodiment of evil the world has ever seen.

{6} I saw the woman put many of the saints to death, in fact, she considered it sport and she used the blood of saints to scare millions into submission. I saw many cowards yield to the whore during this time of persecution. So many died resisting her that the whore became drunk with the blood of those who bore testimony to Jesus. As I watched her, I became terribly ill.

{7} Then the angel said to me: "Why are you so overwhelmed? I will now explain to you the mystery of the woman and of the beast she rides, which has seven heads and ten horns. But before I tell you about the woman and the beast she rides, you must first know something about the appearing of the lamblike beast.

{8} The great red dragon which you saw in Revelation 12, once was in heaven, but he was cast into the Abyss. During the fifth trumpet, he will come up out of the spirit-world of the Abyss and eventually go to his destruction. The inhabitants of the earth whose names have not been written in the book of life from the creation of the world will be astonished when they see the lamblike beast. Mortal eyes have never beheld the glory of such a being. Furthermore, only a very few people anticipate the fact that the devil is going to appear. But when

NIV

{6} I saw that the woman was drunk with the blood of the saints, the blood of those who bore testimony to Jesus. When I saw her, I was greatly astonished.

{7} Then the angel said to me: "Why are you astonished? I will explain to you the mystery of the woman and of the beast she rides, which has the seven heads and ten horns.

{8} The beast, which you saw, once was, now is not, and will come up out of the Abyss and go to his destruction. The inhabitants of the earth whose names have not been written in the book of life from the creation of the world will be astonished when they see the beast, because he once was, now is not, and yet will come.

NIV

{9} "This calls for a mind with wisdom. The seven heads are seven hills on which the woman sits.

Interlaced thoughts

he does, there will great astonishment because he once was visible, but since his expulsion from heaven – he is not visible, and yet, he will fully appear before the people of earth. He will fully appear and walk about upon the earth in various places and the people will be completely surprised. "Watch for him."

{9} John, this information won't be hard to understand when the events happen. However, to understand them *before* they begin to come to pass requires considerable study. So, this calls for a mind with wisdom. The seven heads are seven unholy hills or mountains upon which the woman sits. You already know two things about the seven heads. First, they are blasphemous or anti-Christ. Secondly, the sixth head was wounded in 1798, but when Babylon rises from the sea, that head will be healed. The seven heads are seven religious systems. Now consider why they are figuratively described as seven hills.

Jerusalem is figuratively called, "Mt. Zion," and you know that the temple of God sits on His holy hill in heaven, and you also know that the pagans regularly worship on mountain tops or highest hills because they believe that gods dwell in the mountains. So, the seven religious systems of the world are likened unto hills or mountains because people *look up to them* as

Interlaced thoughts

having the authority of God.[1] In other words, people look up to their religious leaders for instructions from God. Even in the United States, Americans call their most important building, "Capitol Hill" for in that building, the nation's laws are passed.

{10} The seven heads are also seven kings. This means that each head is a kingdom having subjects. Each religious system has its own rulers and its subjects. When Jesus was born, five of these religious systems were exposed as false. They are:

1. Atheism
2. Heathenism
3. Judaism
4. Eastern Mysticism
5. Islam*

*Note: The title of Islam used here refers to the primitive doctrines of the descendants of Ishmael. Even though Mohammed lived in the sixth century A.D., Ishmael is considered the founder of Islam.

So, John, as of today, five heads have been exposed as false. They are fallen. The sixth head is Christianity which will become known as Catholicism in centuries to come. You, John, are a charter member of this great head which in later times, will become blasphemous. This is the sixth head that shall be wounded[2] at the

NIV

{10} They are also seven kings. Five have fallen, one is, the other has not yet come; but when he does come, he must remain for a little while.

NIV

{11} The beast who once was, and now is not, is an eighth king. He belongs to the seven and is going to his destruction.

{12} "The ten horns you saw are ten kings who have not yet received a kingdom, but who for one hour will receive authority as kings along with the beast.

{13} They have one purpose and will give their power and authority to the beast.

Interlaced thoughts

appointed time, but the deadly wound shall be healed in the last days.[3] The seventh head has not yet come; but when Protestantism does come, it will remain for less than 400 years. When you consider that the other six heads will last for 2,000 years or more, Protestantism will only last a short time.

{11} The lamblike beast you saw, once was visible, and then he was cast out of heaven and put in the Abyss so that he is not visible to human beings at the moment, but he will physically appear "here and there"[4] and he will become the eighth king. He will closely identify with the seven heads and he is going to his destruction with them. The reason he is called an eighth king is so that you may draw a comparison from Prophecy 2 where the little horn uprooted three horns and became the eighth. Just as the little horn dominated the remaining seven horns, so the devil shall dominate the religions of the world. This is an important parallel. Watch for it.

{12} The ten horns you saw are ten kings (the ten toes) who will rule over the world in its final days. During the days of the sixth trumpet, the final hour of God's mercy, the devil will set up ten vassals of his one-world empire.
{13} These will have one purpose. They are pawns of the devil. They will give their power and authority

Interlaced thoughts

to him. {14} They will join with the religious leaders and the devil to make war against the Lamb as He appears in the clouds, but the Lamb will overcome them because he is Lord of lords and King of kings – and when Jesus appears in the clouds, the wicked will not only behold Jesus, they will see His 144,000 servants who were taken into heaven at time of the special resurrection in Prophecy 10."[5]

{15} Then the angel said to me, "The waters you saw, where the whore sits, are peoples, multitudes, nations and languages. Like a giant wrestler winning the match, she sits upon the whole world as victor.

{16} After the fifth plague is poured out upon the throne of the devil, Babylon, the beast having seven heads, and ten horns, will hate the dominion of the prostitute. Each religious entity will see that they have been deceived by the devil. The coalition will collapse. They will destroy the religious system set up by the devil. They will see their ruin and leave her naked; they will eat her flesh and burn her with fire – so great will be their wrath. They will be very angry with themselves for having believed the lies of the devil. {17} Whosoever refuses to receive the truth and be saved, the same will obey the devil. God has determined that the contents of every heart shall be revealed. Those who refuse to worship God will,

NIV

{14} They will make war against the Lamb, but the Lamb will overcome them because he is Lord of lords and King of kings - and with him will be his called, chosen and faithful followers."

{15} Then the angel said to me, "The waters you saw, where the prostitute sits, are peoples, multitudes, nations and languages.

{16} The beast and the ten horns you saw will hate the prostitute. They will bring her to ruin and leave her naked; they will eat her flesh and burn her with fire.

{17} For God has put it into their hearts to accomplish his purpose by agreeing to give the beast their power to rule, until God's words are fulfilled.

NIV

{18} The woman you saw is the great city that rules over the kings of the earth."

References

1. Isaiah 2:2; Daniel 9:16,20; Jeremiah 3:6, Psalm 2:6; 15:1; Hosea 4:13
2. Daniel 7:21-25
3. Revelation 13:3
4. Matthew 24:23
5. Revelation 11:12, 19:1-8

Interlaced thoughts

even in their rebellion, accomplish his grand purpose by agreeing to give Babylon their power to rule, until God's appointed time is fulfilled. {18} Watch for the appearing of the great whore. The evil woman you saw is the coming great city that will rule over the kings of the earth."

Prophecy 15

Revelation 18:1-8

Beginning point in time: Shortly before the sixth trumpet
Ending point in time: Shortly before the seventh trumpet
Synopsis: This short prophecy describes the final invitation to salvation. This event begins just before the sixth trumpet war begins and this message ends just before the seventh trumpet sounds. This is God's final call. Two things stand out in this prophecy. First, as high and mighty as Babylon may think she is, she is full of evil and is mortal. Secondly, the devil has no friends. He will use anyone who supports his scheme but, in the end, he loves no one but himself. The reader should read the remainder of Revealtion 18 in his Bible.

NIV

{1} After this I saw another angel coming down from heaven. He had great authority, and the earth was illuminated by his splendor.

Interlaced thoughts

{1} Then I saw another scene. This scene begins just before the sixth trumpet war. I saw a mighty angel come down from heaven. He had even greater power than the three angels with the three messages, and the whole earth heard his powerful message in just a few days. I marveled at the power of his message. I saw him join in with the three angels of Revelation 14 and as a result, the remaining 144,000 were given even more power than before. Then I realized what was taking place. God was sending a final call to save any who would step across the line and submit to His authority. I saw that standing for Jesus required great faith, for now the devil preparing to take control of earth. Soon Jesus would close the door to mercy and because He loves each person so much, and because He does not want one to perish, Jesus sends this angel to earth with His final invitation.

Interlaced thoughts

{2} With a mighty voice the angel shouted: "Fallen! Fallen is Babylon the Great! She has become a home for demons and a haunt for every evil spirit, a cage for every unclean and detestable bird." This language goes back to the days of Jeremiah when Israel had abandoned God.[1] This language means that Babylon is like a cage. And just as men snare birds and fill their cages full for the market, so the devil has snared a cage full of demons and evil men. And as birds do not understand their fate, neither do the victims of the devil understand theirs.

{3} The angel continued saying "For all the nations have drunk the maddening wine of her adulteries. The kings of the earth have committed adultery with her, and the merchants of the earth have grown rich from her excessive luxuries." This phrase comes from the prophets Jeremiah and Ezekiel. It means that under the distressing circumstances of the time, kings and rulers of earth will endorse the deadly aims of the devil's religious systems. They will unite in an unholy alliance. Religious leaders will appeal to civil authorities for laws enforcing false worship upon the people. For the sake of political expediency, the rulers will comply. In return, kings and politicians will maintain their powers. Those who trade in food and the necessities of life will become rich for they will grossly overcharge the people due

NIV

{2} With a mighty voice he shouted: "Fallen! Fallen is Babylon the Great! She has become a home for demons and a haunt for every evil spirit, a haunt for every unclean and detestable bird.

{3} For all the nations have drunk the maddening wine of her adulteries. The kings of the earth committed adultery with her, and the merchants of the earth grew rich from her excessive luxuries."

NIV

{4} Then I heard another voice from heaven say: "Come out of her, my people, so that you will not share in her sins, so that you will not receive any of her plagues; {5} for her sins are piled up to heaven, and God has remembered her crimes. {6} Give back to her as she has given; pay her back double for what she has done. Mix her a double portion from her own cup.

{7} Give her as much torture and grief as the glory and luxury she gave herself. In her heart she boasts, 'I sit as queen; I am not a widow, and I will never mourn.'

{8} Therefore in one day her plagues will overtake her: death, mourning and famine. She will be consumed by fire, for mighty is the Lord God who judges her."

Interlaced thoughts

to the scarcity of basic necessities. The rich will get richer and the poor will despair.

{4} Then I heard Jesus say: "Come out of her, my people, so that you will not share in her sins, so that you will not receive any of her seven plagues; {5} for her sins are piled up to heaven, and God has marked every one of her awful crimes. {6} "Now I will give back to her as she has dealt with my people; I will pay her back *double* for what she has done. I will give her a *double* portion from her own cup for she has not only violated my saints, she has violated Me. I am a great king. I own the earth and the fullness thereof."

{7} She will receive as much torture and grief as the glory and luxury she gave herself for God's vengeance is fair. The leaders of Babylon may think, 'We sit as a queen; We rule over the earth, who shall rule over us?[2] We are not a poor widow having no protector, we will never mourn, we are almighty.' But, they do not know Me. "As ants are to man, so Babylon is to Me. They do not know me or my ways." {8} Therefore, at the appointed time, her plagues will begin and they will overtake her and destroy her. This great organization will receive death, mourning and famine. She will be consumed by fire, for Almighty is

Interlaced thoughts

the God of earth who judges and sentences her.

NIV

References

1. Jeremiah 5:26-28
2. Lamentations 1:1

Prophecy 16

Revelation 19:1-20:6

Beginning point in time: Just before Second Coming
Ending point in time: During the millennium
Synopsis: This prophecy reveals three important truths. First, the 144,000 will be received into heaven before the rest of the redeemed as first fruits of the harvest. Secondly, the *assumed body* of the devil, and Babylon will be destroyed at the Second Coming. Lastly, the saints will determine the *amount* of punishment due each wicked person during the millennium. Everyone who violated God's standards of behavior will receive punishment commensurate with their crimes. Justice will be fully served.

NIV

{1} After this I heard what sounded like the roar of a great multitude in heaven shouting: "Hallelujah! Salvation and glory and power belong to our God,

{2} for true and just are his judgments. He has condemned the great prostitute who corrupted the earth by her adulteries. He has avenged on her the blood of his servants." {3} And again they shouted: "Hallelujah! The smoke from her goes up for ever and ever." {4} The twenty-four elders and the four living creatures fell down and worshiped God, who was seated on the throne. And they cried: "Amen, Hallelujah!"

{5} Then a voice came from the throne, saying: "Praise our God, all you his servants, you who fear him, both small and great!"

Interlaced thoughts

{1} Then, I looked up into heaven and I saw the 144,000 who had been taken up into heaven. They were the first fruits of the great harvest and they were called up to heaven at the time of the special resurrection. I heard them shouting: "Hallelujah! Salvation and glory and power belong to our God, {2} for true and just are his judgments. He has condemned the great prostitute who corrupted the earth by her adulteries and He has avenged our blood and suffering upon her." {3} And again they shouted: "Hallelujah! The smoke from her destruction goes up for ever and ever." {4} The twenty-four elders and the four living creatures fell down and worshiped God, who was seated on the throne. And they cried: "Amen, Hallelujah!"

{5} Then a voice came from one of the four living creatures who attends the throne of God, saying to the 144,000, "Praise our God, all you servants, you who fear him, both small and great!"

Interlaced thoughts

{6} Then I heard the 144,000 sing, like the roar of rushing waters and like loud peals of thunder, shouting: "Hallelujah! For our Lord God Almighty reigns.

{7} Let us rejoice and be glad and give him glory! For the wedding of the Lamb has now come, and His bride, His kingdom of saints, has made herself ready. He will now go to earth and retrieve her into His mansion which He has prepared for all that love His name.

{8} Beautiful clothes made of fine linen, bright and clean, were all laid out for the saints." (Figuratively speaking, fine linen stands for the righteousness of Jesus which the saints received as a gift.)

{9} Then the angel said to me, "Write this down so there can be no misunderstanding: 'Blessed are those who are invited to the wedding supper of the Lamb!' " And he added, "These are the true words of God."

{10} At this I fell at the feet of the angel to worship him. But he said to me, "Do not do it, John! I am a fellow servant with you and with your brothers who hold to the words of Jesus. Worship the living God! For everything that comes out of the mouth of Jesus is His testimony. And His testimony will be fully understood by the 144,000 who shall receive the gift of

NIV

{6} Then I heard what sounded like a great multitude, like the roar of rushing waters and like loud peals of thunder, shouting: "Hallelujah! For our Lord God Almighty reigns. {7} Let us rejoice and be glad and give him glory! For the wedding of the Lamb has come, and his bride has made herself ready.

{8} Fine linen, bright and clean, was given her to wear." (Fine linen stands for the righteous acts of the saints.)

{9} Then the angel said to me, "Write: 'Blessed are those who are invited to the wedding supper of the Lamb!' " And he added, "These are the true words of God."

{10} At this I fell at his feet to worship him. But he said to me, "Do not do it! I am a fellow servant with you and with your brothers who hold to the testimony of Jesus. Worship God! For the testimony of Jesus is the spirit of prophecy."

NIV

{11} I saw heaven standing open and there before me was a white horse, whose rider is called Faithful and True. With justice he judges and makes war.

{12} His eyes are like blazing fire, and on his head are many crowns. He has a name written on him that no one knows but he himself.

{13} He is dressed in a robe dipped in blood, and his name is the Word of God.

{14} The armies of heaven were following him, riding on white horses and dressed in fine linen, white and clean.

{15} Out of his mouth comes a sharp sword with which to strike down the nations. "He will rule them with an iron scepter." He treads the winepress of the fury of the wrath of God Almighty.

Interlaced thoughts

understanding prophecy from the Holy Spirit."

{11} I waited for a short time. A great parade was assembled in heaven. Then, I saw heaven standing open and there before me was a white horse. The Grand Marshal of the parade is a rider called Faithful and True because He is known to keep every promise and judge every deed with truth. With justice He judges the conduct of man and makes war against His enemies.
{12} His eyes are like blazing fire. No one hides from His sight. On His head are seven crowns of victory and authority. He has a name written on Him that no one knows but He himself. This name has been kept secret until the marriage of the Lamb because the devil would have desecrated His name by claiming it if it were
known. {13} He is dressed in a robe dipped in blood for He has been to the tomb of the second death and is alive forever more. His everlasting name is the Word of God for He is the faithful and true
expression of God's will. {14} The armies of heaven were following him. They were riding on white horses as if prepared for battle. They were dressed in fine linen,
white and clean. {15} Jesus speaks, and out of his mouth comes something like a sharp sword with which to strike down the nations. His enemies cannot resist Him. "He will rule them with an iron scepter."

Interlaced thoughts

He is angry. He treads the winepress of the fury of the wrath of God Almighty. {16} On His robe and on His thigh He has this name written: KING OF KINGS AND LORD OF LORDS and no one can argue His claim.

{17} Just as the parade began to move toward earth, I saw Jesus, in glory bright as the sun. He call in a loud voice to all the birds flying in midair, "Come, gather together for the great supper of God, {18} so that you may eat the flesh of kings, generals, and mighty men, of horses and their riders, and the flesh of all people, free and slave, small and great."

{19} The wicked, caught "red-handed" trying to kill His saints, realized their doom. I saw the beast with seven heads and the ten kings of the earth gathered together at a place called Armageddon. They were prepared to make war against the Rider on the white horse and His army. At the command of the devil, the kings of earth agreed to kill all of God's people before He could rescue them. {20} But Babylon and its evil leader, the false prophet, the father of liars, the ancient serpent who performed miraculous signs on Babylon's behalf, were arrested by Jesus. Attending Him were His true prophets, the 144,000, who had so bravely countered the deceptions of the devil. The world quickly saw the

NIV

{16} On his robe and on his thigh he has this name written: KING OF KINGS AND LORD OF LORDS.

{17} And I saw an angel standing in the sun, who cried in a loud voice to all the birds flying in midair, "Come, gather together for the great supper of God,
{18} so that you may eat the flesh of kings, generals, and mighty men, of horses and their riders, and the flesh of all people, free and slave, small and great."

{19} Then I saw the beast and the kings of the earth and their armies gathered together to make war against the rider on the horse and his army.

{20} But the beast was captured, and with him the false prophet who had performed the miraculous signs on his behalf. With these signs he had deluded those who had received the mark of the beast and worshiped his image. The two of them were thrown alive into the fiery lake of burning sulfur.

NIV

{21} The rest of them were killed with the sword that came out of the mouth of the rider on the horse, and all the birds gorged themselves on their flesh.

{20:1} And I saw an angel coming down out of heaven, having the key to the Abyss and holding in his hand a great chain.

{2} He seized the dragon, that ancient serpent, who is the devil, or Satan, and bound him for a thousand years.

{3} He threw him into the Abyss, and locked and sealed it over him, to keep him from deceiving the nations anymore until the thousand

Interlaced thoughts

contrast. The devil who claimed to be God now faced his 144,000 accusers, the true prophets of God. Babylon and the devil were caught in the act of trying to kill God's people. Understand that the false prophet had deceived those who had received his mark and they obeyed his commands for great were his miracle-working powers. The great system of Babylon the beast, and Satan's person—her false prophet, were thrown alive into a fiery lake of burning sulfur that Jesus ignited at the second coming. {21} The rest of the wicked were killed with the sword that came out of the mouth of Jesus, and all the birds of earth gorged themselves on their flesh.

So ended the atrocities of Babylon and its leader. But, here is a mystery. The devil was not destroyed by the wrath of Jesus at the second coming, only his physical body was burned up.

{20:1} After all the saints had been removed from earth, I saw an angel come down out of heaven. He had the key to the Abyss and a great chain in his hand. {2} He seized the dragon, that ancient serpent, who is the devil, or Satan, and bound him for a thousand years.

{3} He threw the devil and his angels back into the invisible world of the Abyss (they had been released during the fifth trumpet), and locked and sealed it over them.

Interlaced thoughts

God decreed that the devil could not influence anyone. They were chained to this desolate earth until one thousand years were ended. After that, the devil and his angels would be set free for a short time.

{4} I then looked up into heaven and I saw thrones on which were seated those who had been given authority to judge. There were many thrones. And I saw those who had been beheaded because of their testimony for Jesus and because of the word of God. They had not worshiped the beast or his image and had not received his mark on their foreheads or their hands. These martyrs came to life and reigned on these thrones with Christ a thousand years.

{5} (Those who were killed by the splendor of Jesus at the Second Coming did not come to life until the thousand years were ended.) But the martyrs who refused the mark of the beast were called to life at the Second Coming. This is the first resurrection. {6} Blessed and holy are those who have part in the first resurrection. The second death which comes at the end of the millennium has no power over them. However, these martyrs will be priests of God and of Christ and will reign with Him for a thousand years.

Note: the righteous will determine the punishment for those who persecuted them. God declares that

NIV

years were ended. After that, he must be set free for a short time.

{4} I saw thrones on which were seated those who had been given authority to judge. And I saw the souls of those who had been beheaded because of their testimony for Jesus and because of the word of God. They had not worshiped the beast or his image and had not received his mark on their foreheads or their hands. They came to life and reigned with Christ a thousand years.

{5} (The rest of the dead did not come to life until the thousand years were ended.) This is the first resurrection.

{6} Blessed and holy are those who have part in the first resurrection. The second death has no power over them, but they will be priests of God and of Christ and will reign with him for a thousand years.

NIV

Interlaced thoughts

vengeance is His, but His people shall determine the amount of punishment. (I Corinthians 6:2,3, Matthew 19:28) Men who have been particularly violent will suffer longer than those who were not so evil. Every man will be fully rewarded according to his deeds. Complete atonement will be made by the wicked: a life for a life, an eye for an eye, a tooth for a tooth.

Prophecy 17

Revelation 20:7-21:1

Beginning point in time: End of the millennium
Ending point in time: Earth made new
Synopsis: This prophecy explains how God will fairly deal with the wicked at the end of the millennium. Even more, this prophecy reveals the great mystery behind the Book of Life, the book sealed with seven seals. The opening of this book exposes the devil as the father of liars and the Father as a confirmed God of love. Throughout all eternity, God's subjects will never again question His honesty or integrity.

NIV	Interlaced thoughts
{7} When the thousand years are over, Satan will be released from his prison	{7} When the thousand years were over, Jesus returned to earth with all the saints in the Holy City. Then, the wicked of all ages were resurrected and Satan was released from his prison in the Abyss.
{8} and will go out to deceive the nations in the four corners of the earth – Gog and Magog – to gather them for battle. In number they are like the sand on the seashore.	{8} Immediately, the devil went out to deceive all the nations in the four corners of the earth – just like in the ancient days when Gog, the ruler of Magog, incited the nations against Israel[1] – to gather them for battle. In number they were like the sand on the seashore.
{9} They marched across the breadth of the earth and surrounded the camp of God's people, the city he loves. But fire came down from heaven and devoured them.	{9} Intent upon capturing the Holy City and destroying the saints therein, the wicked mob marched across the breadth of the earth and surrounded the camp of God's people, the great city He loves. But fire came down from heaven and devoured them.
{10} And the devil, who deceived them, was thrown into the lake of burning sulfur, where the beast and the false prophet had been thrown. They will be tormented day and night for ever and ever.	{10} And the devil, who deceived them, was finally thrown into the lake of burning sulfur, where Babylon and the false prophet had been thrown. There, they will be tormented day and night for as long as there is any

Interlaced thoughts

remaining particle for such is the justice of God and the judgment of the saints.

{11} As I reflected on these scenes, I wondered what this had to do with the ultimate vindication of the Father and the book sealed with seven seals. Then I was shown an impressive scene. When Jesus returned to earth with the Holy City and the saints at the end of the thousand years, I saw the wicked resurrected so that they might behold the reality of God. Most of them had died without fearing God and many denied that He even existed. But, *all* of them refused to submit to His authority. What a crowd. The effect of sin upon human beings was sickening for people from every generation now stood outside the city gate. I saw those who lived before the flood. They were much larger than those who lived at the end of time. But, the contrast between the wicked and their mortal bodies and the saints in their immortal bodies was beyond description. Every person who had ever lived on the earth was alive this day. What a throng! The saints were inside the city and the wicked were outside.

The devil urged the wicked to rush upon the Holy City to destroy it. As they rushed upon the City of God, I saw Jesus stand upon a high balcony and command in the same voice that calmed the angry Sea of

NIV

{11} Then I saw a great white throne and him who was seated on it. Earth and sky fled from his presence, and there was no place for them.

NIV

Interlaced thoughts

Galilee, "Peace. Be still." Instantly, a hush fell over the whole earth.

Then, the sky opened up into a giant screen and every being looked into the sky and beheld the story of his life which the angels of God had faithfully recorded. God required each person to behold three things. First, every person saw the plan of salvation fully explained. They saw the fall of Adam and Eve, they saw the destruction of the flood, they saw scenes from Calvary and the great humility that Jesus suffered to make salvation possible for man. Next, each person saw his life-long response to the promptings of the Holy Spirit. The wicked clearly saw their rejection of the love and salvation of Jesus. They saw, with unvarnished clarity, their rejection of the Holy Spirit and the results of their evil deeds and rebellion. On the other hand, the saints beheld the eternal importance of yielding to the impress of the Holy Spirit. Everyone comprehended the effects of their choices for each record was true and faithful. Lastly, the Father required that every person behold his day in heaven's court. He wanted every person to observe the actions of Jesus as He decided their eternal case. At the end of these three scenes, *every* person confessed that Jesus had faithfully judged them and that His judgment was righteous and true.

Interlaced thoughts

{12} And there they stood. The wicked dead, now resurrected, some great in stature and some small, all were standing before the throne and the open books of record which they had just seen in the heavenly panorama. What could they say? How could they argue with a presentation from God? Jesus stepped forward and kindly asked if anyone had a complaint about the truthfulness of the scenes and His judgment. At this request, every knee bowed before its Maker. What could guilty man say to His Creator? It was a scene that shall never be forgotten. The wicked bowed before Jesus admitting that His sentence of eternal death upon them was just and fair. The saints bowed before their Savior realizing that were it not for the great mercy of God, they would have no right to eternal life. But the devil and his angels, who were standing at the back of the great crowd, refused to bow before Jesus.

Then, Jesus held up the Book of Life which had been sealed with seven seals. Before the assembled hosts of heaven and earth, He broke open the seventh and final seal. Then a powerful display occurred in the heavens. The sound was louder than anything I have ever heard. All the people were frightened at the display of God's glory. I saw the great white throne and the Father was seated on it. Like a curtain call, it seemed that

NIV

{12} And I saw the dead, great and small, standing before the throne, and books were opened. Another book was opened, which is the book of life. The dead were judged according to what they had done as recorded in the books.

NIV	Interlaced thoughts
	earth and heaven fled from His presence, and there was no place for them. Now, there was total silence in the heavens. The Book of Life was opened. Everyone present looked into this book which had been written before the angels and the world were created. Now, the sealed contents of this sensitive book would be revealed. Naturally, billions of good and evil angels watched with great interest. And behold, the book contained a faithful record of everything that had happened since angels were created. The book revealed that God knew before Lucifer was created what he would do. The book revealed the lies that Lucifer would tell about His Creator and his work of deception – both in heaven and on earth. But, what was most fascinating to all present, was that the book of Life was identical to the books of record! As I watched this scene, the meaning of this unfolded to me. This was too wonderful! At last, I saw the exoneration of the Father from the false charges the devil had made about Him before the world was created. Here's a summary of the exoneration: The Father knew, even before Lucifer was created, that one day Lucifer would charge Him with evil and malicious deeds. Lucifer would raise doubt about His honesty and integrity by skillfully asking questions which could not be

Interlaced thoughts

answered by fellow angels. It is not possible for a finite mind to comprehend the actions and works of a infinite God. The Father knew He would be misrepresented and misunderstood. And, at the time Lucifer was questioning Him, He did everything He could to satisfy Lucifer's need. But, the real problem was that Lucifer had become jealous of Jesus. He wanted the position that Jesus held in heaven as archangel. The Father plainly told Lucifer that he would never be able to have that position and bitterness grew in Lucifer's heart until open rebellion took place in heaven.

Now that the end had come, the Father could reveal three things. First, He knew what Lucifer would say about Him even before he was created. He knew that Lucifer would bring rebellion to heaven and ultimately cause one-third of the angels to perish. This was all written down in the book. Secondly, He knew the name of each person who would be born on earth and He knew what their life would be. He also knew what each person's choice for eternal destiny would be, and He wrote these things down before the angels and the world were created. But the one thing that stands out above all others, is that the Father, knowing all this in advance, never manipulated any of His creatures to avoid these problems even though He knew the

NIV

NIV	Interlaced thoughts
	great suffering Lucifer would bring to His house. Lucifer had accused the Father of not being a God of love. He accused God of not giving the power of choice to His creatures. Lucifer proclaimed, "Your creatures are nothing more than servants of your desires. They're not free! They're slaves." Now that every person had seen his life pass before him, now that every person had admitted that God's judgment was fair and true, now that every person admitted that his life was accurately judged, the opening of the Book of Life proves that yes, the Father knows everything but, the Father compels no one to serve Him. He does not force anyone to serve Him. His creatures are truly free to exercise the power of choice. And the Book of Life, now opened, is positive proof that God does not use His great powers to manipulate His creatures. Every being is truly granted the inalienable right to exercise choice. The Book of Life is so called because it contains the names of those who shall live throughout eternity. Even though the record of every life is in the book, the names of those who refused salvation were blotted out when the Father wrote the book. Understand, that God did not blot out their names on the basis of predestination, rather, He blotted out those names on the

Interlaced thoughts

basis of foreknowledge. He knew what all choices would be. He did not create anyone to be destroyed. What an infinite God!

So there we were. The wicked dead, just resurrected, now knew they had been fairly judged according to what they had done as recorded in the record books of heaven. The saints stood in awe of God's mercy to them as sinners. {13} Remember, everyone who has ever lived on earth was present. Those who died in the sea and those who had been in graves, and each person was rewarded according to what he had done. And Lucifer, the Father of liars, was summoned to come to the front to stand before the Father and before Jesus. There, before all angels and human beings, Jesus asked the devil if the records, now exposed in the books of record and the Book of Life, were true. He asked if He had been faithful and true in presenting the events as they were. The devil responded by bowing before the Father and Jesus saying, "I am a liar. You alone are righteous and true." As the wicked beheld this scene, words cannot describe their outrage toward this guilty thug so full of evil. In a murderous frenzy the wicked rushed upon the devil and his demons to destroy them – but what is human strength compared to that of an angel?

NIV

{13} The sea gave up the dead that were in it, and death and Hades gave up the dead that were in them, and each person was judged according to what he had done.

NIV

{14} Then death and Hades were thrown into the lake of fire. The lake of fire is the second death.

{15} If anyone's name was not found written in the book of life, he was thrown into the lake of fire.

{21:1} Then I saw a new heaven and a new earth, for the first heaven and the first earth had passed away, and there was no longer any sea.

References

1. Ezekiel 38
2. Deuteronomy 32:43; Isaiah 34:8; Hebrews 10:30; Malachi 4:1-3
3. 2 Peter 3:13

Interlaced thoughts

{14} Then fire fell from the heavens. The earth seemed as though it were made of flammable material. The great horde of evil people and even death and the grave itself were thrown into the lake of fire. This lake of fire is the second death. {15} If anyone's name was not found written in the book of life, he was thrown into a great lake of fire.

After several days, the wicked were finally consumed by fire. The devil and his angels suffered until the guilt of their sins was fully atoned for.[2]

{21:1} Then I saw a new heaven and a new earth, for the first heaven and the first earth had passed away, and there was no longer any great sea of fire.[3]

Prophecy 18

Revelation 21:2-22:5

Beginning point in time: Descent of the Holy City
Ending point in time: New Earth created
Synopsis: This prophecy describes the installment of Jesus and His people into their new kingdom. It is important to note that Jesus requires His people to be patient but strong, sympathetic to sinners but resisting evil, full of faith and pure in heart. Given the frailty of humanity, the worsening conditions of earth and hour of trial before us, these qualifications can only be developed if we are willing live by faith.

NIV

{2} I saw the Holy City, the new Jerusalem, coming down out of heaven from God, prepared as a bride beautifully dressed for her husband.

{3} And I heard a loud voice from the throne saying, "Now the dwelling of God is with men, and he will live with them. They will be his people, and God himself will be with them and be their God.
{4} He will wipe every tear from their eyes. There will be no more death or mourning or crying or pain, for the old order of things has passed away."

Interlaced thoughts

{2} Then I saw another scene. I saw the Holy City, the new Jerusalem, coming down from God out of heaven. The capital city of the kingdom, New Jerusalem, was prepared as a bride for her husband. {3} And I heard Jesus say in a loud voice: "Now the dwelling of God is with men, and He will live with them. They will be His people, and God Himself will be with them and be their God.
{4} He will wipe every tear from their eyes. There will be no more death or mourning or crying or pain, for the old order of things has passed away."

I understood two wonderful things about this decree. First, God intends to exalt the redeemed of earth as administrators of His universe. And the angels will be honored to serve the saints for such is the kingdom of heaven: the greater the level of service, the greater the servant. God will move His throne to earth which will hereafter serve as the administrative center of the universe.

Interlaced thoughts

This transition does not lessen the glory of God; rather, it elevates the position of human beings, for who can subtract glory from God?

Secondly, I understood that God will remove those feelings from the saints that make them sad, for when the saints beheld the punishment of the wicked, they wept and wept. Jesus and the hosts of heaven also wept. Many, many friends and family perished in the lake of fire. But, when sin and sinners are no more, God will seal out emotional attachments from the past and the joy of the saints will focus on eternal joys. There will be no more tears for the old order has passed away.

{5} Jesus said, "I am making everything new!" Then he said to me, "Write this vision down John, for these words are trustworthy and true." {6} He said to me: "Now you have received a view of what I am going to do and how I shall do it. It will be done just as you saw. I am the Alpha and the Omega, the Beginning and the End. I am Almighty God. Let everyone know that those who are thirsty for heavenly things, I will give them drink without cost from the spring of the water of life. {7} He who overcomes the suffering inflicted by the devil, his image and his mark will inherit all this, and I will be his God and he will be my son forever.

NIV

{5} He who was seated on the throne said, "I am making everything new!" Then he said, "Write this down, for these words are trustworthy and true." {6} He said to me: "It is done. I am the Alpha and the Omega, the Beginning and the End. To him who is thirsty I will give to drink without cost from the spring of the water of life.

{7} He who overcomes will inherit all this, and I will be his God and he will be my son.

NIV

{8} But the cowardly, the unbelieving, the vile, the murderers, the sexually immoral, those who practice magic arts, the idolaters and all liars – their place will be in the fiery lake of burning sulfur. This is the second death."

{9} One of the seven angels who had the seven bowls full of the seven last plagues came and said to me, "Come, I will show you the bride, the wife of the Lamb." {10} And he carried me away in the Spirit to a mountain great and high, and showed me the Holy City, Jerusalem, coming down out of heaven from God.

{11} It shone with the glory of God, and its brilliance was like that of a very precious jewel, like a jasper, clear as crystal.

{12} It had a great, high wall with twelve gates, and with twelve angels at the gates. On the gates were written the names of the twelve tribes of Israel. {13} There were three gates on the east, three on the north, three on the south and three on the west. {14} The wall of the city had twelve foundations, and on them were the names of the twelve apostles of the Lamb. {15} The angel who talked with me had a measuring rod of gold to measure the city, its gates and its walls.

Interlaced thoughts

{8} But mark these words. The cowardly, the unbelieving, the vile, the murderers, the sexually immoral, those who practice magic arts, the idolaters and all liars – their place will be in the fiery lake of burning sulfur. This is the second death."

{9} One of the seven angels of the seven last plagues came and said, "Come with me John, I will show you the bride, the glorious kingdom of the Lamb. Come and behold the saints." {10} And he carried me away in the Spirit to a mountain great and high, and showed me the Holy City, the capital of His kingdom, New Jerusalem, filled with God's saints, coming down out of heaven from the dwelling place of God.

Interlaced thoughts

{16} The city was laid out like a square, as long as it was wide. He measured the city with the rod and found it to reach a distance equal to that between old Jerusalem and Rome (1,400 miles). Like a giant cube, the city was as wide and high as it was long.

{17} He measured its wall and it was 200 feet thick, by man's measurement, which the angel was using. {18} The wall was made of jasper, and the city of pure gold, as pure as glass.

{19} The foundations of the city walls were decorated with every kind of precious stone. The first foundation was jasper, the second sapphire, the third chalcedony, the fourth emerald, {20} the fifth sardonyx, the sixth carnelian, the seventh chrysolite, the eighth beryl, the ninth topaz, the tenth chrysoprase, the eleventh jacinth, and the twelfth amethyst. {21} The twelve gates were twelve pearls, each gate made of a single pearl. The great street of the city was of pure gold, like transparent glass. How can words describe the glory of this city?

{22} I did not see a temple in the city, because the Lord God Almighty and the Lamb are its temple. People in the Holy City will not worship in a temple because they will worship the living God from one Sabbath to another!

NIV

{16} The city was laid out like a square, as long as it was wide. He measured the city with the rod and found it to be 12,000 stadia in length, and as wide and high as it is long.

{17} He measured its wall and it was 144 cubits thick, by man's measurement, which the angel was using. {18} The wall was made of jasper, and the city of pure gold, as pure as glass.

{19} The foundations of the city walls were decorated with every kind of precious stone. The first foundation was jasper, the second sapphire, the third chalcedony, the fourth emerald, {20} the fifth sardonyx, the sixth carnelian, the seventh chrysolite, the eighth beryl, the ninth topaz, the tenth chrysoprase, the eleventh jacinth, and the twelfth amethyst. {21} The twelve gates were twelve pearls, each gate made of a single pearl. The great street of the city was of pure gold, like transparent glass.

{22} I did not see a temple in the city, because the Lord God Almighty and the Lamb are its temple.

NIV

{23} The city does not need the sun or the moon to shine on it, for the glory of God gives it light, and the Lamb is its lamp. {24} The nations will walk by its light, and the kings of the earth will bring their splendor into it.

{25} On no day will its gates ever be shut, for there will be no night there. {26} The glory and honor of the nations will be brought into it.

{27} Nothing impure will ever enter it, nor will anyone who does what is shameful or deceitful, but only those whose names are written in the Lamb's book of life.

{22:1} Then the angel showed me the river of the water of life, as clear as crystal, flowing from the throne of God and of the Lamb {2} down the middle of the great street of the city. On each side of the river stood the tree of life, bearing twelve crops of fruit, yielding its fruit every month. And the leaves of the tree are for the healing of the nations.

Interlaced thoughts

{23} The city does not need the sun or the moon to shine on it, for the glory of God gives it light, and the Lamb is its lamp. {24} The redeemed of all nations will walk by its light, and the 144,000,—the kings of the new earth—will bring their splendor into it. {25} On no day will its gates ever be shut, for there will be no darkness or fear there. {26} The glory and honor of all the redeemed from every nation, kindred, tongue and people will be brought into it. {27} Nothing impure will ever enter it, nor will anyone who does what is shameful or deceitful, but only those whose names are written in the Lamb's Book of Life.

{22:1} Then the angel showed me the river of the water of life, as clear as crystal, flowing from the throne of God and of the Lamb {2} down the middle of the great street of the city. On each side of the river stood the tree of life, bearing twelve crops of fruit, yielding its fruit every month. And the leaves of the tree will be for the healing of the redeemed from all nations. Because of sin, the human family was once separated by language, religions and distance. Now, they will be brought together as one family and they will meet at the tree of life and become acquainted.

Interlaced thoughts

{3} No longer will there be any curse. Sin is gone forever. The throne of God and of the Lamb will be in the city, and his servants will serve him. {4} They will see his face, and his name will be written on their foreheads.

{5} There will be no more darkness. They will not need the light of a lamp or the light of the sun, for the Lord God will give them light. And they will reign for ever and ever.

NIV

{3} No longer will there be any curse. The throne of God and of the Lamb will be in the city, and his servants will serve him.
{4} They will see his face, and his name will be on their foreheads.

{5} There will be no more night. They will not need the light of a lamp or the light of the sun, for the Lord God will give them light. And they will reign for ever and ever.

Epilogue

Revelation 22:6-21

Synopsis: The epilogue introduces three important elements: First, Jesus concludes His testimony to John stressing the promise that He will soon return. Secondly, the book of Revelation is not to be sealed up so that people across the ages can find applications within it to bolster their hopes in the Second Coming of Jesus. Lastly, Jesus concludes with a solemn warning about maintaining the integrity of the message within Revelation. Jesus warns that this message must not be compromised. If it is, there will be a great penalty.

NIV

{6} The angel said to me, "These words are trustworthy and true. The Lord, the God of the spirits of the prophets, sent his angel to show his servants the things that must soon take place."

{7} "Behold, I am coming soon! Blessed is he who keeps the words of the prophecy in this book."

{8} I, John, am the one who heard and saw these things. And when I had heard and seen them, I fell down to worship at the feet of the angel who had been showing them to me. {9} But he said to me, "Do not do it! I am a fellow servant with you and with your brothers the prophets and of all who keep the words of this book. Worship God!"

{10} Then he told me, "Do not seal up the words of the prophecy of this book, because the time is near.

Interlaced thoughts

{6} Then an angel said to me, "Listen carefully, for my words are trustworthy and true. Jesus, the God of truth and holy prophets, has sent me to show His servants the things that must soon take place." {7} These are the words of Jesus, "Behold, I am coming soon! Blessed is he who obeys the words of the prophecy in this book." {8} I, John, am the one who heard and saw these things. And when I had heard and seen them, I fell down to worship at the feet of the angel who had been showing them to me. {9} But he said to me, "Do not do it! I am a fellow servant with you and with your brothers the prophets and of all who keep the words of this book. Worship God only!"

{10} Then he told me, "Do not seal up the words of the prophecy of this book, because the day of preparation and salvation is always near. The Father has designed that this book and its contents should be interpreted by passing generations to keep the mainspring of Christ's

Interlaced thoughts

return alive. However, the 144,000 will fully understand the contents of this book when the appointed time arrives.

{11} Then I saw Jesus was sitting on a cloud. After waving His sickle over the earth, He said, "Let him who does wrong continue to do wrong; let him who is vile continue to be vile; let him who does right continue to do right; and let him who is holy continue to be holy." This decree marked the close of salvation. {12} Then Jesus said, "Behold, I am coming soon! My reward is with me, and I will give to everyone according to what he has done. To those who have done right, I will grant eternal life. To those who have done evil, I will reward with eternal death. {13} I am the Alpha and the Omega, the First and the Last, the Beginning and the End. Who can change my decree? {14} Blessed are those who repent of their sins and overcome sin through faith in my promises, they will have the right to the tree of life and the will go through the gates into the city. But understand this. {15} Outside the city are the degenerate and common, the unholy, those who practice magic arts, the sexually immoral, the murderers, the idolaters and everyone who loves and practices falsehood. I will not have these in my kingdom.

NIV

{11} Let him who does wrong continue to do wrong; let him who is vile continue to be vile; let him who does right continue to do right; and let him who is holy continue to be holy."

{12} "Behold, I am coming soon! My reward is with me, and I will give to everyone according to what he has done.

{13} I am the Alpha and the Omega, the First and the Last, the Beginning and the End.

{14} "Blessed are those who wash their robes, that they may have the right to the tree of life and may go through the gates into the city.

{15} Outside are the dogs, those who practice magic arts, the sexually immoral, the murderers, the idolaters and everyone who loves and practices falsehood.

NIV	Interlaced thoughts
{16} I, Jesus, have sent my angel to give you this testimony for the churches. I am the Root and the Offspring of David, and the bright Morning Star."	{16} John, I, Jesus, have sent my angel to give you this testimony for the seven churches. Make copies and send this to them. As promised in the Old Testament, I am the Root and the Offspring of David, and the bright Morning Star. I am the fulfillment of all the Scriptures."
{17} The Spirit and the bride say, "Come!" And let him who hears say, "Come!" Whoever is thirsty, let him come; and whoever wishes, let him take the free gift of the water of life.	{17} The Holy Spirit and my people must invite others to get ready. Let them say, "Come!" And then, let him who hears repeat the invitation to his friends. Let him say, "Come!" Whoever is thirsty for peace and joy and life eternal, let him come; and whoever chooses, let him take the free gift of the water of life.
{18} I warn everyone who hears the words of the prophecy of this book: If anyone adds anything to them, God will add to him the plagues described in this book.	{18} Now John, here is a most serious warning. I warn everyone who hears the words of the prophecy of this book: If anyone adds anything to them so that their truthfulness is corrupted, I will add to him the plagues described in this book.
{19} And if anyone takes words away from this book of prophecy, God will take away from him his share in the tree of life and in the holy city, which are described in this book.	{19} And if anyone takes words away from this book of prophecy so that their importance is diminished, I will take away from him his share in the tree of life and in the holy city, which are described in this book. I want the message of this book to remain intact. Do not lessen the meaning of my words. Do not corrupt my testimony with vain words.
{20} He who testifies to these things says, "Yes, I am coming soon." Amen. Come, Lord Jesus.	{20} Then Jesus said, "Yes, I am coming soon." Amen. I, John, said, "Come, Lord Jesus.
{21} The grace of the Lord Jesus be with God's people. Amen.	{21} The grace of the Lord Jesus be with God's people." Amen.

Appendix A

Promises that could not be kept

A large number of Bible expositors teach that *all* of God's promises to man are irrevocable, that is, once made – they can never become void. For example, most people correctly believe that God will forever abide by His covenant with man that He will never send another flood to totally destroy the world. Notice the promise: "I establish my covenant with you: Never again will all life be cut off by the waters of a flood; never again will there be a flood to destroy the earth." (Genesis 9:11) This covenant is unilateral, that is, it has nothing to do with man's behavior. God has made an unconditional covenant that He will never again destroy the world with a flood. Therefore, this covenant is irrevocable.

But, the question has to be asked. Are *all* of God's covenants unilateral and therefore, irrevocable? Does God ignore the behavior of man and fulfill His covenants anyway? This subject becomes very interesting whenever people discuss the Jews. Many people hold to the idea that the Jews are still God's chosen people on earth today, even though they reject Jesus Christ as the Messiah and His claim that He was the Son of God. Many popular scholars teach that the book of Revelation predicts the conversion of 144,000 Jews to Christianity after the rapture. These Jewish Christians, they believe, will then evangelize the world during the great tribulation and gather in a great harvest of souls for Christ's second coming. So, does the Bible teach that all of God's covenants are irrevocable?

Possibilities

To explain the covenant that God gave to the Jews, I must ask three things that might be disturbing to some readers. To make the following presentation as simple as possible, I have to ask the reader to *assume the possibility* that the plan of salvation, that is, the means of salvation, has not changed since the day the plan was implemented. In timeless words, "Trust and obey, for there is no other way." (Hebrews 11) Secondly, I ask that the reader *assume the possibility* that the plan of salvation is one thing and the terms and conditions of trusteeship are another. In other words, the plan of salvation is a trust and those who have the responsibility of sharing the good news are trustees of the plan. My second request includes the concept that terms and responsibilities of trustees have changed from age to age as God saw fit. This means that God has required certain things of trustees at certain times which He didn't require at other times. (Acts 15) Lastly, I ask the reader to *assume the possibility* that faithful trustees of God and all who receive salvation through them come to a place where they recognize the sovereignty and righteous authority of God. This means that all who receive God's salvation joyfully submit to God's laws—not as a means to salvation, but in response to His great mercy. (John 14:15, Ephesians 2:8)

With these three items addressed, we shall investigate the administration of the plan of salvation.

God sets up a trust

In the simplest of terms, a trust is an arrangement whereby one person transfers something of value to a second person for the benefit of a third person. In this definition, a trust involves three distinct parties. First, the person creating the trust is called the grantor because he owns an asset that he wants to distribute. But, instead of distributing the asset himself, he asks another to do it for him. In this case, the person responsible for the distribution of the asset is called a trustee. His responsibility is to carry out the wishes of the grantor and in so doing, the trustee is rewarded for his services. Lastly, the person designated to receive the asset is called the beneficiary.

A trust is quite different than a will. A testamentary will is a document whereby one person declares that his assets are to be transferred to another person after he dies. The major difference between a will and a trust is that a will takes effect upon the death of the testator whereas a trust can take effect as soon as it is set up.

The reader may already guess what my next comment will be. The plan of salvation, from its inception, was set up as a trust instead of a will. God established the plan of salvation as a trust so that mankind could *immediately benefit* from it the day sin should appear. Further, it has ever been God's plan that some people would serve the plan of salvation as trustees. Clearly, He intended that His trustees would faithfully discharge their duties, and as a result, all the world could become beneficiaries of His assets. These last two concepts are no small points and the reader should give this due consideration.

God chooses trustees

As stated earlier, a simple trust involves three parties: the grantor, the trustee and the beneficiary. The plan of salvation was designed as a trust because God designed that certain human beings should work for the salvation of other human beings. In other words, God has from the beginning, entrusted certain people with advanced knowledge about the conditions and blessings of salvation and in turn, these have been responsible for disseminating the benefits of God's salvation to the rest of the human race. If it is a privilege to serve as a trustee of a wealthy trust, what is the honor of serving as a trustee of the plan of salvation?

The first trustee of the plan of salvation was Adam. God revealed to him the basic elements of the plan. Adam was commissioned to teach his offspring about sin and God's plan for salvation. In turn, the firstborn male of each succeeding generation was to inherit the privilege of trusteeship as part of his birthright. If each trustee was faithful to his responsibility, then every person on earth would have knowledge of God's wonderful plan to redeem man and restore him to his Eden home. But alas, Cain, the firstborn of Adam, wanted nothing to do with God or His plans. He didn't want the responsibility of being a trustee. And, in anger, Cain killed his younger brother, preventing him from receiving this special opportunity.

To replace Abel, Eve gave birth to Seth. (Genesis 4:25) By studying Adam's ancestry down to the time of the flood, we find that with the exception of Cain, trusteeship was passed to the firstborn of each generation. The trustees were known as patriarchs for a patriarch is a person who inherits the property of the family according to paternal right, that is, the rights that go with being the first born male. We also read in the Bible that the trustees began to openly proclaim the teachings of the Lord when Enosh was born to Seth. (Genesis 4:26) By the time we reach Noah, we find that most of the people who lived before the flood wanted nothing to do with God's plan of salvation. In fact, 1,656 years after Adam sinned, we find only one trustee living upon the earth. His name was Noah, and the total number of antediluvian beneficiaries turned out to be seven. Notice the lineage of the patriarchs up to the time of the flood:

Ten patriarch trustees

Adam - Seth - Enosh - Kenan
Mahalalel - Jared - Enoch
Methuselah - Lamech - Noah.

Note: Paternal rights could be, under certain circumstances, redirected. In the case of Adam, paternal rights were transferred to Seth. Centuries later, paternal rights were fraudulently obtained by Jacob, but they need not have been. God would have provided an honorable way to transfer the birthright from Esau to Jacob, for in God's plan, no one must bear the responsibility of being a trustee if he doesn't want to.

Two things stand out about the trusteeship of the patriarchs. First, there are only ten trustees between the expulsion from Eden and the flood, a span of 1,656 years. Because each of these men lived to be several centuries old, and because they had many offspring, the world must have been populated by thousands of people at the time of the flood. Secondly, the significance of being the firstborn son back then was much different than today. God used the special love and affection given the *firstborn* as an object lesson to teach that one day Jesus, His only begotten Son, the faithful and true Trustee of the plan of salvation, would come to earth and redeem mankind.

Another beautiful object lesson is also found in the fact that in those days, the firstborn inherited everything. Today, this would seem most unfair, but in those days, the firstborn received everything owned by his father. Of course, the firstborn then distributed any or all of the estate as he saw fit. Again, the object lesson here is that someday, Jesus, the firstborn of God, will receive the kingdom of the earth. And, as was the option of the firstborn, Jesus will freely distribute the wealth of His kingdom among His brothers and sisters.

God seeks more trustees

Noah was the last of the patriarch trustees. None of Noah's sons walked with God as did their father. We cannot even be sure who the firstborn of Noah was, although some think it was Japheth. (The Hebrew language leaves room for uncertainty as to whether Shem or Japheth was the eldest. Genesis 10:21) Even with the uncertainty of who was the firstborn of Noah, the history that follows shows that none of the three boys walked in their father's steps. It's also sad to note that even though the flood cleansed the earth of sin, the stain of sin remained in the hearts of the survivors. In fact, about a century after the flood, the descendants of Noah built the tower of Babel in defiance of God's covenant that He would never again destroy the world with a flood!

At the Tower of defiance, God separated the people of earth into groups by language. This simple act caused the dispersion of mankind upon the face of earth. At that time, there are no known trustees of the plan of salvation.

The Bible traces the genealogy of Noah through Shem down to Abraham. If I've calculated correctly, Abraham was about 58 years old when Noah died. If Noah lived out the remainder of his life in the area around the mountains of Ararat, then Abraham probably never met the ancient patriarch. When God called Abraham to move to the land of Canaan, Abraham lived out on the eastern frontier of civilization. Ur of the Chaldees was more than 800 miles from the mountains where the ark had rested. God's call to this descendant of Noah literally turns out to be, "Go West, young man, go westward to the land of Canaan".

When Noah died, so did the trusteeship begun with Adam. Since the chain was broken, God started over. About 375 years after the flood, He looked down upon the earth and chose an open-hearted man named Abram as a trustee of the plan of salvation and Abram favorably responded to the invitation. It is important to note that Abram (later, Abraham) was not in line to receive the trusteeship. In fact, it is highly doubtful that Abraham was the firstborn of Terah. But, God sought new trustees of the gospel and Abraham was, for the most part, an honest man. (Genesis 20)

Abraham walked with God. He was a friend of God. And, after a period of testing the faith of Abraham, God purposed to make Abraham the father of many nations. (Genesis 17:4) So, the trust, originally given to Adam, was implemented again. God called Abraham and he responded. However, with this new beginning, trusteeship continued much as it was before the flood, that is, the firstborn still inherited all the land and the wealth upon the death of the father. This lineage of trustees is called the Abrahamic trustees. Notice their progression:

The Abrahamic trustees

Abraham - Isaac - Jacob Judah - Er

The lineage outlined here ends rather quickly. You can see firsthand the degenerating consequences of sin. Because Abraham failed to trust in God, Isaac was not his first born, Ishmael was. Then, Jacob was not the firstborn of Isaac, Esau was. And, Jacob tried to obtain the birthright through deceit only to discover that God would not accept his treachery. And Reuben, the firstborn of Jacob, was emotionally unstable. Neither did he conduct himself as worthy of the sacred trust granted to the firstborn. Jacob denied him the birthright for sexual promiscuity. (Genesis 49:4,35:22) Jacob also denied the privileges of birthright to his next-born sons, Simeon and Levi, because of their violence and cruelty. So, Judah, the fourth in line, was given paternal rights and the sacred trust. Then God killed Judah's firstborn, Er, for his wickedness. (Genesis 38:7) From there, God's attempt to deliver the plan of salvation to the inhabitants of earth fell apart again. When trustees fail to discharge the wishes of the grantor, the beneficiaries cannot receive the gifts of the grantor. As a consequence of delinquency, God sent the descendants of Abraham down into Egypt. It is ironic that Joseph, a "grand-son of Abraham", is the one who set the stage for his family to become slaves. (Genesis 47:21) God permitted the Hebrews to become slaves of Pharaoh and they summarily lost their opportunity to serve the God of their fathers for the next 400 years.

God seeks new trustees

One day at a burning bush in the Arabian desert, God called Moses to be a trustee of the gospel. (Hebrews 3:17-4:2) Moses was neither the firstborn of his family nor of the tribe of Judah, the tribe to which paternal rights belonged. (Note: The lineage of Jesus is reckoned through Judah. See Matthew 1 and Luke 3) At this point, the lineage didn't matter for God was starting over. When God's initial plan failed because of human stubbornness, He resorted to "Plan B." Therefore, God, keeping His promise to Abraham, needed a man to deliver the Hebrews out of Egypt. And Moses, the murderer-turned-shepherd, became a trustee of the gospel. But, the Israelites were unwilling to become trustees of the gospel. At Mt. Sinai, God was prepared to cancel the covenant given to Abraham. But, Moses prevailed with God. (Exodus 32:10)

What God wanted to do was to offer the entire nation of Israel an opportunity to become trustees of the plan of salvation. The population of the world had significantly multiplied. There were many tribal nations scattered upon the face of earth, and most of them did not know the God of heaven, nor His great love for man.

God knew that the best way to demonstrate to the world that He loves mankind, and that He wants to restore mankind to the Garden of Eden, was to take a nation of underdogs and make them greater than all other nations. God also knew that a nation of underdogs had certain bad habits and attitudes that had to be removed if they were going to reach the high and lofty stature He had in mind.

So, working through His newly appointed trustees, Moses and Aaron, God set out to make of Israel a great nation of trustees. God even promoted one tribe above all the others to be special representatives of Him before the people. This tribe was the tribe of Levi. But, after a few centuries, it became impossible to tell who was leading who. The Levites were no different than the people, They did the same evil things in the sight of the Lord. Time after time, God sent prophets to the kings and priests of Israel so that the nation was reminded of the conditions upon which the blessings of God were based. But, the Israelites hated the prophets and killed most of them. Century after century the Israelites were chastised and rebuked for their rebellion. In 605 B.C., God even sent the whole nation to Babylon as captives for their rebellion. But, their captivity did not produce long-term repentance. So, the story of Israel ends on a sad note. For 1,470 years God tried everything possible to make Israel into a great nation. But, they refused to measure up to the conditions of being trustees of the gospel. In the end, God sent the Roman army against Jerusalem and they completely destroyed Israel. All this happened just as He had warned from the very beginning. (Deuteronomy 28)

God seeks new trustees

Jesus, knowing that Israel was beyond redemption, chose a new group of trustees when He was upon earth. Yes, to facilitate rapid deployment of the gospel throughout the world, He chose some men who already knew a number of things about the dealings of God in the past. He chose twelve men who could draw upon an extensive body of knowledge that had already been revealed about God and His character. He chose twelve men who would, when the right time came, step out of Judaism and become known as Christians. And, all but one of the original twelve lived up to the calling!

With the establishment of the Christian Church, the conditions for trusteeship were no longer restricted to lineage or paternal rights. Nor was it necessary to exalt a nation of underdogs. That plan had failed. The world had changed and God changed the terms of trusteeship to meet the needs of man. After all, the ultimate purpose of a trust is to benefit the beneficiaries. So, the flood-gates were thrown open and anyone who wanted to be a trustee of the gospel could be a trustee. There are many names for this new arrangement, but Christians call it "the priesthood of the believer." In effect, it means that any person, male or female, Jew or Gentile can now become a trustee of the gospel of salvation if they want to. Historically, we call the twelve disciples of Jesus the first trustees of this arrangement.

Remember, the duty of a trustee is to carry out the wishes of the grantor of the trust. The point here is that God wanted the world to know of His merciful salvation. God wants the world to know of His power to save. God wants everyone in the world to know they can have victory over sin. God wants the world to know they will have joy, happiness and peace if men and women will only obey His commands.

God seeks more trustees

The history of the Christian Church is not envious. Within a period of 1,800 years, the Church went from purity of purpose to persecutor of the saints. In short, the Christian Church repeated the rebellious history of the Jewish nation: it forgot God, it hated those who served God, and it destroyed many who firmly stood for God's truth about salvation. Why is it that sin consistently ruins the plans of God? Trustees may forget their responsibility to the trust and begin to think that they own the assets that belong to their grantor. Trustees may wrongfully appropriate the benefits of their position to themselves. They may misrepresent the truth; however, God has clearly shown that the position of trustee is revokable if the trustee is not faithful. This is exactly what happened to the Christian Church. The leaders of the Church made themselves the beneficiary of God's assets instead of distributing the assets of God's mercy. The Church made service to God a very burdensome experience, and it threatened those who disagreed with it with death. History says that millions died for refusing to obey the laws of the Church. So, God raised up another body of people as trustees.

God again seeks trustees

When the strong-arm of the papacy was broken in 1798, this gave rise to a new group of people that would take the gospel commission seriously. Just as Christianity rose out of the cradle of Judaism, Protestantism rose from the libraries of Christianity. God transferred all rights, honors and privileges to those among the Protestants who would serve Him as trustees of His gospel. Still, the basic trust remains intact: The Grantor wants the world to benefit from the plan of salvation. And, the Grantor wants faithful trustees who will accomplish His will.

But, in less than 250 years, Protestantism has floundered. She has become derelict in the fulfillment of her duties. She has lost her vision and her purpose. No longer does she seek to save that which is lost. She has grown indifferent to the great truths of God through materialism and humanism. Prosperity has destroyed Protestantism. Today, the powerful movement of 18th and 19th century Protestantism is dead. Many claim the name of Protestantism but few remember her mission.

America the great, America the superpower, America the rich and increased with goods, Protestant America is no longer Protestant America. America is floundering. Her insurmountable problems are mounting by the day. She cannot restart her economy. She cannot find jobs for her people. She cannot solve inner city problems. Drugs, crime, violence, sexual immorality and dishonesty stain her glorious past. She was the home of the free and the brave. Today, she is the home of the tired, the poor and huddled masses and for most of these, she can no longer offer the fulfillment of the American dream. Today, she is a nation crumbling from within. Her leaders, once the pride of the nation, are now an embarrassment to her people. Few respect and fewer trust the self-serving leaders of America's government. Politics has turned negative. Politicians don't talk about ideals and high goals because dirt about each other is more interesting. Protestant America has lost her right to be the trustee of God's salvation and she will receive the same consequences as all nations who have failed before. The judgments of God are soon to come upon America.

One last time, God seeks new trustees

Just in case the reader has forgotten, a few words are repeated. In the simplest of terms, a trust is an arrangement whereby one person transfers something of value to a second person for the benefit of a third person.

The world now has more people living upon it than at any other time in its history and as a percentage of people living, it is fair to say that fewer people know about the plan of salvation than at any other time in earth's history. What does this say about all the dealing of God with mankind? Is God's unhappiness with man justified? Have we consistently failed God, our benevolent Creator?

Soon, the fourth seal will be opened. (See Appendix C.) The seven trumpets of Revelation shall begin to sound, and the world will know of God's great displeasure. The world, in a corporate sense, and every person in particular, will immediately learn that everything that has happened upon earth has been done before the eyes of the Lord. He missed nothing. Every person is going to hear that God's great day of judgment has begun.

When the trumpets begin, God will send throughout the world 144,000 trustees of the gospel. These faithful men and women will come from the pews of Protestantism. These will understand the Word of God, the Bible, and God will empower them with the Holy Spirit so that they might tell the world of His plan of salvation. These will accomplish in a very short time, all that God desires. The world will hear the eternal, unchanging gospel of Jesus Christ. And, every person will have to make a decision for or against the eternal truth of salvation. Then, the end will come. Jesus will return to earth and gather His faithful trustees, the 144,000, and the beneficiaries of His trust: the numberless multitude.

God's final trustees will live forever

The story doesn't end with the second coming. The reader should know that the final trustees of God will be the redeemed of all ages. These will serve God throughout His far-flung universe as Priests and Kings. Because the redeemed of all ages have shown themselves to be faithful and obedient to the King of kings, He will greatly honor them in the age to come just as they honored Him on earth. They will be positioned above the realms of angels and they will sing praises to God throughout eternity. I find it very wonderful that the redeemed should be so recognized as the 7th and final group of trustees. As the number seven signifies a full and complete number, so the redeemed will testify of the fullness of God's love forever. Again, the trusteeships of God's trust are:

1. The patriarchs
2. The lineage of Abraham
3. The nation of Israel
4. The Christian Church
5. The Protestants
6. The 144,000 servants of God
7. The redeemed of all ages

Summary

The distinction between the terms of God's everlasting covenant and the terms of trusteeship requires careful investigation. This is not a subject for the casual student even though the concept is quite simple to understand.

The reader is therefore encouraged to affirm or deny the point that God has continued to extend the plan of salvation to the world in spite of the behavior of those chosen to accomplish the mission.

The bottom line is that the plan of salvation is an irrevocable covenant with mankind. And, ever since its beginning, the means to salvation has been faith. (See Hebrews 11.) But, that's not the question. The real question centers on who will receive the terms and conditions of salvation by faith and be saved. The next most important question centers on who will respond to the gracious call of our Lord and become a trustee of the plan of salvation so that others may receive its benefit?

Appendix B

How near is soon or how soon is near?

If the reader will review Prophecy 1 (Daniel 2), he will notice that although the passage of time is represented in the vision, there is no indication of *how much time* is involved. And, it is not unreasonable to suggest that Daniel and Nebuchadnezzar anticipated the fulfillment of the king's vision within a few generations of their day. Knowing that it takes time for something as large as a world empire to rise and fall, they probably didn't anticipate fulfillment of the entire vision during their lifetime; however, they may have speculated that the vision could have been fulfilled within a few centuries.

"Wolf, wolf"

Across the ages, God has prevented man from knowing how much time is involved in His sovereign plans. We might say that the amount of remaining time has been one of Heaven's best kept secrets. God has wisely kept this matter a mystery for the knowledge of remaining time is a double- edged sword. On one side, suppose God told us the end of the world would occur on July 1, 3015. This date is so far from now that Christians would lose heart. Think about it. If you asked a girl to marry you and she said she would in 50 years, what would you do in the meantime?

If you knew for a fact that the second coming of Jesus was 1,024 years away, how much effort would you put forth *right now* to encourage others to get ready to meet the Lord? And Jesus, understanding human nature all too well, addressed this matter in a parable to his disciples:

{35} "Be dressed ready for service and keep your lamps burning, {36} like men waiting for their master to return from a wedding banquet, so that when he comes and knocks they can immediately open the door for him. {37} It will be good for those servants whose master finds them watching when he comes. I tell you the truth, he will dress himself to serve, will have them recline at the table and will come and wait on them. {38} It will be good for those servants whose master finds them ready, even if he comes in the second or third watch of the night. {39} But understand this: If the owner of the house had known at what hour the thief was coming, he would not have let his house be broken into. {40} You also must be ready, because the Son of Man will come at an hour when you do not expect him." (Luke 12:35-40)

Jesus knows that the other side of this double-edged sword is just as dangerous. By withholding knowledge about the amount of remaining time, Jesus also knew that the "Wolf, wolf" cry would desensitize more and more people as time passed. In other words, as time passed and the return of Christ did not materialize, rational people would naturally become skeptical of any message specifying the nearness of Christ's return.

Jesus respects our skepticism about any message concerning the time of His appearing for two reasons. First, the passage of time suggests the continuation of time. In other words, our world has been traveling around the sun for thousands of years and what new evidence is there to suggest that it won't keep traveling around the sun for thousands of years to come? Secondly, hundreds have declared the amount of remaining time to be this or that down through the centuries, and they have been proven false. This repeated failure suggests that it is not possible to know the amount of remaining time and therefore, any discussion on remaining time is nothing more than idle speculation.

Remaining time cut short

Jesus clearly reveals that it is impossible to calculate the date of His coming because the time of the second advent has been changed! Yes, the time that was *first* allotted for the duration of the great tribulation has been cut short. Jesus said, "For then there will be great distress, unequaled from the beginning of the world until now—and never to be equaled again. {22} If those days had not been cut short, no one would survive, but for the sake of the elect those days will be shortened." (Matthew 24:21-22)

To appreciate the meaning of Jesus' words, the reader must consider a couple items. First, this text (and several others) indicate a sublime truth: God has appointed a quantity of time for the duration of the world. And in mercy, looking at the severity of the great tribulation which happens at the end of the world, He has shortened it. For the sake of His people, He has cut short the appointed time for no one could live through the ordeal if it were not shortened. This suggests that the Father has shortened the quantity of time *first* allotted to the tribulation and we cannot know the amount of reduction in time. Therefore, the time of Christ's return cannot be closely calculated.

The reader may wonder, "Why would God set a time and then change it?" This writer can't provide a good answer to this question except to say that God is merciful. Remember Sodom and Gomorrah? God showed that he was negotiable about the number of righteous people necessary to spare the city. (See Genesis 18.) And, in the case of Nineveh, God spared the city for forsaking their evil ways. (Jonah 3:10) The point is that sometimes God lays out a plan, and then adjusts it for the sake of those who love Him.

Date of second coming cannot be known

Some apply Matthew 24:36 to the second coming. Jesus said, "No one knows about that day or hour, not even the angels in heaven, nor the Son, but only the Father." While this verse may apply to the second coming, there is evidence suggesting that this text compliments Revelation 14:14-20; 22:11. If so, it then applies to something even more important than the date of the second coming: the close of salvation. In either case, we have to understand that humans aren't allowed to know the exact amount of remaining time that earth shall have. The element of anticipation remains. Therefore, we have to be on our toes, watching and waiting.

More than future-telling

Jesus told His disciples, "You will hear of wars and rumors of wars, but see to it that you are not alarmed. Such things must happen, but the end is still to come. {7} Nation will rise against nation, and kingdom against kingdom. There will be famines and earthquakes in various places. {8} All these are the beginning of birth pains. " (Matthew 24:6-8) Did you notice that Jesus told His disciples to not be alarmed by wars and rumors of wars in the first sentence?

During the Iraqi war of January 1991, a radio talk-show host on WLW in Cincinnati made this remark: "Ever notice how apocalypse people come out of the woodwork whenever terrible things happen?" He was referring to all the "end of the world" types that came forward with prophetic utterances as America was going to war. He reasoned that if the Iraqi war was in Bible prophecy, why were we just *now* hearing about it? He noted that the Bible was written thousands of years ago, and if the Iraqi war was prophetically significant, prophecy expositors should have predicted this specific war *before* Iraq invaded Kuwait in August of 1990. He asked, "isn't the purpose of Bible prophecy—knowledge about the future?"

Yes, one of the purposes of Bible prophecy is knowledge about the future. But there is much more. God has a larger purpose behind Bible prophecy than future-telling. Bible prophecy allows us to understand something of the plans and purposes of God. Bible prophecy deals with more than the rise and fall of world empires—a spectacular sight indeed. But the grandest view that Bible prophecy offers is beholding the actions of God. Watching God work through the plans and actions of men to accomplish His will and purpose is one of the greatest insights we can have about God. This is what Bible prophecy is all about.

Does *soon* mean thousands of years?

Because God has kept the amount of remaining time a secret, many people run into a problem with the understanding of inspiration. Here's the problem: down through the ages prophets have been shown scenes of the second advent of Christ, but these prophets are not shown *when* the Day of the Lord occurs. As a result, they have consistently interpreted the Great Day of the Lord as being near, soon or imminent. Notice the consistency of their words even though they lived centuries apart:

Paul thought the end was imminent: "What I mean, brothers, is that the *time is short*. From now on those who have wives should live as if they had none." (1 Corinthians 7:29)

"And do this, understanding the present time. *The hour has come* for you to wake up from your slumber, because our salvation is nearer now than when we first believed. {12} The night is nearly over; *the day is almost here.* So let us put aside the deeds of darkness and put on the armor of light." (Romans 13:11-12)

"...But now he (Jesus) has appeared once for all *at the end of the ages* to do away with sin by the sacrifice of himself." (Hebrews 9:26)

John thought the end was imminent: "Dear children, *this is the last hour*; and as you have heard that the antichrist is coming, even now many antichrists have come. This is how we know it is the last hour." (1 John 2:18)

"The revelation of Jesus Christ, which God gave him to show his servants what must *soon* take place. He made it known by sending his angel to his servant John." (Revelation 1:1)

Peter thought the end was imminent: "For you know that it was not with perishable things such as silver or gold that you were redeemed from the empty way of life handed down to you from your forefathers, {19} but with the precious blood of Christ, a lamb without blemish or defect. {20} He was chosen before the creation of the world, but was revealed in *these last times (years)* for your sake." (1 Peter 1:18-20)

At Pentecost, Peter said, "These men are not drunk, as you suppose. It's only nine in the morning! {16} No, this is what was spoken by the prophet Joel: {17} '*In the last days*, God says, I will pour out my Spirit on all people. Your sons and daughters will prophesy, your young men will see visions, your old men will dream dreams.' " (Acts 2:15-17)

Isaiah thought the end was imminent: "Wail, for *the day of the Lord is near;* it will come like destruction from the Almighty." (Isaiah 13:6)

Ezekiel thought the end was imminent: "For *the day is near,* the day of the Lord is near–a day of clouds, a time of doom for the nations." (Ezekiel 30:3)

Joel thought the end was imminent: "Alas for that day! For *the day of the Lord is near*; it will come like destruction from the Almighty." (Joel 1:15)

"Multitudes, multitudes in the valley of decision! For *the day of the Lord is near* in the valley of decision." (Joel 3:14)

Obadiah thought the end was imminent: "*The day of the Lord is near* for all nations. As you have done, it will be done to you; your deeds will return upon your own head." (Obadiah 1:15)

Zephaniah thought the end was imminent: "Be silent before the Sovereign Lord, for *the day of the Lord is near*. The Lord has prepared a sacrifice; he has consecrated those he has invited." (Zephaniah 1:7)

"*The great day of the Lord is near–near and coming quickly.* Listen! The cry on the day of the Lord will be bitter, the shouting of the warrior there." (Zephaniah 1:14)

A day is as a thousand years?

To defend the idea that everything written by the prophets is inerrant, some scholars argue that God represents time as short to His prophets because in His sight, a day is like a thousand years and a thousand years as a day. I find no value in this argument for two reasons. First, the only infallible person to ever live was Jesus Christ. Prophets are forgiven sinners just like the rest of us and even though they are inspired, they remain fallible and they do make mistakes. See Galatians 2:11-14; Acts 21:4-14 and 1 Kings 13.

Secondly, and more importantly, God has not revealed the amount of remaining time to *any* person. For example, in Nebuchadnezzar's vision, no time was specified for the fulfillment of the vision. In the visions of John, Peter, Paul, Joel and others, God showed them scenes which they describe to the best of their ability, but without any knowledge of remaining time, they all conclude (without exception) that they must be living at the end of time. We find this phenomenon to be consistent among the prophets across the centuries. For example, John was taken into vision to see scenes about the end of the world. He clearly saw them and wrote them down in the book of Revelation, but God did not reveal anything to him about the amount of time between his day and the end of the world. Consequently, John was left with the impression that the end must be very near and he wrote accordingly.

I also find no value in the argument that the Bible uses words such as *near* or *soon* to refer to a time span of thousands of years. Don't misunderstand. We know that time is nothing to God – a thousand years are as a day and a day as a thousand years. (Psalm 90:4) But, my point is that God does not mislead humanity by using *His* perception of time. He would not represent something as imminent for the sake of deceiving people into believing something untrue. As Paul said, "...Let God be true and every man a liar..." Romans 3:4 Fact is, *God has never said that the remaining time on earth was short.* This was the conclusion of the prophets. And three thousand years of history proves that it was their perspective and not a revelation from God. Keep in mind, the subject here is quantity of time. Because God has not revealed the quantity of time, prophets have consistently reached for the same conclusion – time is short. But, the quantity of elapsed time proves that the prophets were simply mistaken. They had no information on the amount of remaining time and they simply concluded that time was short. However, when God declares something is about to be fulfilled, He knows how to use our language, and He uses words we understand, He tells us what He is going to do and it happens just as declared. For example, see Ezekiel 24:14.

How does inspiration work?

If God gave you, an ordinary person, a vision about the end of the world, would that make everything you say thereafter infallible? No. If you thought your vision was soon to be fulfilled and plainly said so, and then a thousand years pass by, would that mean the vision was a hoax? No. This is a delicate matter and some people may not be able to resolve this. But, the answer is quite simple as I see it. At various times God reveals things to ordinary people. They are then free to write down what they have seen and make comments about the meaning. The point is that the vision comes from God but the comments about the vision come from the prophet. (1 Corinthians 13:9) So, we must apply two tests to the statements of the prophets regarding chronology. First, we can look at history and see if their conclusions were correct. Secondly, we can look at the 18 apocalyptic structures of Daniel and Revelation and chronologically determine where their visions belong in the long sweep of time.

My point is that all of the prophets we have investigated were shown scenes about the Great Day of the Lord and not one of them had the faintest idea that it was still thousands of years away. God did not allow them to understand *when* the end was coming. Everyone of them, without exception, thought the end was about to happen in their day.

In God's time

Another problem arises from the study of time. If we conclude that thousands of years can exist between two verses of the Bible, how can we know when a long period of time exists between verses and when no time exists between verses? There is only one way to answer this question that I know of. The answer is found in the prophetic matrix of Daniel and Revelation. *When all 18 stories of Daniel and Revelation are properly aligned, we discover the chronological location and relative timing of each part.*

Progression towards fulfillment shows where we are in the prophetic process. Because God lays out a few periods, this is the *only way* we can know when the end is near. Wars, famines and earthquakes are not positive proof that the end of the world has come. Civilizations come and go. Famines come and go and earthquakes happen frequently. But, there has to be clear evidence that the end of the world has been reached if we are going to believe such a claim. So where can we find such evidence? Only through confirming the progressive fulfillments of apocalyptic prophecies with historical records can we find our place in God's allowance of time. Now that the mystery of Daniel and Revelation has been understood, we discover that remaining time is short. Perhaps less than 7 years.

Bottom line

Can the final generation positively know they are the last generation? Yes, but only when they know the amount of remaining time. Is there evidence in the Bible suggesting that the 1990's are earth's final years? I think so. While the evidence is not *solid,* it nonetheless is there if you are looking for it and it makes 1994 and the years that follow appear to be quite important. (See Appendix D.)

Appointed time of the end

The Bible clearly says there is an appointed time of the end. Notice these two verses:

Daniel 8:17 "As he came near the place where I was standing, I was terrified and fell prostrate. 'Son of man,' he said to me, '*understand that the vision concerns the time of the end.*' "

Daniel 8:19 "He said: 'I am going to tell you what will happen later *in the time of wrath*, because the vision concerns *the appointed time of the end.*' "

In these verses we find that the vision of Daniel 8 reaches down to the time of the end. We also find that there is an appointed time of the end. And, we also find that the appointed time of the end is a time of wrath.

Now, add these four verses to the equation:

Daniel 11:27 "The two kings, with their hearts bent on evil, will sit at the same table and lie to each other, but to no avail, because an end will still come at *the appointed time.*"

Daniel 11:35 "Some of the wise will stumble, so that they may be refined, purified and made spotless until the time of the end, for *it will still come at the appointed time.*"

Daniel 11:40 "*At the time of the end* the king of the South will engage him in battle, and the king of the North will storm out against him with chariots and cavalry and a great fleet of ships. He will invade many countries and sweep through them like a flood."

Daniel 12:4 "But you, Daniel, close up and seal the words of the scroll *until the time of the end.* Many will go here and there to increase knowledge."

Can there be any doubt from all six verses in Daniel that God has appointed a time of the end? How long is it? When does it begin? When does it end?

When does the end begin?

The reader probably noticed that all six quotes are taken from Daniel 8-12. We know that the 2,300-day prophecy of Daniel 8 reaches from 457 B.C. to A.D. 1844. (See Appendix E.) If we literally apply the words of Gabriel, he says that the vision concerns [events] occurring during *the time of the end.*

It appears that the time of the end began in 1798, at the end of the 1,260 years of little horn domination because the judgment of human beings identifies the final phase of Christ's ministry in heaven before the second coming. The scenes in Revelation 4-5 which John observed and the court scene in Daniel 7:9,10 which Daniel observed identify the same process in heaven which began in 1798. The key that connects these two scenes is the exaltation granted to Jesus. Compare Daniel 7:13,14 with Revelation 5:1-12.

We also find that end of the little horn power's 1,260 years is connected to the beginning of the judgment scene in heaven. See Daniel 7:20,21,26.

Add to the above, the opening of the third seal in 1844 and we find our chronological position in time awaiting the opening of the fourth seal. If my calculations and conclusions are correct, the judgment of the living will begin about 1994. (Appendix D) Since it can be reasonably shown from the Bible that 1998 marks the 6000th year of sin's existence, it therefore appears that from 1798 to 1998 is the appointed time of the end.

From the beginning, God appointed the time of the end. He set the limits by His own authority. Have we reached the end? Is it possible to know?Yes.

Appendix C

The coming wrath of God

"I the Lord have spoken. The time has come for me to act. I will not hold back; I will not have pity, nor will I relent. You will be judged according to your conduct and your actions, declares the Sovereign Lord." (Ezekiel 24:14)

"The Lord will march out like a mighty man, like a warrior he will stir up his zeal; with a shout he will raise the battle cry and will triumph over his enemies. {14} For a long time I have kept silent, I have been quiet and held myself back. But now, like a woman in childbirth, I cry out, I gasp and pant. {15} I will lay waste the mountains and hills and dry up all their vegetation; I will turn rivers into islands and dry up the pools." (Isaiah 42:13-15)

When God breaks His silence with sin, it will happen suddenly. But, there is one thing that separates the wrath of God from violent, random acts of nature. God reveals what He is going to do before He does it. Historically, God's wrath severs yesterday from today. I believe we are going to experience the wrath of God within the next three years. Life as we have known it will immediately and irrevocably change. The world has never witnessed anything like the coming judgments of God, nor could it sustain another visitation. God will act suddenly and powerfully and all peoples in every nation will be awed by His swiftness and severity. What is Jesus about to do? He is about to open the 4th seal:

"When the Lamb opened the fourth seal... I looked, and there before me was a pale horse! Its rider was named Death, and Hades was following close behind him. They were given power over a fourth of the earth to kill by sword, famine and plague, and by the wild beasts of the earth." (Revelation 6:7,8)

Beginning of the tribulation

The opening of the fourth seal marks the beginning of the great tribulation. So extensive will be the cataclysm, that God has promised that this tribulation shall not exceed 1335 days (Daniel 12:11,12). But, during this time period, 25% of Earth's 5.4 billion will perish. Such an assault on human beings will begin with nothing less than a direct order from God. So, why will He do this to us?

Isaiah explains, "See, the Lord is going to lay waste the earth and devastate it; he will ruin its face and scatter its inhabitants... The earth will be completely laid waste and totally plundered. The Lord has spoken this word... The earth is defiled by its people; they have disobeyed the laws, violated the statutes and broken the everlasting covenant. Therefore a curse consumes the earth; its people must bear their guilt. Therefore earth's inhabitants are burned up, and very few are left." (Isaiah 24:1-6)

Symbolic or literal - past or future?

Some people argue that the four judgments of the fourth seal are symbolic and therefore, not to be taken literally. Others say that the fourth seal happened long ago. Many argue that God does not kill people anyway. Let the Bible speak. Notice this: "Son of man, if a country sins against me by being unfaithful and I stretch out my hand against it to cut off its food supply and send *famine* upon it and kill its men and their animals... Or if I send *wild beasts* through that country and they leave it childless and it becomes desolate so that no one can pass through it because of the beasts... Or if I bring a *sword* against that country and say, 'Let the sword pass throughout the land,' and I kill its men and their animals... Or if I send a *plague* into that land and pour out my wrath upon it through bloodshed, killing its men and their animals... For this is what the Sovereign Lord says: How much worse will it be when I send against Jerusalem *my four dreadful judgments - sword and famine and wild beasts and plague* - to kill its men and their animals... 'They will come to you (Ezekiel), and when you see their conduct and their actions, you will be consoled regarding the disaster I have brought upon Jerusalem - every disaster I have brought upon it. You will be consoled when you see their conduct and their actions, for you will know that I have done nothing in it without cause,' declares the Sovereign Lord." (Ezekiel 14:13-23) (Emphasis mine.)

No one can reasonably say after reading these verses that God's four judgments of plague, famine, sword and wild beasts are symbolic. Furthermore, God personally claims responsibility for sending "His four dreadful judgments" upon man. God also justified Himself to Ezekiel for doing such things by saying, "I have done nothing in it without cause." Understand that God has used these four judgments in the past and He is going to use these four judgments in the near future.

The full cup principle

What brings a loving God to the point where He will send horrific judgments upon human beings? Sin. Today, many people interpret God's silence or passiveness with sin to mean that He is either indifferent to what we do, or He depends on the inescapable consequences of sin to deal with our evil ways. Others assume that His silence is proof that He does not hold us accountable for our day-to-day activities. For this reason, people are committing horrible deeds of evil all the while thinking that God does not care or see. But, the truth is that each one of us will have to render to our Maker a full accounting for every action!

Solomon warned: "Now all has been heard; here is the conclusion of the matter: Fear God and keep his commandments, for this is the whole duty of man. For God will bring every deed into judgment, including every hidden thing, whether it is good or evil." (Ecclesiastes 12:13,14) Paul affirms the judgment saying, "For we must all appear before the judgment seat of Christ, that each one may receive what is due him for the things done while in the body, whether good or bad." (2 Corinthians 5:10)

Christians talk and sing about God's mercy – His saving grace, but few openly talk about God's anger or wrath. Why? Are we afraid to know what makes God angry? Have we made a religious caricature of God by separating His justice from His mercy?

To put God's wrath into perspective, we have to review a little Bible history to observe that God follows a consistent principle in dealing with humanity. This principle is called the "full cup principle." The concept is so simple that even a child can understand it. In essence, when a person, city, nation or body of people reach a certain level of decadence or wickedness, God's patience expires and He breaks his silence with divine judgments. If the situation is redeemable, His judgments are redemptive. If the situation is beyond redemption, His judgments are utterly destructive.

Examples

In the days of Noah... "The Lord saw how great man's wickedness on the earth had become, and that every inclination of the thoughts of his heart was only evil all the time. The Lord was grieved that he had made man on the earth, and his heart was filled with pain. So the Lord said, 'I will wipe mankind, whom I have created, from the face of the earth – men and animals, and creatures that move along the ground, and birds of the air – for I am grieved that I have made them.' " (Genesis 6:5-7)

God destroyed the world with a flood in Noah's day because the antediluvian's cup of iniquity had reached full measure. God broke His silence by first warning the world through Noah of what He was going to do, and then, He proceeded to destroy the inhabitants of the world as promised. When divine love and mercy no longer produced repentance and reformation in the antediluvians, God demanded destructive action. Please notice in Genesis 8:21 that God took full responsibility for destroying the earth.

Amorite's fill up their cup: "Then the Lord said to him (Abraham), 'Know for certain that your descendants will be strangers in a country not their own, and they will be enslaved and mistreated four hundred years. But I will punish the nation they serve as slaves, and afterward they will come out with great possessions. You, however, will go to your fathers in peace and be buried at a good old age. In the fourth generation your descendants will come back here, for the sin of the Amorites has not yet reached its *full measure.*' " (Genesis 15:13-16)

Notice the last sentence of this text. God would only give the land of Canaan to Abraham's offspring *after* the sins of the Amorites had reached full measure! Make no mistake about this. God does not steal land from one nation to give to another. All the earth belongs to our Creator and He would only give it to Abraham's descendants *after* the Amorites had exhausted their opportunity of possessing that beautiful land. Also keep in mind that ancient Israel's possession of Canaan was based on the *same* conditions applicable to the Amorites. Moses knew that possession of Canaan was conditional. So, he warned Israel:

"But be assured today that the Lord your God is the one who goes across ahead of you like a devouring fire. He will destroy them; he will subdue them before you. And you will drive them out and annihilate them quickly... After the Lord your God has driven them out before you, do not say to yourself, 'The Lord has brought me here to take possession of this land because of my righteousness.' No, it is on account of the wickedness of these nations that the Lord is going to drive them out before you. It is not because of your righteousness or your integrity that you are going in to take possession of their land; but on account of the wickedness of these nations..." (Deuteronomy 9:3-5)

Don't miss this

Here is an extremely important point: The Canaanites were driven out of Canaan and destroyed when their cup of wickedness became full! When God's patience with the Canaanites reached its limit, God broke His silence with them by sending His wrath upon them!

Israel & Babylon filled up cups At the time of the Babylonian captivity, God told Israel:

"But you did not listen to me... and you have provoked me with what your hands have made, and you have brought harm to yourselves... Because you have not listened to my words, I will summon all the peoples of the north and my servant Nebuchadnezzar king of Babylon... and I will bring them against this land and its inhabitants and against all the surrounding nations. I will completely destroy them and make them an object of horror and scorn, and an everlasting ruin... This whole country will become a desolate wasteland, and these nations will serve the king of Babylon seventy years. But when the seventy years are fulfilled, I will punish the king of Babylon and his nation, the land of the Babylonians, for their guilt... and will make it desolate forever. " (Jeremiah 25:7-12)

Notice a critical point in these verses. Israel was to be destroyed for provoking God, *and* eventually, so was Babylon! This is proof that God deals with the heathen just as He deals with those who know Him! In God's eyes, wickedness is wickedness. Each person, city, nation or kingdom has a cup and when it becomes full - God breaks His silence.

One more brief point about ancient Babylon must be made. When the mysterious handwriting appeared on the palace wall, Belshazzar, king of Babylon, suspected that the God of heaven was sending the sword against him and He summoned the prophet Daniel to interpret the handwriting. Before interpreting the handwriting on the wall, Daniel recounted the divine judgments the Most High had sent upon his arrogant grandfather, Nebuchadnezzar. Then Daniel said:

"But you his son, O Belshazzar, have not humbled yourself, though you knew all this. Instead, you have set yourself up against the Lord of heaven... But you did not honor the God who holds in his hand your life and all your ways... This is what these words mean: ***Mene*: God has numbered the days of your reign and brought it to an end. *Tekel*: You have been weighed on the scales and found wanting. *Peres*: Your kingdom is divided and given to the Medes and Persians."** (Daniel 5:22-28)

New Testament examples

The full cup principle is also found in the New Testament. Paul warned the sexually immoral Romans:

"...You are storing up wrath against yourself for the day of God's wrath, when his righteous judgment will be revealed. God will give to each person according to what he has done... But for those who are self-seeking and who reject the truth and follow evil, there will be wrath and anger." (Romans 2:5,6,8)

Paul clearly understood why the wrath of God was coming. He told the believers in Colosse, "Put to death, therefore, whatever belongs to your earthly nature: sexual immorality, impurity, lust, evil desires and greed, which is idolatry. Because of these, the wrath of God is coming." (Colossians 3:5,6)

On the other side of the coin, Paul encouraged the believers in Thessalonica to be patient in their suffering until the enemies of Jesus had filled up their cup.

"...You suffered from your own countrymen the same things those churches (in Judea) suffered from the Jews, who killed the Lord Jesus and the prophets and also drove us out. They (the Jews) displease God and are hostile to all men in their effort to keep us from speaking to the Gentiles so that they may be saved. In this way they always heap up their sins to the limit. The wrath of God has come upon them at last." I (Thessalonians 2:14-16)

When Paul wrote this epistle, he knew that the Jews had filled up their cup of sin and that they were doomed to destruction by the Romans. The anticipated destruction occurred in 70 A.D.

Jesus predicts wrath

Jesus spoke of the full cup principle in a discourse with the Pharisees. After pronouncing 7 curses upon them for religious bigotry and hypocrisy, Jesus said: "Fill up, then, the measure of the sin of your forefathers! You snakes! You brood of vipers! How will you escape being condemned to hell?" (Matthew 23:32,33)

Again, the point is made. When a nation or individual reaches the limit of divine forbearance, God breaks his silence. His mercy with sin and sinner has a limit. Jesus concluded his denunciation of the Jews saying: "O Jerusalem, Jerusalem, you who kill the prophets and stone those sent to you, how often I have longed to gather your children together, as a hen gathers her chicks under her wings, but you were not willing. Look, your house is left to you desolate." (Matthew 23:37,38)

God's four judgments

Israel was fully warned about the consequences of violating God's laws at the time of the Exodus. God said: "But if you will not listen to me and carry out all these commands... then I will do this to you: I will bring upon you sudden terror, wasting diseases and fever that will destroy your sight and drain away your life... I will break down your stubborn pride and make the sky above you like iron and the ground beneath you like bronze. Your strength will be spent in vain, because your soil will not yield its crops... I will send wild animals against you... destroy your cattle and make you so few in number that your roads will be deserted... I will bring the sword upon you to avenge the breaking of the covenant... I will send a plague among you... I will lay waste the land... I will scatter you among the nations..." (Leviticus 26:14-33)

Look closely at this text and see if you can find God's four judgments identified. They are specifically mentioned. In addition to the four judgments, notice that they come in the form of sudden terror. This is how God breaks His silence. His judgments come with sudden terror upon nations when their cup of sin and rebellion becomes full. Paul saw that God's wrath will suddenly break out upon the world in the last days. He says, "While people are saying, 'Peace and safety,' destruction will come on them suddenly, as labor pains on a pregnant woman, and they will not escape." (1 Thessalonians 5:3)

Bible history says

The Bible does not leave us guessing how God implements His four judgments. Notice these instances:

Sword: God raises up military leaders to send the sword wherever He wants it. From Jeremiah 25:9 we learn that God sent His *servant,* King Nebuchadnezzar, against Jerusalem. Nebuchadnezzar did not know that he was a servant of the Most High God at the time! Nevertheless, God used the pagan king to accomplish the destruction of Jerusalem. In the same way, God overthrew the empire of Babylon through Darius, another unwitting servant of God. (Daniel 5:30,31) The Bible also says that King Cyrus was a servant of God. See Ezra 1:1; Isaiah 44:28, 25:1. It is especially interesting to know that God is able to accomplish His plans without forcing His will upon any individual! The point is that God raises up military leaders to take the sword wherever He wants, even though generals choose to do what they want to do! And if human agency is not available, the Lord will send His own angels as necessary. The largest known number of people to be killed by the death angel was 185,000 soldiers of Sennacherib's army, although this number may be less than the first-born killed in Egypt at the time of the Exodus. See Isaiah 37:36 and Exodus 11.

Famine: God sends famine at times and in places to accomplish His purposes. In Genesis 41, God sent seven years of famine to Egypt and in the process, removed Joseph from prison and put him on the throne. This amazing promotion for Joseph opened the way for the descendants of Abraham to move down into Egypt! See Genesis 15:12-16.

In 2 Samuel 21:1, the Bible says, "During the reign of David, there was a famine for three successive years; so David sought the face of the Lord. The Lord said, 'It is on account of Saul and his blood-stained house; it is because he put the Gibeonites to death.' " Clearly, the three year famine came as a direct result of Saul's disobedience.

In 2 Kings 8:1 we learn of another seven-year famine sent by the Lord, "Now Elisha had said to the woman whose son he had restored to life, 'Go away with your family and stay for a while wherever you can, because the Lord has decreed a famine in the land that will last seven years.' " Perhaps one of the best known famines recorded in the Bible happened during the days of Elijah and King Ahab. Notice what James says, "Elijah was a man just like us. He prayed earnestly that it would not rain, and it did not rain on the land for three and a half years. Again he prayed, and the heavens gave rain, and the earth produced its crops." (James 5:17,18) The combined evils of violence, idolatry and sexual immorality have reached epic proportions and God has not only noticed, He is about to rise up in response!

Plague: Plagues can come in numerous forms. We think of bubonic plague or of cholera as a plague, but the word plague means anything troublesome or afflicting. God sent several plagues upon Pharaoh and Egypt to impress them that He wanted His people set free. These plagues included frogs, blood-water, gnats, flies, boils, hail, locusts, darkness, etc. See Exodus 7-10. The Lord killed 10 of the 12 spies with a plague for giving a bad report about the Promised Land! See Numbers 14:37 More than 14,700 people died of a plague in a wilderness rebellion started by Korah. See Numbers 16:49. On one occasion, God sent a plague that killed 24,000 people for sexual immorality! See Numbers 25:9. On another occasion, God sent a plague upon Israel and killed 70,000 people because King David disobeyed the Lord and took a census. (1 Chronicles 21:14-16) The point here is that God does send plagues upon people to kill them when they continually insist on disobeying His commands.

Wild beasts: Wild beasts, like plagues, come in many forms. Peter described them saying, "I looked into it (the sheet) and saw four-footed animals of the earth, wild beasts, reptiles, and birds of the air." (Acts 11:6) The creatures of earth are wild beasts. So how does God use them? The Lord clearly warned Jeremiah how wild beasts would be used to accomplish His deadly purpose upon Israel. He said, " 'I will send four kinds of destroyers against them (Israel),' declares the Lord, 'the sword to kill and the dogs to drag away and the birds of the air and the beasts of the earth to devour and destroy.' " (Jeremiah 15:3) The Bible also says that God sent poisonous vipers into the camp of Israel when they complained against Him. See Numbers 21. One family of "wild beasts" that may be very influential in the future is insects. Killer bees, fleas, fire ants, swarms of locusts and other tiny creatures can cause unbelievable damage! It is important to notice that God promised Israel that He would restrain the wild beasts if they would repent of their idolatry and love and obey Him. God said, "I will make a covenant of peace with them (Israel) and rid the land of wild beasts so that they may live in the desert and sleep in the forests in safety." (Ezekiel 34:25)

A Review of the 4th seal

"When the Lamb opened the fourth seal, I heard the voice of the fourth living creature say, 'Come!' I looked, and there before me was a pale horse! Its rider was named Death, and Hades was following close behind him. They were given power over a fourth of the earth to kill by sword, famine and plague, and by the wild beasts of the earth." (Revelation 6:7,8)

The evidence is clear and abundant all through the Bible that God has used His four judgments to deal with peoples and nations of the world when their cup of sin becomes full. The Bible is also clear that He only uses these judgments when sin and rebellion reach a point where His love and mercy have no redeeming effect. See Ezekiel 5. So, the judgments described in the fourth seal are literal and are to be taken seriously. As a matter of fact, the 25% figure mentioned in the fourth seal should be taken very seriously. If the population of earth is 5.4 billion today, then 25% of that number would be 1.3 billion casualties! We can only begin to conceptualize the excessiveness of our sins by considering such extensive destruction.

How will the four judgments come?

Revelation's story explains how and when the four judgments of the fourth seal will be suddenly released. Without getting lost in all the prophetic parts, here's a brief explanation.

Right now, God has special angels holding back the four winds of His judgments. When 144,000 people are prepared to proclaim the everlasting gospel, the angels will let go of the four winds. These winds symbolize the forthcoming destruction of His four judgments—sword, famine, plague and wild beasts.

144,000 evangelists, located around the earth since 1844, will explain the purpose of God's judgments and they will proclaim a comprehensive message of salvation which includes the imminent return of Jesus. The everlasting covenant and the terms of salvation will be seen in their glorious beauty. Of course, the powerful proclamation of the gospel will anger the devil and those who love evil. Because of the severity of the judgments, world leaders will unite to appease God. Eventually, the devil himself will appear claiming to be God in the flesh. To make his control of earth complete, the devil will demand that his followers destroy the God-sent evangelists and those who follow them. The net effect is that everyone on earth will be caught in a great tribulation.

Seven trumpets

Here are some important things to know. The judgments mentioned in the fourth seal will begin suddenly according to I Thessalonians 5:3. The four judgments of the fourth seal will come in the form of seven trumpets. In other words, sword, famine, plague and wild beasts are implemented by the seven trumpets. The reason that the four judgments are symbolized as trumpets is that God's judgments will be used as harbingers of the arrival of His holy Son, Jesus Christ.

The seven trumpets of Revelation are designed to awaken the people of earth that Jesus is coming. The first trumpet will be a great meteoric shower of burning hail. This burning hail will ignite enormous, unquenchable fires. The second and third trumpets will be horrific asteroid impacts, and the fourth trumpet may be great bands of darkness upon our globe, caused by millions of tons of ejecta, ash and debris put into the atmosphere by volcanoes. The fifth trumpet marks the physical appearing of the devil claiming to be God. The sixth trumpet is a global civil war that the devil incites to take control of all the earth. And the seventh trumpet marks the end of God's salvation.

I believe the fourth seal will open sometime in 1994 or 1995. Before the sudden destruction of the first trumpet begins, there will be an enormous global earthquake. Then, a short time later, the first trumpet will sound and showers of fiery meteors will rain down upon earth. This destruction may come from the effect of earth passing through some asteroid belt or a meteor field. This shower of burning rocks will ignite large, unmanageable fires all around the world. Thousands of square miles of rain forests and crops will be burned up. Food will become scarce overnight and global famine will immediately follow. The famine will affect every person living on earth.

Listen up

The 144,000 of Revelation 7 are servants to whom God will give special powers. See Luke 9 for an example of this. The Two Witnesses of Revelation are the Bible and the Holy Spirit. The 144,000 servants will be the human vehicles through whom the Two Witnesses will communicate with every person. Like Moses and Elijah of old, the 144,000 will perform many miracles to convince people that their message is sent from God. They will explain what God is doing and why. But, just as Pharaoh hardened his heart when Moses stood before him, many in our day will harden their hearts against God's messengers. On the other hand, many will turn from rebellion and be saved when they hear the gospel call from God's Word.

The Holy Spirit will attempt to win every heart and signs and wonders will add credibility to the truth of God's Word. Revelation 11:6 clearly says that the Two Witnesses (the personification of the 144,000) will perform miracles, even striking the earth with every kind of plague as often as they want! BUT, (and this is an emphatic but) don't be fooled by miracles and false prophets. Jesus clearly said, "For false Christs and false prophets will appear and perform great signs and miracles to deceive even the elect – if that were possible." (Matthew 24:24)

The devil is coming

The Bible predicts that Satan will physically appear as a dazzling being upon the earth before the second coming of Jesus. See 2 Corinthians 11:14 and 2 Thessalonians 2:1-9. Satan is the man of lawlessness. When He appears on earth, he will make up his own laws. His laws will have no regard for human rights or human dignity. He will claim that he is God and to demonstrate his divinity, he will call fire down from heaven in full view of men. (Revelation 13:13) The appearance of Satan will not come as a surprise to those understanding Revelation, for the appearing of the devil occurs during the 5th trumpet. See Revelation 9:1-12.

After Satan has appeared on earth for a few months, he will unite all his followers from the nations. When he has gained enough influence, he will move deftly and swiftly to take control of the entire world by motivating his followers to take the sword and gain control of earth. This war, described in Revelation 9, is the 6th trumpet. This world war will be like the civil war that consumed America last century, except it will involve every nation.

Satan's followers intend to dominate their respective nations on behalf of the one they believe to be God! Millions upon millions will die as a result of this war. (Some translations of the Bible say the number of soldiers mentioned in Revelation 9:16 will be 200,000,000. Currently, the entire world has less than 8 million troops in uniform. Examine this horrible war in Revelation 9.) As a result of the carnage, wild animals will rapidly multiply. They will literally feed upon the dead.

Seven last plagues

But wait, there's more. The seven *last* plagues follow the seven *first* plagues (seven trumpets) and the seven last plagues also include the same four judgments! These judgments are described in Revelation 16 and are reserved for those who shall receive the mark of the beast. The first judgment is a plague of sores that falls upon those receiving the mark of the beast. The second, third and fourth plagues deplete what food supplies remain.

Famine will then be pandemic. The fifth plague marks the unmasking of Satan. God will fully expose to the world that they have been following the devil himself. The sixth plague is Satan's final attempt to destroy the people of God. And the seventh plague is a great hailstorm of fire that attends the second coming of Jesus.

When Jesus appears during the seventh and final judgment, the Bible says, "Out of his mouth comes a sharp sword with which to strike down the nations..." (Revelation 19:15) In other words, the nations will mourn at the appearing of Jesus, for He overthrows them by His Word and the splendor of His glory. "At that time the sign of the Son of Man will appear in the sky, and all the nations of the earth will mourn..." (Matthew 24:30) A lake of blazing fire will consume Babylon and those not thrown into the lake of fire will be slain by the brightness of Christ's coming. Birds will gorge themselves on the flesh of the slain. See 2 Thessalonians 2:8 and Revelation 19:21.

Summary

The destruction of 25% of the earth (1.3 billion people) is beyond our comprehension. And today, it seems like a horrible fairy tale. But, be assured of two things. First, God does nothing without purpose and cause. Secondly, the Bible points out that God's judgments come in two phases. The first phase is redemptive. That is, God awakens people so that they may realize the sinfulness of their course - and indeed, many will repent and be saved. The second phase of God's judgments is utter destruction. God will send his wrath, without mercy, upon all those who receive the mark of the beast. Understand that God is justified in these actions. These things will be examined in later chapters.

If you already know Jesus as your Savior, you have no reason to be afraid. The Psalmist wrote, "Even though I walk through the valley of the shadow of death, I will fear no evil, for you are with me..." (Psalm 23:4) If you haven't given yourself to Jesus, surrender your life now by obeying the teachings of Jesus and living by faith in His promises. Be willing and obedient to the prompting of the Holy Spirit. Covenant with God to bring your life in harmony with His wonderful truths and God will take care of you. Earth's cup of iniquity is almost full. God is about to break His silence. The end of this old earth is here and the beginning of the New Earth lies just around the corner.

Appendix D

Jubilee cycles explain a year for a day

The purpose and beauty of the ancient Jubilee Calendar is now beginning to unfold. Its purpose has been shrouded in mystery for centuries, but now the secrets of the Jubilee calendar are becoming known. Dating back to the days of the Exodus, this time mechanism was given to Moses for some very interesting reasons.

A rest for the land

Upon entering the Promised Land, God had Joshua divide the land of Canaan into twelve "parcels." Each tribe was given a parcel according to its size and the families within a tribe were given a tract of land. All were free to use the land as they saw fit. They could even sell the land to fellow Hebrews in other tribes, but when the Year of Jubilee arrived, the land had to revert back, at no charge, to the original tribe and family that received it from Joshua. The exception to this rule was city property. (Joshua 14, Leviticus 25:10,29)

The Year of Jubilee was celebrated at the end of each Jubilee cycle. Study the chart on the next page and notice that each day of the week represents a year. (A complete full sized chart can be obtained for $2 by calling (513) 848-3322.) Notice that at the end of each week, the seventh year is a sabbatical year for the land. Understand that the sabbatical year *was not a sabbatical year for the people,* but for the land. (Leviticus 25:2) After seven weeks of 49 years had fully ended, the Year of Jubilee commenced. You will notice that the 50th year celebration occurs during the first year of the next cycle of 49 years (See 1388 B.C.). At first, this confuses many people. How can the 50th year of celebration also be the first year of the next cycle? Consider the mechanism: The Jews marked off 49 days (seven weeks) from the Feast of Unleavened Bread to observe Pentecost. If Passover occurred on a seventh-day Sabbath, then seven Sabbaths and one day later, the 50th day, the Day of Pentecost fully arrived. (Leviticus 23:15,16) Understand that in this case, the 50th day, the day of Pentecost, is also the first day of the week. The point here is that God's Jubilee calendar is based on recurring cycles of seven weeks. And, the 50th year of the old cycle falls at the same time as the first year of the new cycle. (For those who are thinking ahead, this is the only way that the 70 weeks of Daniel 9 can equal 490 years.)

Not man's calendar

The Jubilee Calendar was given to Israel for two wonderful reasons. First, God made Israel His time-keepers for mankind. They were the only people to receive the perpetual responsibility of marking

The first two Jubilee cycles

W	Day	Yr	Jubilee Cycle	Jubilee Cycle
			1	2
	Sun	1	The Exodus 1437 B.C.	1st 50th Yr 1388 B.C.
	Mon	2	1436	
	Tue	3	1435	
	Wed	4	1434	
	Thu	5	1433	
	Fri	6	1432	
1	**Sat**	7	1431	1382
	Sun	8		
	Mon	9		
	Tue	10		
	Wed	11		
	Thu	12		
	Fri	13		
2	**Sat**	14	1424	1375
	Sun	15		
	Mon	16		
	Tue	17		
	Wed	18		
	Thu	19		
	Fri	20		
3	**Sat**	21	1417	1368
	Sun	22		
	Mon	23		
	Tue	24		
	Wed	25		
	Thu	26		
	Fri	27		

chart continued

4	**Sat**	28	1410	1361
	Sun	29		
	Mon	30		
	Tue	31		
	Wed	32		
	Thu	33		
	Fri	34		
5	**Sat**	35	1403	1354
	Sun	36		
	Mon	37		
	Tue	38		
	Wed	39		
	Thu	40	Canaan!	
	Fri	41		
6	**Sat**	42	1396	1347
	Sun	43		
	Mon	44		
	Tue	45		
	Wed	46		
	Thu	47		
	Fri	48		
7	**Sat**	49	1389	1340

1 Jubilee cycle
= 7 weeks
= 49 years

the passage of time as God sees time. And, to prevent Israel from guessing at time, God synchronized His eternal calendar on two occasions. First, He told Moses *when* to start counting. (Exodus 12:2) Then, for forty years, He constantly verified the days of the week in the minds of His people by doubling the amount of manna that fell on the sixth day and withholding manna on the seventh day of the week. (Exodus 16:26)

In addition to synchronizing His people with His calendar, God required the perpetual observance of the seventh-day Sabbath to mark the passage of the weekly cycle. This observance would distinguish His people from others. God declared that His seventh-day Sabbath would be a sign between Him and His people. (Exodus 31:17) But keeping up with the weekly cycle was only part of His larger purpose. God also required the observance of new moons to mark the passage of monthly cycles (2 Chronicles 2:4). He required the observance of the Passover on the 15th day of the new year to mark their yearly anniversary of deliverance. He required the observance of each seventh-year sabbatical to mark seven year cycles within the Jubilee. And God required the observance of the Year of Jubilee to mark the completion of each 49 year cycle. (Leviticus 26:14-44)

Not observed now

Because Jubilee cycles aren't observed today, many people depreciate the importance of these timing cycles. When Jesus died on Calvary, the observances of feast days and ceremonies became unnecessary (Colossians 2:11-16, Galatians 4:9-11), but the time-periods they marked remain with us. As far as God is concerned, the weekly cycle, the monthly cycle, the yearly cycle, the week of years and the Jubilee cycle are still intact. (This assertion will be demonstrated later.) The point here is that when Jesus died, the ceremonial services that occurred at these specific times became unnecessary, but the cycles of time remain. In fact, the cleansing of the heavenly sanctuary is directly connected to 2,300 day/years which have their origin in the Jubilee calendar!

A starting point

A day in the Jubilee calendar represents a year. Verify this point by looking at the chart on page 236. The Jubilee Calendar marks the passage of time by counting "weeks of years." That is, a week of seven days represents seven years. This may sound complicated, but remember, the Jews did not have a fixed date by which to mark their calendars like we do today. When we say 1992, what are we referring to? We are saying that there have been 1,992 years since the birth of Jesus (actually, 1,992 years is incorrect but this is beside the point). Because our calendar dates from an event that is recognized by all nations, we can keep track of the years quite easily. But suppose the Japanese did not base their calendar on the birth of Jesus, what year Honda would they be selling in the U.S.A. right now?

The weekly cycle is a template

God foreknew the problems of keeping track of time, so he created a calendar *based on the template* of the weekly cycle. Many people understand the importance of the cycle of the week, but few understand the importance of the other cycles. We'll investigate two.

The sabbatical

God declared that a sabbatical year must occur every seventh year (Leviticus 25:3-7). Every seventh year, the land was not to be planted or harvested. In His divine wisdom, God accomplished two important things with the seventh-year sabbatical. First, the land itself received a much needed rest. Secondly and more importantly, He wanted to test Israel's faith every seventh year. He wanted to see if they would trust Him enough to provide for their needs. Think about this, would it take considerable faith for an agricultural nation to let the land lay fallow for a whole year? So, God declared that years 7, 14, 21, 28, 35, 42 and 49 were perpetual Sabbatical years. The land was to receive its rest.

The Year of Jubilee

The 49th year was the last sabbatical of a Jubilee cycle. It was considered a high year because it was the seventh sabbatical. And the high sabbatical of the 49th year was followed by the once-per- generation Year of Jubilee. Again, the immediate purpose of the Year of Jubilee was the test of faith. God wanted His people to realize that the land they enjoyed was a gift from Him. He wanted them to know that they did not work for it, earn it, nor deserve it. Therefore, it was to be given back to its original owner every 50 years with the same cheerful spirit that He gave it to them because the land was not theirs to own. He wanted them to know that they were only stewards of it. And, if they were faithful, they could remain upon the land. If they were unfaithful to Him, He promised to throw them out. (Joshua 24:13, Leviticus 18:24-28; 25:23 and Jeremiah 2:7). He also required that they were not to plant or harvest their fields during the Year of Jubilee, for it was a holy year (Leviticus 25:11,12).

The harmony of time

The observance of the seventh-day Sabbath kept the weekly cycle intact. The observance of new moons kept the monthly cycle intact. The observance of the Passover kept the yearly cycle intact. The observance of seventh-year sabbaticals kept the week of years intact. And, the observance of the Jubilee cycle kept the land in the hands of its original owner.

Note: In all but the very first Jubilee cycle, there were eight sabbatical years per Jubilee cycle. These include the Year of Jubilee (year 1) plus seven sabbaticals (years 7, 14, 21, 28, 35, 42, 49). See charts on pages 236 and 272.

Warning

When God gave Israel the Jubilee Calendar, He made clear their responsibility. He warned, **"But if you will not listen to me and carry out all these commands... then I will do this to you: I will bring upon you sudden terror, wasting diseases and fever that will destroy your sight and drain away your life... Your land will be laid waste, and your cities will lie in ruins. Then the land will enjoy its sabbath years all the time that it lies desolate and you are in the country of your enemies; then the land will rest and enjoy its sabbaths. All the time that it lies desolate, the land will have the rest it did not have during the sabbaths you lived in it."** (Leviticus 26:14-35).

If we look carefully at the penalty for violating the sabbatical years we may correctly estimate their value in God's sight. *The penalty for violating the sabbatical years was severe because God wanted Israel to live by faith. He also wanted Israel to perpetuate His calendar.* Since the Jubilee Calendar was initiated at the time of the Exodus (Exodus 12:2), God designed that Israel should never forget their deliverance, their benevolent Creator and God. He required them to observe His sabbatical years. Anything God calls holy has an important lesson in it. He does not declare something holy to tempt man with disobedience.

The Bible almost silent

The silence regarding sabbatical or Jubilee celebrations in the Bible leads me to conclude that Israel didn't often measure up to God's ideal. In fact, only one Year of Jubilee is mentioned in all the Bible: Isaiah 37:30 and II Kings 19:29. Here we find that the 49th sabbatical year and the Year of Jubilee occurred during the 14th and 15th years of Hezekiah's reign (II Kings 18:13) which fell on 703/702 B.C. This small point will become very vital when we try to identify the year of origin for the Jubilee cycle.

God's patience = 70 units

God's patience with Israel's backsliding is beyond human understanding. For centuries He tried to get Israel to shape up and accomplish all that He had in mind. But they refused. Eventually, Israel filled up their cup of iniquity. God's patience expired when Israel violated a total of 70 sabbatical years.

When the number 70 was fully reached, Israel was expelled from Jerusalem and hauled off to Babylon by King Nebuchadnezzar. They had to remain in Babylon for 70 years because the land had gone without 70 sabbaticals of rest! Remember God's warning? **"All the time that it lies desolate, the land will have the rest it did not have during the sabbaths you lived in it"** (Leviticus 26:35). In other words, God's patience with Israel reached its limit with 70 years of sabbatical violations and He had them evicted from the land. Notice what the Bible says about their captivity, **"The land enjoyed its sabbath rests; all the time of its desolation it rested, until the seventy years were completed in fulfillment of the word of the Lord spoken by Jeremiah"** (II Chronicles 36:21).

How are 70 sabbaticals counted?

How do we know that Israel was placed in captivity because they had violated 70 sabbatical years? **"Now, son of man, take a clay tablet, put it in front of you and draw the city of Jerusalem on it. Then lay siege to it... You are to bear their sin for the number of days you lie on your side. I have assigned you the same number of days as the years of their sin. So for 390 days you will bear the sin of the house of Israel. After you have finished this, lie down again, this time on your right side, and bear the sin of the house of Judah. I have assigned you 40 days, a day for each year"** (Ezekiel 4:1-6).

Notice how the math works. If we add the 390 years of Israel's sin to the 40 years of Judah's sin, we obtain a sum of 430 years of sinful living. This is why Ezekiel had to lay on his right and left sides for a total of 430 days – a day for each year. In 430 years, there are eight Jubilee cycles plus a partial cycle (the 9th) which contains 38 years. The point is that 430 years contain exactly 70 sabbaticals! (Keep in mind that there are 8 sabbaticals in a Jubilee cycle of 49 years.) Here's how the total of 70 sabbaticals is found:

Jubilee Cycle	Years	Sabbaticals
1	49	8
2	49	8
3	49	8
4	49	8
5	49	8
6	49	8
7	49	8
8	49	8
9	38	6
Total	430	70

Day/Year again

While in Babylonian captivity, God spoke to the prophet Daniel and told him that He was going to give Israel another chance. This opportunity would also have a limit of 70 units. However, instead of granting Israel 70 sabbaticals of time, God used the next larger unit within the calendar. He granted Israel 70 sevens (70 weeks of years). This, God hoped, would be enough time for Israel to become all that He wanted. Note the progression within the Jubilee Calendar. God moved from 70 sabbaticals of patience to 70 weeks of patience. Seventy weeks in the Jubilee calendar contain 490 literal years. See 457 B.C. to A.D. 33 on the chart on pages 272 and following.

According to Daniel 9, the 70 weeks were to begin with the decree to restore and rebuild Jerusalem. In the Jubilee year of 457 B.C., Artaxerxes, the world monarch of the Persian empire, issued a decree granting the Jews complete sovereignty as a nation. Nehemiah carried the declaration to the Jews in Jerusalem. He arrived in Jerusalem in early fall and probably read the declaration on the Day of Atonement in the Year of Jubilee, because the land was officially theirs at the sounding of the trumpet on the Day of Atonement in the Year of Jubilee. (Leviticus 25:9-10)

Note: for a careful explanation of the 70 weeks and how the appearing of Jesus Himself confirmed the timing of these events, the reader is referred to *The Revelation of Jesus,* another book by this writer.

When A.D. 33 arrived, the 70 weeks expired. The Jews had not progressed as God desired. Israel had greatly rebelled against the Holy One of Israel Himself. So, in A.D. 70, God sent the Romans upon Jerusalem and it was completely destroyed again.

7 x 10 = 70

Have you begun to notice that God's patience may be measured in units of 70? Consider this: When Israel violated 70 sabbaticals, God had them removed from the land by Babylonian King Nebuchad- nezzar so that the land might receive its rest. When Israel violated the 70 weeks, God had Jerusalem destroyed by Rome's army in A.D 70. Again, the land got its rest.

If you are a student of the Old Testament, you know that judgment day, the most important day of the sanctuary service, was the Day of Atonement. It occurred on the tenth day of the seventh month. The month and day of this service combine to form 70. It may be that seven represents the fullness of God's patience and ten represents the limit of His mercy. One thing is certain, 70 units seem to indicate a time for judgment. You may have already considered the possibility that the total existence of sin will be 7,000 years, which just happens to be 70 centuries. And, the length of life itself is often called threescore and ten which of course, is 70 years. Psalms 90:10 Are these numbers just coincidental?

Kindness has a limit, too

The first use of 70 sevens is found in Genesis 4:24. But, the finest explanation is found in the New Testament. **"Then Peter came to Jesus and asked, 'Lord, how many times shall I forgive my brother when he sins against me? Up to seven times?' Jesus answered, 'I tell you, not seven times, but seventy-seven times' "** (Matthew 18:21,22). The NIV and other translations of this verse seem to say 77 times. Actually, Jesus didn't say 77 times. Rather, He turned to Peter and said, "seventy-sevens." Peter immediately understood the phrase. Just as Israel had been forgiven by God and granted seventy-sevens (490 years) of redemptive opportunity, Peter was to forgive his brother and grant him the same redemptive grace.

Prophetic time periods

It is beyond the scope of this article to examine all the prophetic time periods in the Bible. However, this point must be made: *All apocalyptic time periods occurring within the operation of Jubilee cycles are to be interpreted in Jubilee units of time. Under this system, a day represents a literal year.* This also means that prophetic time periods outside of Jubilee cycles are to be interpreted as they are given, i.e., literal units of time. This concept becomes very interesting when we consider the possibility that there may be a finite number of Jubilee cycles. That number could be 70.

Notice how the Jubilee principle works with respect to prophetic time periods. Before Jubilee cycles were given, prophetic time periods were literal. Therefore, Noah's 120 years of warning (Genesis 6:3) were 120 literal years because they happened *before* Jubilee cycles began. The 1260 days of Daniel 7:25, Revelation 12:6,14 are to be interpreted using Jubilee units. Therefore, they represent a 1,260 year time period. The 1,000 years of the seventh millennium will be literal years because they occur *after* the expiration of Jubilee cycles.

One other point. Some ask why the 70 years prophesied by Jeremiah were literal since they occur during Jubilee cycles. Answer: The 70 years of Babylonian captivity were payment-in-kind for violating the 70 seventh-day sabbaticals. So, Israel spent a year in captivity for each seventh-day sabbatical violation.

Consider this twice

Suppose there is a week of millenniums, that is, each day of creation stands for a period of 1,000 years. Suppose that the millennium of Revelation 20 is not a random number, but actually the 7th millennium or sabbatical millennium for earth. The idea here is that the whole earth gets its rest for 1,000 years because the wicked are dead and the saints are in heaven. Suppose that the second coming of Jesus is on or about the 6,000th year. If the reader will consider this possibility, this simple concept will clear up several problems regarding time periods in Daniel and Revelation.

A most interesting possibility develops. Assume there are 70 Jubilees of time. The 70th Year of Jubilee would be 1994. Add to this date, the 1,335 literal days of Daniel and something very interesting happens: Now, the Jubilee calendar and the millennial calendar reach to 1998 which can be reasonably shown to be the 6,000th year!

The real point here is that after the Jubilee expires, prophetic time becomes literal. This simple mechanism explains why some time periods are day/year and others are literal time.

Jubilees continue after A.D. 34

Two prophecies confirm the perpetuity of Jubilee cycles long after the demise of ancient Israel in A.D 70. The first prophecy is found in Daniel 7:25. Here the Bible foretells that the little horn power would persecute the saints of God for a time, times and dividing of time. This time period of 1,260 day/years began in A.D. 538 and ended in 1798. History clearly confirms the duration of this time period and even more, verifies the presence and operation of the day/year principle. But even more, the fulfillment of this prophecy confirms the operation of the Jubilee Calendar, for without it there is no hermeneutical reason to apply the day/year mechanism. In other words, the operation of the Jubilee calendar is clearly confirmed by historical events.

Some argue that in symbolic prophecy, a day always equals a year. This is not true. Look at Daniel 4:16. Seven times are sentenced upon king Nebuchadnezzar who is symbolized as a tree in this prophecy. Furthermore, the Hebrew word *'iddan* in Daniel 4:16 is identical with Daniel 7:25 and Daniel 12:7. As far as I know, only Jehovah Witnesses apply the day/year principle to Daniel 4:16 and Daniel 7:25 and Daniel 12:7. But, the reader should require some principle to determine when time is literal and when time is day/year and the answer is simple. If the time period is part of apocalyptic prophecy *and* occurs during the operation of the Jubilee calendar, the time period must be interpreted as Jubilee units, i.e., day/years.

The second prophecy that confirms the perpetuity of the Jubilee cycle long after the demise of ancient Israel is found in Daniel 8:14. Whatever question may have existed about the use of day/years within the Jubilee Calendar is eliminated by the fulfillment of this prophecy. Because this prophecy begins in 457 B.C. and reaches down to A.D. 1844, two impressive points must be recognized. First, the day/year principle is clearly at work here because the time (70 sevens = 490 literal years = 10 Jubilee cycles) granted to Israel is "cut off" from this larger prophecy. In other words, if the 70 sevens are reckoned in Jubilee units of weeks, then the 2,300 days of Daniel 8:14 must also be reckoned in Jubilee units of day/years because the 2,300 days start at the *same* time as the 70 sevens. Secondly, and maybe even more importantly, this prophecy clearly points out that Jesus connected His ministry in the heavenly sanctuary to the timing mechanism established by Jubilee cycles. If Jesus reckons the operation of the Jubilee calendar as important, shouldn't we?

70 Jubilee cycles end in 1994

The Jubilee chart beginning on page 272 is a pictograph covering 3,431 years. It begins with the Hebrew Exodus in 1437 B.C. and ends in A.D. 1994. Notice the two shaded blocks of time. The first block identifies the 70 weeks of Daniel 9. This block of time demonstrates the synchronism of Jubilee cycles. The second block identifies the 1,260 years of papal dominion. This block demonstrates the operation of the Jubilee calendar after A.D. 33.

Exodus dating

Often the first question raised by the Jubilee chart is its beginning date. Debate on the date of the Exodus from Egypt has gone on for centuries and considerable diversity of opinion exists. So, how can the date of the Exodus be determined?

First, no one can prove with absolute certainty the date of the Exodus. Given the lack of solid evidence, most scholars will grant a small variance to whatever date they settle on. For this reason, 1437 B.C. is not an extraordinary date. But, it is a *calculated* date using three well respected events whose dating has been verified outside the Bible.

Secondly, 1437 B.C. is not only historically plausible, it is the *only* date that compliments the weekly cycle of years without difficulty. If the reader can tolerate the idea that the Jubilee cycle serves a greater purpose than marking the passage of time, the end result will be a new appreciation for the intricate workings and plans of God.

70 Jubilee cycles

Notice that the Jubilee chart is divided into 70 columns of Jubilee cycles. Each column represents one

Jubilee cycle of 49 years. To improve readability, only the sabbatical years are printed. You will notice them at intervals of seven years. In addition, special dates are also included for perspective. You will also notice that the first year of each cycle is printed. This is done because the *Year of Jubilee* is a sabbatical year.

Ultimate purpose

The Jubilee calendar offers a simple solution to the problem of which prophecies are day/year and which are not. In essence, the calendar operates like this: if a prophetic time period falls within the time period of 70 Jubilees and that prophecy belongs to the family of 18 apocalyptic prophecies found in Daniel and Revelation, it must be interpreted by the day/year principle. After the expiration of the Jubilee calendar, all prophetic time periods are to be interpreted as literal time. Thus the 1,000 years of the millennium are literal years and not 1,000 years of day/years.

As said before, if we add 1,335 literal days to the end of 70 Jubilee cycles, we reach into 1998 which can be reasonably demonstrated to be on or about the 6,000th year. (See *Day Star* Volume 2, Number 10.) As a bonus, it can be easily shown that all time periods in Daniel and Revelation will harmoniously fit together if Jubilee units are applied to those time periods within the Jubilee calendar and literal units are applied to those time periods after the expiration of the Jubilee calendar.

How 1437 B.C. is calculated

The calculation of 1437 B.C. is not complicated. Basically, the process requires assembling 4 known dates with one uncertain time period. After placing them on a chart, we then impose the Jubilee scheme upon them. Here's the mathematical process:

- 1 Kings 6:1 says that the temple of Solomon was begun during the 480th year after the Exodus.

- The seventy years of captivity in Babylon have been confirmed outside of the Bible as 605 B.C. to 536 B.C. Also, the destruction of Jerusalem (compare II Kings 25:8,9 with Jeremiah 52:5; 32:1,2) during Nebuchadnezzar's 19th year has been confirmed as August, 586 B.C. from sources outside the Bible. Zedekiah was taken as a prisoner to Babylon in his eleventh year.

- The beginning of the 70 weeks found in Daniel 9 occurs in 457 B.C. during the 7th year of the reign of Artaxerxes. This means that the 70th week of years occurred between 27 (the first year) and 33 A.D. (the seventh year). Jesus Himself confirmed the timing of this prophecy by appearing and dying in the middle of the week. (See Galatians 4:4, Daniel 9:27.)

- The 70 weeks of Daniel 9 are synchronous with the weeks of the existing Jubilee calendar from which they are taken. In fact, the 457 B.C. decree of Artaxerxes is the only decree of four decrees made, which occurs during a Jubilee year. Given the purpose of the Jubilee year and the condition of Israel at the time, this is particularly important. The shadow covering 457 B.C. to A.D. 33 demonstrates the synchronisms of the Jubilee calendar. In other words, the 70 weeks of years (490 years) are synchronous with the Jubilee cycles that were already operating at the time.

- The 1,260 day/years of persecution found in Daniel 7:25 ended in February, 1798, when Napoleon captured the pope and sent him into exile in France as a prisoner. The time allotted for this persecution began in A.D. 538 and ended in 1798. This specific time period is also mentioned two more times in the Bible: Revelation 12:6 and 12:14. Because this time period is not connected to the 70 week prophecy of Daniel 9, and because this time period begins five centuries after the fall of Jerusalem, the historical fulfillment of this prophecy demonstrates the continued operation of the Jubilee calendar. The shaded area covering A.D. 538 to 1798 demonstrates the continued operation and presence of the Jubilee calendar. Please note that 1798 was to Protestants what A.D. 34 was to Christians: a Jubilee year!

The larger scheme

Look at the years 1437, 457, 34, 1798 and 1994. Notice that all of the these except 1437 are Jubilee years. Is it just a coincidence that each of these five dates marks the beginning of a new trusteeship of God's truth? When God called Israel out of the bondage of Egypt in 1437 B.C., He made them trustees of His everlasting gospel. They were to be a light on a hill, the salt of the earth, BUT, they failed. God then turned to Christians. In A.D. 34 the trusteeship of the everlasting gospel was transferred and God marked the transition by converting Saul into an apostle to the Gentiles (Acts 9) and by sending Peter to the home of a Gentile (Acts 10). *These things happened in the Jubilee Year of A.D. 34.*

After a while, the Christians repeated the same mistakes as their Jewish forefathers. The persecuted became the persecutor. And in February, 1798, according to divine decree (Daniel 7:25), the rule of the Catholic Church was broken when Napoleon took the pope captive. *This happened in the Jubilee year of 1798!* From this time, Protestantism has had unrestricted freedom to accomplish the task of carrying the everlasting gospel to all the world.

But, the Protestants have lost their mission and purpose. They have fallen away from the truths of the everlasting gospel just as their forefathers did and their trusteeship is about to be taken from them and given to the final generation: the remnant. This could happen in the upcoming Jubilee year of 1994!

If we add up the trusteeships in units of Jubilee cycles, we find an interesting balance. The Jews received 30 full Jubilees of opportunity. Christians received 36 full Jubilees of opportunity. Protestants, I believe, will receive 4 full Jubilees of opportunity and finally, the 144,000 will achieve in a mere 1260 days what the others failed to do. Could this be a Gideon-like miracle?

The $6.40 question

When all of the above are added together, we are left with one uncertainty. If our dating scheme of the calendar is correct, we have to account for the years between 957 B.C. (the building of the temple which began in Solomon's 4th year, 1 Kings 6:1) and 586 B.C. (the year Zedekiah was taken captive, II Kings 25). This is a total of 371 years.

It is impossible to precisely account for the 371 years between these two events because of co-regent reigns. A co-regent reign occurs when two kings reign at the same time. For example, the old king may continue his reign while the young king is getting established. Even more, sometimes an ascension year is counted and at other times, we cannot be sure if the ascension year is counted as part of the reign of kings or not.

Scholars who have painstakingly reviewed the Biblical list of forty kings in Judah and Israel during this time generally concur that the allotted time period between the building of the temple and the capture of Zedekiah falls somewhere between 369 and 389 years. This variance is very ample for our need because 371 years falls *within* that range. Further, we can reduce some of the uncertainty of the 371 years by reaching back to 703/702 B.C. This reduces the time in question to only 254 years. The Bible says that Hezekiah was in his 14th year when the Year of Jubilee took place and the only one that happened during his reign is 702 B.C. Isaiah 36:1

When the data is brought together, the 1437 B.C. date easily falls within widely accepted dating schemes for the Exodus. In addition, 1437 B.C. date of the Exodus compliments the synchronous operation of the weekly cycles of seven years which God put in motion at the time of the Exodus. If we accept the presence and operation of the Jubilee calendar, we have a simple but profound explanation for why some prophecies use the day/year mechanism and others do not. This little key opens up a whole new world of discovery about the timing of end-time events.

Summary

No one can prove something that has not happened. Neither does God ask us to believe something without first giving us substantial evidence upon which to build our faith. Therefore, we have a wonderful opportunity to study these things and see if they are of any value. In spite of all that has been said, this point is true: 1994 will soon be here. We'll soon know if this date marks the end of God's patience with human beings and the beginning of the seven trumpets of Revelation! Be on your toes.

Appendix E

How 1798 marks the beginning of the end

The Bible identifies the existence of many time periods. And if we carefully examine them, we can find most of them in history. It is also true that God made the meaning of certain prophetic passages obscure, but we find an interesting mechanism occurring throughout recorded history. *On or about the time of fulfillment, cryptic passages from prophecy make sense just as they read.*

Literal time begins at creation

The book of Genesis mentions four time units. They are: day, week, month and year. (Genesis 1:5; 2:2, 29:27; 7:11; 1:14) These units are used to describe time in two ways:

Time past / Time to come

In Genesis 2:2, the first time period reviewed *in the past* is the week. On the other hand, the first time period mentioned *to come* is the probationary 120 years before the flood. (Genesis 6:3) Just like the seven days of creation, the 120 years mentioned in Genesis 6:3 must be literal time, because Noah was 600 years old when the flood came. (Genesis 7:6) It is believed that Noah not only built the ark during this 120 years, he also warned the world of impending destruction. (Hebrews 11:7) Even more, the seven days predicted before the flood are also seven literal days. (Genesis 7:4)

Certainly the ages of the patriarchs are given in literal time. For example, we know that Abraham was 100 and Sarah was 90 when Isaac was born. (Genesis 17:17, 21:5) We also find that when God spoke to Abraham of time to come, He spoke of literal time. He said, "Then the LORD said to him, 'Know for certain that your descendants will be strangers in a country not their own, and they will be enslaved and mistreated four hundred years.' "

(Genesis 15:13) We also find the seven years of plenty and seven years of famine in Egypt during the days of Joseph to be literal time. (Genesis 41:29,30)

The point here is that during the first two and a half millenniums of earth's existence, both time periods – time past and time to come – were always reckoned in literal time. Why would it have been any other way?

Then came the Jubilee Calendar

When God took Israel out of Egypt, He created two new units of time – the week of years and the Jubilee cycle. These units of time were added to the four existing units mentioned above. (The reader is referred to Appendix D for a larger discussion on the Jubilee Calendar.) The purpose of these new timing schemes is wonderful to behold. In effect, God's purpose with the week of years was to test the faith of Israel. This was done by requiring Israel to give the land rest every seventh year. By this method, God would test them to see if they would trust enough in Him to provide for their needs. God's purpose for the Jubilee cycle was to teach each generation of Israel that the land they had been given was not theirs. It, like His salvation, was a gift. He wanted Israel to know that they were only stewards of the land, and if they failed to live up to the terms of His covenant, they would be expelled from the land. (Leviticus 26:14-46)

It is important to know that God synchronized the deliverance of Israel with the operation of His Jubilee calendar by establishing the first day of the first month of the first year. (Exodus 12:2) From that time forward, all religious services were to be reckoned from the first day of each year. For example, the Passover began on the 14th day of the first month. (Leviticus 23:5-8)

Israel's rebellion

God's first demonstration of Jubilee time occurred about two years after the Exodus from Egypt. After many wonderful and marvelous demonstrations of His love for them, He had lead Israel to the gates of the Promised Land. There, He told Moses to send spies into the Promised Land so that the people could receive a report of what the land was like. After forty days, the spies returned and ten of them spread a bad report about the land among the Israelites. (Numbers 13:32) Their contempt for God led them to criticize Him before the people and rebellion broke out in the camp. This made God very angry and He almost destroyed the whole camp. (Numbers 14:12) Moses interceded and God relented somewhat. "The Lord replied [to Moses], 'I have forgiven them, as you asked. {21} Nevertheless, as surely as I live and as surely as the glory of the Lord fills the whole earth, {22} not one of the men who saw my glory and the miraculous signs I performed in Egypt and in the desert but who disobeyed me and tested me ten times– {23} not one of them will ever see the land I promised on oath to their forefathers. No one who has treated me with contempt will ever see it.'" (Numbers 14:20-23)

Then the Lord sentenced the Israelites to death in the wilderness. He said, "In this desert your bodies will fall–every one of you twenty years old or more who was counted in the census and who has grumbled against me." (Numbers 14:29) Afterwards, the Lord explained their punishment: "For forty years–one year for each of the forty days you explored the land–you will suffer for your sins and know what it is like to have me against you." (Numbers 14:34)

A stand alone principle?

Some scholars see this last verse as a stand alone, unique implementation of the day/year principle. From this and Ezekiel 4:5,6, they claim that the day/year principle must be used throughout apocalyptic prophecy. Such a conclusion is misleading for there is *nothing* in Numbers 14:34 (or Ezekiel 4:5,6) that indicates that a day equals a literal year in the apocalyptic prophecies of Daniel and Revelation. Rather, these texts demonstrate that God, for a valid reason, uses the day/year principle. So we ask, what is the reason underlying God's use of the day/year principle? The answer: the Jubilee Calendar.

Under the Jubilee Calendar, a week of seven days represents seven years. The number of days the spies spent investigating the Promised Land was forty. So when the spies returned and cast contempt upon God by giving a bad report, they violated God's covenant to give them the Promised Land. (See Numbers 14:23) Because God's covenant is directly connected to His plan of salvation, and because God's covenant is directly connected to the Jubilee calendar (Leviticus 26:15-35), Israel was punished accordingly. The point here is that God did not create the day/year principle just to punish the children of Israel. Rather, He used the *existing* day/year principle which had been given to Israel through the Jubilee Calendar.

But we must ask, how can we tell when the day/year principle is to be used?

Seven times for Nebuchadnezzar

In Daniel 4, a vision was given to Nebuchadnezzar. This vision, like the others recorded in Daniel, was symbolic in nature. Daniel was summoned to explain the mysterious vision and Daniel told the king that he was the great tree in the vision that was to be cut down. Daniel explained that the vision was going to be implemented because the king had become too haughty and arrogant. Daniel also suggested that the king repent of his ways so that the judgment could be stayed.

The vision specified that the king was to be punished for seven *times*. Sure enough, twelve months later, the predicted judgment fell upon the king and he was removed from his throne. According to verse 34, the time predicted had passed and the king's sanity and his throne were returned to him.

Now three points have to be made. First, this event occurred around 575 B.C., well after the Jubilee Calendar had been implemented. Secondly, most expositors of prophecy, except Jehovah's

Witnesses, are convinced that the period of time called, "seven times," refers to seven literal years. This understanding is also supported by first century historian Flavius Josephus in *Antiquity of the Jews,* book 10, chapter 10, section 6. But, the point can be made from Scripture that the time period was fulfilled during the life of the king, for "at the end of that time," his sanity returned to him. (Daniel 4:34) Lastly, the Chaldean word, *'iddan,* from which the word "times" is translated (see Strong's Hebrew word 5732) means a year, as in "one *time* around the sun." So, seven times means seven years. This point can also be supported by comparing Revelation 12:6 with 12:14.

Now the question: What excludes the seven times of Nebuchadnezzar from the day/year principle? Answer: Time periods mentioned in the 18 apocalyptic prophecies occurring under the operation of the Jubilee Calendar must be interpreted as a day for a year, on the other hand, time periods not mentioned in the 18 apocalyptic prophecies but occurring during the operation of the Jubilee calendar must be interpreted as literal units of time. Therefore, Nebuchadnezzar's time period is to be interpreted as literal time for it is not part of an apocalyptic prophecy.

Jeremiah's prophecy

Jeremiah predicted that Israel would go into Babylonian captivity for seventy years. "This whole country will become a desolate wasteland, and these nations will serve the king of Babylon seventy years." (Jeremiah 25:11) This prophecy was given around 700 B.C. Further, we know that the Jubilee calendar is in effect because Isaiah himself predicted the bounty of the coming Jubilee year (702 B.C.) would serve as a sign to Hezekiah. (Isaiah 37:30, cf Leviticus 25:21,22) We know from numerous historical sources that the Babylonian captivity of the Jews began with Nebuchadnezzar's first siege in 605 B.C. We also find that Daniel, toward the end of his life, understood that the seventy years predicted by Jeremiah was about to end and he prayed for the deliverance of his people. (Daniel 9:2-20) When we add these items together, we find the following: the seventy years of Jeremiah are literal because they are not within any of the 18 apocalyptic structures in Daniel and Revelation. We also find that Daniel, who was contemporary at the time, understood the prophecy to cover seventy literal years.

Ezekiel's experience

In Appendix D, we examined the operation of the Jubilee Calendar as it pertained to the 70 years of Babylonian captivity. We found that Ezekiel had to lay on his left and right sides for a total of 430 days. The Lord said to Ezekiel, "Then lie on your left side and put the sin of the house of Israel upon yourself.

You are to bear their sin for the number of days you lie on your side. {5} I have assigned you the same number of days as the years of their sin. So for 390 days you will bear the sin of the house of Israel. {6} 'After you have finished this, lie down again, this time on your right side, and bear the sin of the house of Judah. I have assigned you 40 days, a day for each year.' " (Ezekiel 4:4-6)

Again, the point is made that a number of scholars try to demonstrate from these verses that in apocalyptic prophecy, a day always equals a year. Again, I say, this event has nothing to do with the apocalyptic prophecies of Daniel and Revelation! Rather, this text reveals that God is punishing Judah and Israel with 70 years of Babylonian captivity because they violated 70 sabbatical years. Thus, the 70 years of captivity in Babylon is not a random number of years. It is a fulfillment of His covenant with them. Notice what the covenant says: "I will scatter you among the nations and will draw out my sword and pursue you. Your land will be laid waste, and your cities will lie in ruins. {34} Then the land will enjoy its sabbath years all the time that it lies desolate and you are in the country of your enemies; then the land will rest and enjoy its sabbaths." (Leviticus 26:33-34) The Jews knew why they were in Babylonian captivity. God made sure of that fact. Notice how the Bible confirms the relationship between the covenant and its fulfillment: "The land enjoyed its sabbath rests; all the time of its desolation it rested, until the seventy years were completed in fulfillment of the word of the Lord spoken by Jeremiah." (2 Chronicles 36:21)

The little horn power

In Daniel 7:25 we read, "He will speak against the Most High and oppress his saints and try to change the set times and the laws. The saints will be handed over to him for a time, times and half a time." The time period in this prophecy refers to three and a half times "around the sun." This time period is given in literal units, but it is to be interpreted in Jubilee units, that is, a day equals a year. In other words, this time period satisfies both elements of the rule. First, it occurs during the operation of Jubilee cycles and secondly, it is located within the 18 apocalyptic prophecies. Furthermore, this prophecy can be historically verified as having been fulfilled!

An important point must be brought up. The Chaldean word *'iddan* is used both in Daniel 4:16 and in Daniel 7:25. In the first case it represents literal time (seven years) and in the second, it represents Jubilee time (1,260 years). How can the same word have two different applications? Simple. It depends on the action of the rule of interpretation. This should not be too hard to understand. Think of it this way. The word "yes" can have many different applications. Its application depends on the questions.

Lunar months – solar years

The ancients used the sun and moon for timing cycles. This works well for days and weeks, but the monthly and yearly cycles cannot be measured in full days or weeks. A lunar month (one complete orbit of the moon about the earth) is 29.53 days and a solar year (one complete orbit of the earth about the sun) is 365.242 days. The ancients must have recognized that a lunar month is a little less than 30 days, but they apparently regarded the monthly cycle as having 30 days anyway and marked the passage of the month by new moons. This point can be demonstrated from Genesis 7 & 8. In verse 3, we learn that the waters of the flood dissipated after 150 days after the rain began. In verse 4, the ark rests on mountains of Ararat on the 17th day of the seventh month. In Genesis 7:11 we learned that the flood began on the 17th day of the second month. If the information written can be taken literally, then the distance between the 17th day of the second month and the 17th day of the seventh month is five months. Therefore, each month has 30 days. This calculation agrees with verse 3 which says the total lapsed time is 150 days.

The ancients approximated the length of a solar year by dividing the year into twelve months. In fact, we find mention of a 12th month both in 2 Kings 25:27 and Esther 2:12. But, a problem still remains. A lunar year (12 orbits of the moon) is about 10 days shorter than a solar year. So, the cycles of the moon rarely synchronize with the beginning of a new year. To compensate for this problem, the Jews, after their Babylonian captivity, apparently inserted a 13th month into their cycles of years to keep the solar year and lunar year reasonably synchronized. This adjustment amounted to seven intercalary months every 19 years so that the spring harvest synchronized with Pentecost.)

Where did the 360 day year come from?

How does three and half times equal 1,260 years? Where does the 360 day year come from? Some scholars speculate that it came from the ancient Egyptians. But, the Egyptian calendar contained 12 months of 30 days and a 13th month of 5 days called Epagomenae. Others believe that the Babylonians may have maintained a "business" calendar of 360 days which they used for the sake of consistent dating. And, since Daniel was in Babylon when this vision was given, God may have used such a calendar in the vision. But, no such calendar has been found. In fact, no 360 day calendar from an ancient civilization has ever been found. So, there must be another reason why God used a term that reckoned a year as having 360 days even though

He created a year to have 365.242 days.

The Jews, Egyptians and Babylonians had calendars of slightly different lengths because no one knew that the length of a solar year was 365 days, 5 hours, 48 minutes and 46 seconds. In fact, archeology shows that prior to the time of Julius Caesar, there were many different calendars. Some started in the fall. Others started in the Spring. And, Julius Caesar tried to eliminate the never ending confusion between calendars by installing his own on January 1, 45 B.C. But, God knew that *when* the time period predicted in Daniel 7 would become important, intimate knowledge of ancient calendars would be lost or at best, very obscure. So, why did He use a 360 day year?

The answer may be very simple. In fact, God may have used a measurement which was as true then as it is today. And the neat thing about this measurement is that the Egyptians, Babylonians and Jews knew this truth long before Daniel received the vision. This truth is that a circle contains exactly 360 degrees.

Ancient mathematicians believed the orbit of the sun about the earth was circular instead of elliptical. (Remember, they believed the sun circled the earth.) So, the word translated, "a time," refers to one *time around the earth.* Indeed, this is the root meaning of the Chaldean word *'iddan* from which we get the word "time."

So, the representation of time by geometry may solve the problem. In other words, since a circle has 360 degrees, a truth that was well known, then the orbit of the sun about the earth must also be 360 degrees. Thus, the word, *'iddan* represents one orbit of the sun (a solar year) and not the number of literal days in a year. Evidence has been found showing that the ancients knew the length of a solar year was one complete time around the sun. So, a common, although inaccurate 360 day year is not far fetched when you consider that traders of the ancient world did not have to keep up the idiosyncracies of each nation's calendar as they travelled between countries. One "time" was one year. Just like one moon represented one month, more or less, to American Indians.

Before the reader think the use of 360 days to represent a year is quite strange, consider that we do the same thing today. When someone asks how far you live from the grocery store, do you say "4.172 miles" or would you say, "about 4 miles?"

Whatever the reason that God chose to represent these things to Daniel, this fact is known: The time period of a time, times and half a time represents 1,260 days. This point is proven in Revelation 12:6 and 12:14 where John interchanges the two terms. Knowing that 1,260 days and three and a half times are interchangeable, we then conclude that the three and a half times of Daniel 7:25 represent 1,260 years because the rule says it must be interpreted in Jubilee time units.

Other time periods

The book of Daniel mentions six time periods that have to do with apocalyptic prophecy. They are:

1,260 days Daniel 7:25
2,300 days Daniel 8:14
70 weeks Daniel 9:24
1,260 days Daniel 12:7
1,290 days Daniel 12:12
1,335 days Daniel 12:13

For reasons covered in Appendix D, this author understands the first three time periods to fall within the operation of the rule. Therefore, the first three time periods are to be interpreted in day/year units. The last three units of time are literal because they occur after 1994.

The time of the end

The Bible speaks of a specific time period that exists at the end of the world. Throughout the Bible, it is called "the Great Day of the Lord." In most cases, this term refers to a time period when the authority and glory of Almighty God shall be revealed. In the book of Daniel, this time period is also called "the appointed time of the end." Notice these texts (emphasis mine):

Daniel 8:17 As he [Gabriel] came near the place where I was standing, I was terrified and fell prostrate. "Son of man," he said to me, *understand that the vision concerns the time of the end.*

Daniel 8:19 He said: "I am going to tell you what will happen later *in the time of wrath*, because the vision concerns *the appointed time of the end.*"

Daniel 11:35 Some of the wise will stumble, so that they may be refined, purified and made spotless *until the time of the end, for it will still come at the appointed time.*

Daniel 11:36 The king [of the North] will do as he pleases. He will exalt and magnify himself above every god and will say unheard-of things against the God of gods. He will be successful *until the time of wrath is completed, for what has been determined must take place.*

Daniel 11:40 *At the time of the end the king of the South* will engage him [the king of the North] in battle, and the king of the North will storm out against him with chariots and cavalry and a great fleet of ships. He will invade many countries and sweep through them like a flood.

Daniel 12:9 He replied, "Go your way, Daniel, because the words [of this prophecy] are closed up and *sealed until the time of the end.*

These six verses clearly reveal that God, long ago, determined *when* the end should come. This is good news. God's never sleeps even though we may think the hour is late or overdue.

Paul knew that the Father had appointed a time for the end: "For he has *set a day* when he will judge the world with justice by the man [Jesus] he has appointed. He has given proof of this to all men by raising him from the dead." (Acts 17:31)

Lastly, Jesus clearly confirms the fact that the Father has *pre-set* the time allotted for sin much like a cook sets the time allotted for roasting something in the oven. He said to the apostles shortly before His ascension, "It is not for you to know the times or dates the Father *has set* by his own authority." (Acts 1:7)

Two points must be made from this text since it is widely misunderstood. First, Jesus affirms that the Father has set times and dates by His own authority. Even before sin began, the Father had already decided what the time limits of sin would be. But, the next point is more difficult to understand. Jesus told His disciples that it was not for them to know dates and times *that were not relevant* to them. In His statement to the disciples, Jesus did not mean that His disciples in centuries to come could not know the dates and times that were relevant to them; rather, Jesus is revealing an important principle. This principle is that *on or about the time of fulfillment, specific prophecies are understood.*

This is a critical point. The 1,260 and 2,300 year time periods of Daniel 7 and 8 were far from fulfillment when Jesus made this statement to His disciples. *He did not want them to know* that the 1,260 years of Daniel 7 were yet future. He did not want them to know that the 2,300 years of Daniel 8:14 were under way either. Jesus knew that such information would have destroyed the early church before it got started. This principle helps to explain why the book of Daniel was sealed up until the time of the end because time *only becomes important* when the time for prophetic fulfillment arrives.

If I were to paraphrase the thoughts of Jesus in Acts 1:7, I would say, "My friends, it is not for you to know about specific dates and times the Father has set by His own authority until some specific date or time shall arrive. Then, the Holy Spirit will lead you to understand the timing and what is yet to come." See John 16:13 for support of this conclusion.

1798 marks the beginning of the end

In the prophecy of Daniel 7, an apocalyptic sequence unfolds that reveals when the beginning of the end occurs. Read Daniel 7:1-11 and notice the following progression:

1. Lion
2. Bear
3. Leopard
4. Terrible monster
5. Ten horns - little horn

6. Judgment scene in heaven
7. Beasts destroyed in fire

According to the rules of interpretation (page 4), (and confirmed by history) these events occur in their order. According to Daniel 7:20,21 the judgment scene *begins at the end* of the 1,260 years of little horn terror. The proof of this statement is found in two selections of text. First, Daniel says, **"I also wanted to know about the ten horns on its head and about the other horn that came up, before which three of them fell—the horn that looked more imposing than the others and that had eyes and a mouth that spoke boastfully. {21} As I watched, this horn was waging war against the saints and defeating them, {22}** *until the Ancient of Days came* and pronounced judgment in favor of the saints of the Most High, and the time came when they possessed the kingdom." (Daniel 7:20-22) When did the Ancient of Days come to the court described in verse 9? Also notice that this verse says persecution will resume and last until the saints possess the kingdom.

Secondly, Daniel says, **"He [the little horn] will speak against the Most High and oppress his saints and try to change the set times and the laws. The saints will be handed over to him for a time, times and half a time. {26} But the court will sit, and his power will be taken away and completely destroyed forever."** Daniel 7:25-26 Here, the saints are handed over to the little horn until the court sits. Again we ask, when did the court sit?

The reader will notice from verse 21 that the little horn wages war against the saints *until* the Ancient of Days, the Father, came and convened the heavenly court which is described in Daniel 7:9,10. Again, in verse 25, the Bible says the saints will be persecuted for 1,260 years but the court **will sit** and **take away** the great authority of the little horn. *The court brings the persecution of the little horn to an end.* The point here is that the court in heaven convenes at the end of the 1,260 years. At this point in time, the Father grants a restraining order against the little horn power and the saints are freed for a season (until the deadly wound is healed). And, we know from Revelation 13, the persecution of the saints will resume when the trumpets begin. This coming persecution will last until the saints will possess the kingdom. (Revelation 13:5-7)

We can't see into heaven

Consider this. When Jesus gave the prophecy to Daniel recorded in Daniel 7, He connected the end of the little horn's power with the Ancient of Days convening the court scene. Knowing that human beings cannot look up into heaven and see events taking place there, Jesus tells us to watch for certain events on earth so we can know the timing of events in heaven. Isn't this neat?

Again, the point is made: The judgment scene in Daniel 7:9,10 began in 1798 – at the end of the 1,260 years. The little horn power was wounded – not because 1,260 years had passed – but because the Ancient of Days pronounced a restraining judgment in favor of the saints. In other words, the papacy received the deadly wound because the Father ordered it. The 1,260 year time period tells us when to look for the end of papal persecution so that we can know that heaven's court has convened.

Revelation helps to solve the mystery

If the reader will consider the possibility that the scenes in Daniel 7:9 and Revelation 4 and 5 began in 1798, two things will make a lot of sense. First, just assume that Daniel and John saw the *same* service. John's attention is focused on the book sealed with seven seals and the search for someone worthy to open the book. Daniel is focused on the persecution of the saints and the court scene. Now observe how these two elements are directly connected! Daniel reveals the timing of the court (at the end of 1,260 years). Daniel also tells us that after the court convenes, the books are opened and judgment begins. (But, Daniel doesn't say how long after court convenes that the books are opened.)

On the other hand, John reveals the test of worthiness that our High Priest must pass before He can officiate on behalf of human beings. And, we know from Leviticus 16 that the High Priest had to be found worthy before he could officiate on behalf of Israel only on the Day of Atonement. In short, we can therefore say that Jesus was determined worthy to receive the book sealed with seven seals when the court convened in 1798.

Now, three elements come together that confirm that Daniel and John saw the same scene.

1. Both prophets saw Jesus promoted and highly exalted like never before. Jesus was given *sovereign* power for the first time in Daniel 7:13,14, and John saw Jesus declared worthy to receive the book sealed with seven seals *and* the seven attributes of divine authority. (Revelation 5:7,12) **Note:** These powers had not been in Christ's possession since the plan of salvation was implemented.
   We know from ancient Day of Atonement services, that the worthiness of the High Priest was only an issue on the Day of Atonement. (Leviticus 16:6, Hebrews 5:3; 7:27; 9:7) Therefore, the worthiness of Jesus in Revelation 5 is directly connected to heaven's judgment day whose services commenced in 1798. Because, after being found worthy to judge humanity in heaven's Day of Atonement, Jesus

opened the books and began to cleanse the sanctuary in 1844!

2. As the heavenly court room service progressed, John saw Jesus begin to open the seals. (More about them in a moment.) When the third seal was opened in 1844, the judgment of human beings began. In other words, Jesus had to be found worthy to officiate as the Judge of humanity shortly before 1844.
3. Lastly, there is widely-known historical evidence which demonstrates that the seven seals began opening shortly after 1798. In fact, the third seal opened right on time in 1844, and the fourth seal is about to open.

Summary

The seven seals bring the timing of these events into focus. They are progressive and additive in nature. Each broken seal reveals a brighter and clearer understanding of who Jesus really is and the powers that He has. The first seal reveals the salvation of Jesus. This stands in contrast to the salvation controlled by the Roman Church for 1,260 years. The opening of this seal brought a great spiritual revival to Europe and North America between 1798 and 1844. The second seal reveals the supremacy of the Bible, the Word of God, which was translated and distributed to the far corners of earth. This stands in contrast to the ecclesiastical demands of the Church. And the formation of numerous Bible Societies between 1800 and 1844 confirm the operation of the second seal. The third seal reveals Christ's ministry in heaven's sanctuary. This stands in contrast to the vicarious ministry of human priests. The proclamation of the "judgment hour message" since 1844 confirms the operation of this seal. The fourth seal will reveal the authority of Jesus over all men. This seal is the next to open, perhaps in 1994. The fifth seal reveals the faith of Jesus. The operation of this seal will be seen in those who die for their testimony. And the sixth seal physically reveals the King of Kings. With the opening of each seal, Jesus becomes brighter.

Lastly, the first six seals relate to each other in a special way. Think of the first three seals as *causes,* and the next three seals are their *effects*. For example, the first seal describes the work of Jesus impressing upon man the need of salvation through Jesus and the sixth seal is the full realization of that salvation. The second seal describes the distribution of the Bible all over the world and the fifth seal culminates with martyrdom over Bible truth. Finally, the investigative judgment of the dead begun in 1844 during the third seal will move to the living (in 1994?) during the horrific destruction under the fourth seal.

Appendix F

Understanding the apocalyptic chart

The apocalyptic chart on pages 270-271 serves a two-fold purpose. First, it attempts to identify the order and timing of all apocalyptic elements—both past and future. Secondly, it demonstrates the controlling operation of a large prophetic matrix. (A much larger chart can be obtained for $2 by calling (513) 848-3322.) This matrix of Daniel and Revelation has two dimensions. First, there is the passage of time (left to right). Secondly, there is collaboration between the prophecies (top to bottom). Because apocalyptic prophecy follows a consistent pattern, the discovery of the rules that makes this matrix possible now brings a new level of understanding to the prophecies of Daniel and Revelation. For the first time, the messages contained in these two books of the Bible combine to make sense just as they read and when the prophecies are properly combined, they reveal 18 extraordinary stories.

Review the chart twice

To appreciate the meaning of the chart, view the chart from left to right. For example, notice that Story 1 lists the elements of Daniel 2 as: Head, Chest, Thighs, Legs, Feet, Toes, and Rock. *These elements are laid out according to their order given in the prophecy.* In other words, the kingdom symbolized by the head is followed by a kingdom symbolized by the chest, etc. By following the order of elements as they are given, we not only mark the passage of time, we can find our chronological position within the prophecy. By finding our chronological position, we can then see what is going to happen next!

After observing the horizontal flow of the chart, study the vertical alignment of the chart. For example, notice the alignment of the chart below Medo-Persia. You will find: Chest, Bear and Ram. These elements, aligned from different prophecies, combine to form a solid matrix about Medo-Persia, the second world empire of apocalyptic prophecy. History confirms that the Chest of Daniel 2, the Bear of Daniel 7 and the Ram of Daniel 8 represent the same entity and that this entity came to power about 538 B.C. Because these three symbols represent *the same entity*, we can align three prophecies and the resulting matrix helps us understand things about the Medo-Persian empire that could not be otherwise understood.

For example, Daniel was shown a sequence of events. This vision is recorded in Daniel 7 (Story 2). The sequence is as follows: Lion, Bear, Leopard, Monster, Ten Horns, Little Horn, Judgment Day and Beasts thrown into lake of fire. The problem with this sequence of events is that we can historically demonstrate the fulfillment of the Lion, Bear, Leopard, Monster and Little Horn, but we can't historically demonstrate *when* the Judgment Day scene occurs except to say that it occurs after the Little Horn power. This is because the Judgment Day scene doesn't happen on earth. (See Daniel 7:9,10.) However, if we correctly align Daniel 7 with Daniel 8 and Daniel 9 (Stories 3 and 4), we discover the timing of the judgment scene to be 1844. (See *Day Star* Volume 2, Numbers 3 - 6.) From this simple alignment and other supporting data, we can easily calculate *when* the judgment scene began.

Be careful

None of the 18 apocalyptic prophecies are complete within themselves. No one prophecy tells the whole story. In fact, the full story is only revealed after *all* 18 prophecies of Daniel and Revelation are correctly aligned. Many students of prophecy yield to the temptation of minimizing some element as unimportant if they don't know what it means. Even worse, some people will concoct elaborate conclusions without first solving the whole equation. In other words, until the full story is known, we can't have a complete understanding of any of the 18 prophecies. Therefore, be careful in your study. We can be sure that God did not include nonessential elements in apocalyptic prophecy.

Puzzle solving

Prophetic study requires patience and effort, for it is similar to the assembly of a picture-puzzle. If we correctly assemble the obvious parts first, the obscure pieces will finally fall into their right places. Bible prophecy also unfolds like a flower. Ever since the first apocalyptic prophecies of Daniel were written, the people of God have understood *those portions of prophecy that related to them*. But, only the final generation will understand the full story. God designed that apocalyptic prophecy should operate this way for three reasons:

First, apocalyptic prophecy has kept hope alive for almost 2,000 years. That hope, of course, is the glorious return of Jesus. Even though claims of prophetic fulfillment have been declared and proven defective in centuries past, the fact remains that hope in the second advent is still alive.

Secondly, God had apocalyptic prophecies written down in such a way that their messages could not be fully understood until the final generation should arrive. Soon, signs in the heavens and on earth will draw attention to the Bible as never before. By hiding the meaning of the prophecies until the end of time, the discovery of their understanding will generate global attention as people learn that the Bible clearly explains what is taking place! In turn, the Bible will be greatly exalted before the world as the unfailing Word of God.

Lastly, the apocalyptic prophecies of Daniel and Revelation bring all themes of the Bible into crisp focus. Apocalyptic prophecy exposes the comprehensiveness of God's salvation as nothing else can. In the context of last-day fulfillments, the essential doctrines that support Bible prophecy combine to form a wonderful view of God's true character. Divine love is His balance of mercy and justice and everything that God does is fair. The five doctrines that form the foundation of apocalyptic interpretation are the truth about:

1. The authority of God
2. The temple of God
3. The return of God
4. The salvation of God
5. The condition of man in life and death

The more you know about these five doctrines, the better you will understand the prophecies and of course, the stronger will be your appreciation of the goodness and love of God. Few people realize it, but the events predicted in Revelation will soon expose all false doctrines and prophetic interpretations for what they really are. God has carefully designed the closing events of Earth's history so that every person may behold what His truth really is. Also, understand that God is particularly interested in reaching those who don't want to know what the truth is. As in the days of Pharaoh, the Bible predicts that many will harden their hearts in the face of God's truth and when nothing more can be done to save them, the door of mercy will close.

Not an infallible chart

This chart represents the synthesis of my prophetic study for 20+ years. The possibility of error is ever present for I am human. My desire is that this chart will stimulate deeper study and if it serves as a springboard for better understanding, I shall be pleased. So, I respectfully submit these conclusions as "something to consider."

To be sure, many pastors and religious leaders will oppose the placement of events and therefore, the predictions of this chart. To these I can only extend the ultimate prophetic challenge: "Do as I have done. Distribute a detailed copy of *your* chart." By so doing, we can be impartially judged in the near future. The presence or absence of the things we put in print will clearly prove which views are true and which are false. A printed chart will serve as an unchanging witness between us.

While it is not necessary that the reader agree with all of my prophetic views, God desires that every Christian place the prophetic elements somewhere and in some order. Earth is not going to last much longer – signs confirm this every day. Soon, like the springing of a trap, the great tribulation is going to break out upon all inhabitants of Earth and if our prophetic anchor is not carefully grounded in the Word of God, we shall be overwhelmed and blown away by winds of fear and confusion.

The fear of Almighty God is about to fall upon all inhabitants of Earth with sudden calamities. Then the world will see just how terrible it is to fall into the hands of the living God. The Lord will be fearfully exalted throughout the earth as never before in the history of man. Those who understand *what* God is doing will go forth to tell others *why* He is sending judgments of destruction. At that time, the earth will be so distressed that the inhabitants will be forced to give consideration to the things taking place. Even though God's actions are often misunderstood, He does not suddenly break into our daily activities without cause. Human beings today have either forgotten or chosen to ignore the fact that God's visitation is promised. Each of us will face our Creator and give account for our words and deeds.

If we refuse to live holy lives, if we neglect to search for prophetic truth, we shall be left with nothing but spiritual darkness. And what excuse for darkness shall we offer God on that day if our ignorance has been willful?

18 Apocalyptic Stories

The books of Daniel and Revelation contain a total of 18 apocalyptic stories (prophecies). Each story is identified by having a beginning point and ending point in time. For this reason, all 18 stories will neatly fit into time-lines forming a tight and comprehensive matrix of events.

It is most important that we identify where each story begins and ends. For this reason, all 18 apocalyptic stories of Daniel and Revelation are chronologically presented on the chart.

The reader is reminded that the original manuscripts of Daniel and Revelation did not include chapter and verse designations. These "helps" were added centuries after the manuscripts were written to facilitate the study of the Bible. By having a chapter and verse, students can quickly find a sentence or group of sentences for further investigation. These well-intentioned helps can create a superficial problem. Since we normally think of a chapter as a complete unit, it is possible to overlook the presence of the 18 stories because they are grouped differently than chapter units represent. So, do not be confused by the fact that stories can begin and end anywhere within a chapter.

Start and stop

How can we tell when one story ends and another begins? One story ends and another begins when the next event chronologically occurs before the previous event. For example, suppose you are reading about the six seals in Revelation 6. As you read verses 12-17, the sixth seal is described. This seal describes the second advent of Jesus and the sixth seal ends with verse 17. After you finish reading verse 17, the next verse begins talking about four angels holding back the four winds. See Revelation 7:1. Since the four angels hold back the four winds *before* the second coming of Jesus, the beginning of a new story is detected. (It just so happens in this case that a chapter break also occurs at the end of the six seals story.) Remember though, a story does not begin because a new chapter ends or begins. *A new story only begins when the next event chronologically occurs before the previous event.* This simple process never fails.

Here is another essential point: The elements of each story happen in the order in which they are given. This means that each story progresses from its beginning point to its ending point just as it was written. On a few occasions, the order of a story is momentarily broken so that important details can be given to the reader. However, these momentary breaks do not affect the obvious sequence of the story.

Rules of interpretation

Rules of interpretation are inseparable from the study of prophecy for conclusions are directly connected to the methods used during interpretation. If we interpret prophecy using faulty rules, we end up with faulty conclusions. It's that simple.

Since rules of interpretation are not written down in the Bible, they must come from careful research and observation. *The unknown cannot be determined without valid rules.* This is true of every science.

This is critical: Man does not make up the rules of interpretation; rather, man can only discover the presence of rules. Rules are detected when we find consistent behavior within prophetic elements. Once consistency is recognized, we can then state the rule. In other words, if we observe certain things to always be true, only then do we identify the presence of a rule.

Consider this example. Sir Isaac Newton researched the effects of gravity. He studied the behavior of gravity using different experiments. After observing that gravity behaved in certain consistent ways, he wrote down a formula expressing how it works. In other words, Sir Isaac Newton did not make up the rules governing gravity. God did that. But, Sir Isaac Newton was able to discover the rules by which gravity operates and he was able to state the rules of gravity in such a way that the effect of gravity could be accurately calculated and understood by others.

The study of apocalyptic prophecy is very similar to the study of gravity. We reason from the known to the unknown. Before we can interpret those parts of prophecy that are unknown, we have to discover the rules by which fulfillments occurred in the past. By carefully observing the behavior of apocalyptic prophecies that have been fulfilled, we can discover the rules by which they work. After we understand the rules at work, we can then begin to solve those portions of apocalyptic prophecy that are unfulfilled by using rules of interpretation that are always consistent.

One more point. There is a world of difference between prophetic truth and prophetic faith. Prophetic truth refers to those prophecies or those portions of prophecy that qualify as fulfillments. Prophetic faith, on the other hand, refers to those prophecies that are yet to be fulfilled. Since no one can prove something that hasn't happened, our prophetic faith should be carefully built upon the truth that comes from solid principles of interpretation.

What is a prophetic fulfillment?

So, how can we know if a prophecy has been fulfilled? A fulfillment is a full-filling of the prophecy. In other words, a fulfillment occurs when all the specifications of a prophecy are met. Every detail of the prophecy must be satisfied before a fulfillment can be declared. This also means that the chronological order of the prophecy must also be satisfied. For example, some people may claim that the fourth trumpet of Revelation 8 has already been fulfilled. If their claim is true, they not only have to demonstrate that all of the details of the fourth trumpet have been fulfilled, they also have to demonstrate that the fulfillment of the first three trumpets has occurred in their order.

Personal observations

I have observed the presence of three rules of interpretation for apocalyptic prophecy. Keep in mind, there are different types of prophecy and each type has its own rules for interpretation.

1. Each apocalyptic story is identified by the presence of a beginning point and an ending point in time. Further, events within each story are given in chronological order.
2. A prophecy or prophetic element is not fulfilled until

all the specifications of the prophecy are met. This includes the chronology of the sequence.

3. Students of prophecy cannot make up their own interpretations of symbols. If some portion of a prophecy is declared symbolic, the Bible must clearly interpret the meaning of the symbol with applicable scripture.

Supremacy of apocalyptic prophecy

All other prophecies of the Bible are subordinate to apocalyptic sequencing. This means that apocalyptic prophecy determines the chronological placement of non-apocalyptic prophecies. For example, Amos, Ezekiel, Joel, Obadiah and many New Testament prophets believed that the great and awful day of the Lord was "near" and plainly said so. There's no question that what they saw in vision led them to conclude that the "Great Day of the Lord" was at hand. In Revelation, John indicates that the fulfillment of the things he saw was *near or soon.* The problem is that the ancient prophets did not understand how their visions fit into the larger chronology of God's plan.

No one prophet was shown *everything* that God intends to bring about. No disciple of Jesus expected that time would last almost 2,000 years. Paul sums up the process of prophetic revelations saying, "In the past God spoke to our forefathers through the prophets at many times and in various ways... For we know in part and we prophesy in part." Hebrews 1:1, I Corinthians 13:9 Each time God spoke to a prophet about the end of time, more detail was provided. But, without the vehicle of apocalyptic structures, prophecies about the "Great Day of the Lord" cannot be chronologically placed nor can their content be fully appreciated.

The point of all this is that apocalyptic prophecy serves as the backbone of God's chronology. Because this backbone has not been correctly understood in times past, people across the centuries have declared prophecies to be fulfilled, when in reality fulfillment did not occur. Remember, fulfillment requires two affirming actions: first, all specifications of the prophecy must be met; and secondly, the event must happen in its chronological order. If this little system of checks and balances is ignored, the result will be prophetic confusion.

Conclusion

It is my conviction that the judgments predicted under the fourth seal will begin on or about 1994. We don't have to wait long to see if this is true. Even if they don't begin in 1994, the whole world will soon behold His signal displeasure with our corporate behavior. While I may be wrong about the timing, there is no error about His coming wrath. So, why not try to understand this? Either way, you don't have to wait very long to see if it is true.

The 18 Prophecies

Locate each story on the apocalyptic chart and then read its contents. Even better, compare what is taking place in the other stories at the same time. Then, the value of the prophetic matrix can be appreciated.

Story 1. Daniel 2:31-35

Story 2. Daniel 7:1-11

Story 3. Daniel 8:1-12

Story 4. Daniel 9:24-27

Story 5. Daniel 11:2-35

Story 6. Daniel 11:36-12:2

Story 7. Revelation 4:1-6:17

Story 8. Revelation 7:1-8:1

Story 9. Revelation 8:2-9:21

Story 10. Revelation 10:1-11:13

Story 11. Revelation 11:14-19

Story 12. Revelation 12:1-14:5

Story 13. Revelation 14:6-15:4

Story 14. Revelation 15:5-16:21

Discussion. Revelation 17:1-18

Story 15. Revelation 18:1-8

Story 16. Revelation 19:1-20:6

Story 17. Revelation 20:7-21:1

Story 18. Revelation 21:2-22:5

Epilogue. Revelation 22:6-21

Apocalyptic and Jubilee Charts

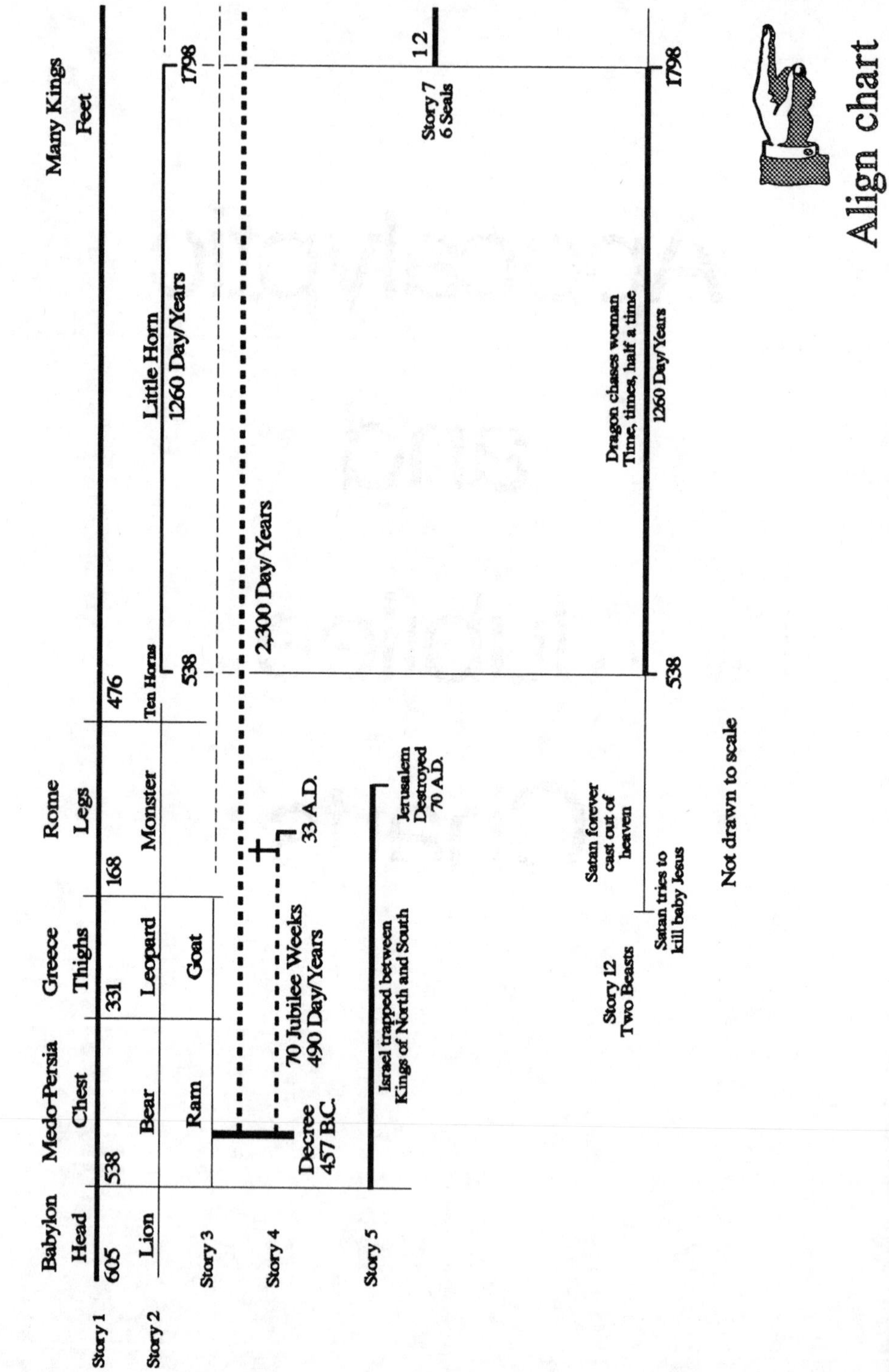
Story 1
Babylon
Head
605
Medo-Persia
Chest
538
Greece
Thighs
331
Rome
Legs
168
476
Many Kings
Feet
Story 2
Lion
Bear
Leopard
Monster
Ten Horns
Little Horn
1260 Day/Years
538
1798
Story 3
Ram
Goat
Story 4
Decree
457 B.C.
70 Jubilee Weeks
490 Day/Years
33 A.D.
2,300 Day/Years
Story 5
Israel trapped between
Kings of North and South
Jerusalem
Destroyed
70 A.D.
Story 7
6 Seals
12
Story 12
Two Beasts
Satan tries to
kill baby Jesus
Satan forever
cast out of
heaven
Dragon chases woman
Time, times, half a time
1260 Day/Years
538
1798
Not drawn to scale
Align chart

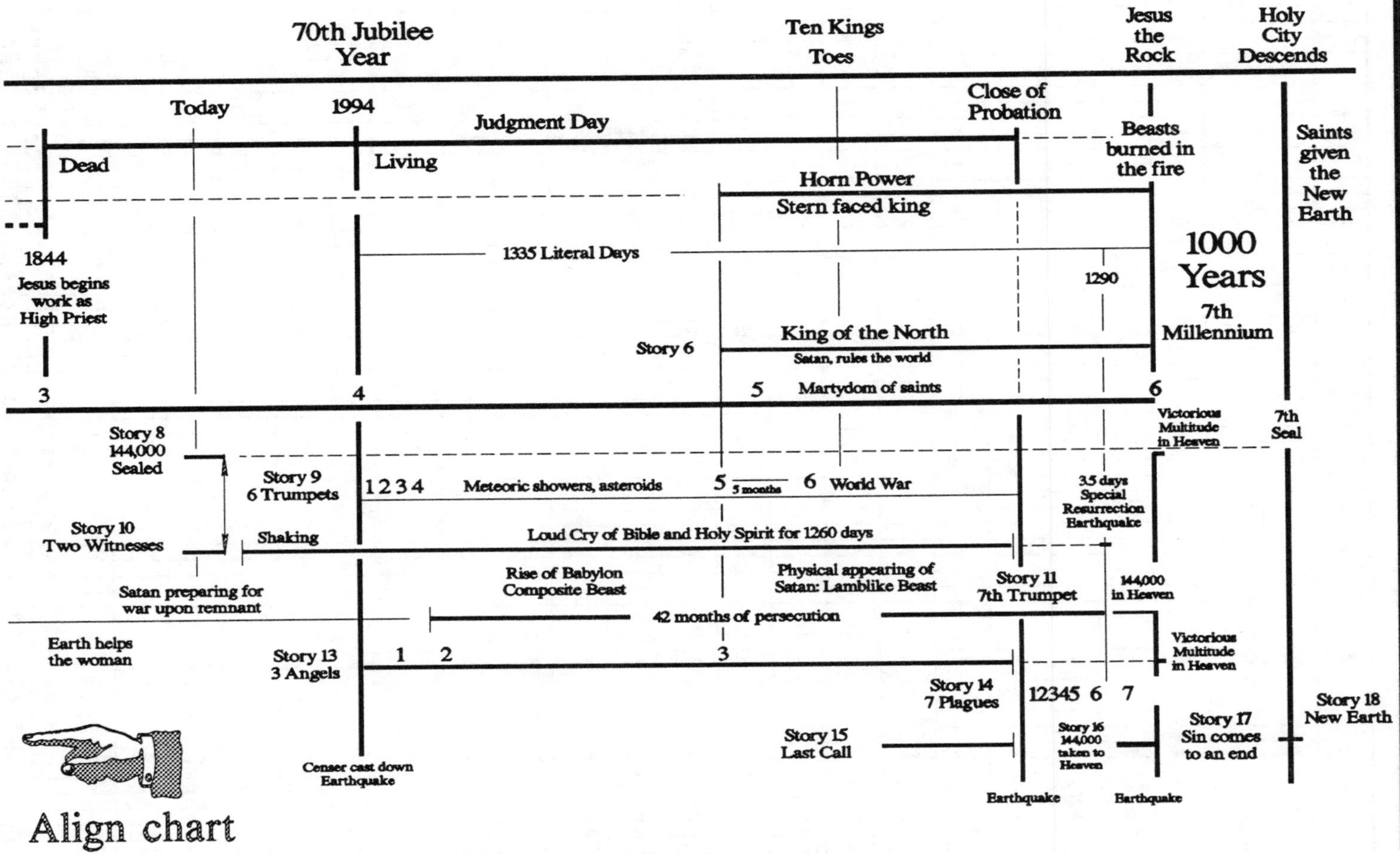
70th Jubilee Year
Ten Kings Toes
Jesus the Rock
Holy City Descends
Today
1994
Judgment Day
Close of Probation
Beasts burned in the fire
Saints given the New Earth
Dead
Living
Horn Power
Stern faced king
1844
Jesus begins work as High Priest
1335 Literal Days
1290
1000 Years
7th Millennium
Story 6
King of the North
Satan, rules the world
3
4
5
Martydom of saints
6
Victorious Multitude in Heaven
7th Seal
Story 8 144,000 Sealed
Story 9 6 Trumpets
1 2 3 4
Meteoric showers, asteroids
5 months
World War
3.5 days Special Resurrection Earthquake
Story 10 Two Witnesses
Shaking
Loud Cry of Bible and Holy Spirit for 1260 days
Rise of Babylon Composite Beast
Physical appearing of Satan: Lamblike Beast
Story 11 7th Trumpet
144,000 in Heaven
Satan preparing for war upon remnant
42 months of persecution
Earth helps the woman
Story 13 3 Angels
1
2
3
Victorious Multitude in Heaven
Story 14 7 Plagues
12345 6 7
Story 17 Sin comes to an end
Story 18 New Earth
Story 15 Last Call
Story 16 144,000 taken to Heaven
Censer cast down Earthquake
Earthquake
Earthquake
Align chart

Wk	Day	Yr	Jubilee Cycle 1 The Exodus	Jubilee Cycle 2 1st 50th Yr	Jubilee Cycle 3 2nd 50th Yr	Jubilee Cycle 4 3rd 50th Yr	Jubilee Cycle 5 4th 50th Yr	Jubilee Cycle 6 5th 50th Yr	Jubilee Cycle 7 6th 50th Yr	Jubilee Cycle 8 7th 50th Yr	Jubilee Cycle 9 8th 50th Yr	Jubilee Cycle 10 9th 50th Yr	Jubilee Cycle 11 10th 50th Yr	Jubilee Cycle 12 11th 50th Yr	Jubilee Cycle 13 12th 50th Yr	Jubilee Cycle 14 13th 50th Yr	Jubilee Cycle 15 14th 50th Yr	Jubilee Cycle 16 15th 50th Yr	Jubilee Cycle 17 16th 50th Yr	Jubilee Cycle 18 17th 50th Yr	Jubilee Cycle 19 18th 50th Yr	Jubilee Cycle 20 19th 50th Yr	Jubilee Cycle 21 20th 50th Yr	Jubilee Cycle 22 21st 50th Yr	Jubilee Cycle 23 22nd 50th Yr	Jubilee Cycle 24 23rd 50th Yr
	Sun	1	1437 BC	1388	1339	1290	1241	1192	1143	1094	1045	996	947	898	849	800	751	702	653	604	555	506	457	408	359	310
	Mon	2	1436																							
	Tue	3	1435															Jubilee Year					Decree to	Temple Finished		
	Wed	4	1434															in Bible					Rebuild			
	Thu	5	1433																	Second						
	Fri	6	1432																	Seige						
1	Sat	7	1431	1382	1333	1284	1235	1186	1137	1088	1039	990	941	892	843	794	745	696	647	598	549	500	451	402	353	304
	Sun	8																								
	Mon	9																								
	Tue	10																								
	Wed	11																								
	Thu	12																								
	Fri	13																								
2	Sat	14	1424	1375	1326	1277	1228	1179	1130	1081	1032	983	934	885	836	787	738	689	640	591	542	493	444	395	346	297
	Sun	15																								
	Mon	16																								
	Tue	17																				Babylon				
	Wed	18																	Third		538	Falls				
	Thu	19																	Seige	586						
	Fri	20																			536	Cyrus' Decree				
3	Sat	21	1417	1368	1319	1270	1221	1172	1123	1074	1025	976	927	878	829	780	731	682	633	584	535	486	437	388	339	290
	Sun	22																								
	Mon	23																								
	Tue	24																								
	Wed	25																								
	Thu	26																								
	Fri	27																								
4	Sat	28	1410	1361	1312	1263	1214	1165	1116	1067	1018	969	920	871	822	773	724	675	626	577	528	479	430	381	332	283
	Sun	29																							331	
	Mon	30																							Medo-Persia	
	Tue	31																							Falls	
	Wed	32																								
	Thu	33																								
	Fri	34																								
5	Sat	35	1403	1354	1305	1256	1207	1158	1109	1060	1011	962	913	864	815	766	717	668	619	570	521	472	423	374	325	276
	Sun	36																								
	Mon	37																								
	Tue	38																								
	Wed	39											Solomon													
	Thu	40										957	Begins													
	Fri	41											Temple													
6	Sat	42	1396	1347	1298	1249	1200	1151	1102	1053	1004	955	906	857	808	759	710	661	612	563	514	465	416	367	318	269
	Sun	43																								
	Mon	44																								
	Tue	45												Ahab Killed												
	Wed	46									1000			in Battle					First Seige -							
	Thu	47									King Saul Dies			852			Sign to		Babylonian							
	Fri	48															Hezekiah		Captivity Begins							
7	Sat	49	1389	1340	1291	1242	1193	1144	1095	1046	997	948	899	850	801	752	703	654	605	556	507	458	409	360	311	262

Wk	Day	Yr	Jubilee Cycle 25 24th 50th Yr	Jubilee Cycle 26 25th 50th Yr	Jubilee Cycle 27 26th 50th Yr	Jubilee Cycle 28 27th 50th Yr	Jubilee Cycle 29 28th 50th Yr	Jubilee Cycle 30 29th 50th Yr	Jubilee Cycle 31 30th 50th Yr	Jubilee Cycle 32 31st 50th Yr	Jubilee Cycle 33 32nd 50th Yr	Jubilee Cycle 34 33rd 50th Yr	Jubilee Cycle 35 34th 50th Yr	Jubilee Cycle 36 35th 50th Yr	Jubilee Cycle 37 36th 50th Yr	Jubilee Cycle 38 37th 50th Yr	Jubilee Cycle 39 38th 50th Yr	Jubilee Cycle 40 39th 50th Yr	Jubilee Cycle 41 40th 50th Yr	Jubilee Cycle 42 41st 50th Yr	Jubilee Cycle 43 42nd 50th Yr	Jubilee Cycle 44 43rd 50th Yr	Jubilee Cycle 45 44th 50th Yr	Jubilee Cycle 46 45th 50th Yr	Jubilee Cycle 47 46th 50th Yr	Jubilee Cycle 48 47th 50th Yr
	Sun	1	261	212	163	114	65	16	34	83	132	181	230	279	328	377	426	475	524	573	622	671	720	769	818	867
	Mon	2							Christian									476								
	Tue	3							Trusteeship									Rome								
	Wed	4							Begins									Falls								
	Thu	5																								
	Fri	6																								
1	Sat	7	255	206	157	108	59	10	40	89	138	187	236	285	334	383	432	481	530	579	628	677	726	775	824	873
	Sun	8																								
	Mon	9																								
	Tue	10																								
	Wed	11																								
	Thu	12							Jesus																	
	Fri	13						4	Born																	
2	Sat	14	248	199	150	101	52	3	47	96	145	194	243	292	341	390	439	488	537	586	635	684	733	782	831	880
	Sun	15						2											538							
	Mon	16						1											Little Horn Power							
	Tue	17						1											Reigns - 1260 Yrs.							
	Wed	18						2																		
	Thu	19						3																		
	Fri	20						4																		
3	Sat	21	241	192	143	94	45	5	54	103	152	201	250	299	348	397	446	495	544	593	642	691	740	789	838	887
	Sun	22																								
	Mon	23																								
	Tue	24																								
	Wed	25																								
	Thu	26																								
	Fri	27																								
4	Sat	28	234	185	136	87	38	12	61	110	159	208	257	306	355	404	453	502	551	600	649	698	747	796	845	894
	Sun	29																								
	Mon	30																								
	Tue	31																								
	Wed	32																								
	Thu	33																								
	Fri	34																								
5	Sat	35	227	178	129	80	31	19	68	117	166	215	264	313	362	411	460	509	558	607	656	705	754	803	852	901
	Sun	36								Jerusalem																
	Mon	37							70	Destroyed																
	Tue	38								by Rome																
	Wed	39																								
	Thu	40																								
	Fri	41																								
6	Sat	42	220	171	122	73	24	26	75	124	173	222	271	320	369	418	467	516	565	614	663	712	761	810	859	908
	Sun	43						27	Jesus Begins																	
	Mon	44							Ministry																	
	Tue	45		168					Jesus Dies																	
	Wed	46		Grecia				30	on Calvary																	
	Thu	47		Falls				Jewish																		
	Fri	48						Probation Ends																		
7	Sat	49	213	164	115	66	17	33	82	131	180	229	278	327	376	425	474	523	572	621	670	719	768	817	866	915

Wk	Day	Yr	Jubilee Cycle 49 48th 50th Yr	Jubilee Cycle 50 49th 50th Yr	Jubilee Cycle 51 50th 50th Yr	Jubilee Cycle 52 51st 50th Yr	Jubilee Cycle 53 52nd 50th Yr	Jubilee Cycle 54 53rd 50th Yr	Jubilee Cycle 55 54th 50th Yr	Jubilee Cycle 56 55th 50th Yr	Jubilee Cycle 57 56th 50th Yr	Jubilee Cycle 58 57th 50th Yr	Jubilee Cycle 59 58th 50th Yr	Jubilee Cycle 60 59th 50th Yr	Jubilee Cycle 61 60th 50th Yr	Jubilee Cycle 62 61st 50th Yr	Jubilee Cycle 63 62nd 50th Yr	Jubilee Cycle 64 63rd 50th Yr	Jubilee Cycle 65 64th 50th Yr	Jubilee Cycle 66 65th 50th Yr	Jubilee Cycle 67 66th 50th Yr	Jubilee Cycle 68 67th 50th Yr	Jubilee Cycle 69 68th 50th Yr	Jubilee Cycle 70 69th 50th Yr	70th 50th Yr
	Sun	1	916	965	1014	1063	1112	1161	1210	1259	1308	1357	1406	1455	1504	1553	1602	1651	1700	1749	1798	1847	1896	1945	1994
	Mon	2																			Protestant				
	Tue	3																			Trusteeship				
	Wed	4																			Begins				
	Thu	5																							
	Fri	6																							
1	Sat	7	922	971	1020	1069	1118	1167	1216	1265	1314	1363	1412	1461	1510	1559	1608	1657	1706	1755	1804	1853	1902	1951	
	Sun	8																							
	Mon	9																							
	Tue	10																							
	Wed	11																							
	Thu	12													Martin Luther										
	Fri	13													Nails 95 Theses										
2	Sat	14	929	978	1027	1076	1125	1174	1223	1272	1321	1370	1419	1468	1517	1566	1615	1664	1713	1762	1811	1860	1909	1958	
	Sun	15																				1861			
	Mon	16																				Civil War			
	Tue	17																				Begins			
	Wed	18																							
	Thu	19																					1914	WW I	
	Fri	20																							
3	Sat	21	936	985	1034	1083	1132	1181	1230	1279	1328	1377	1426	1475	1524	1573	1622	1671	1720	1769	1818	1867	1916	1965	
	Sun	22																							
	Mon	23																							
	Tue	24																							
	Wed	25																							
	Thu	26																		Declaration of					
	Fri	27																		Independence					
4	Sat	28	943	992	1041	1090	1139	1188	1237	1286	1335	1384	1433	1482	1531	1580	1629	1678	1727	1776	1825	1874	1923	1972	
	Sun	29																							
	Mon	30																							
	Tue	31																							
	Wed	32																							
	Thu	33																							
	Fri	34																							
5	Sat	35	950	999	1048	1097	1146	1195	1244	1293	1342	1391	1440	1489	1538	1587	1636	1685	1734	1783	1832	1881	1930	1979	
	Sun	36																							
	Mon	37																							
	Tue	38																							
	Wed	39																							
	Thu	40																							
	Fri	41																							
6	Sat	42	957	1006	1055	1104	1153	1202	1251	1300	1349	1398	1447	1496	1545	1594	1643	1692	1741	1790	1839	1888	1937	1986	
	Sun	43																		French					
	Mon	44																		Revolution					
	Tue	45																		1793					
	Wed	46																					1941		
	Thu	47																		2300 Day	1844		WW II Begins		
	Fri	48																		Prophecy Ends					
7	Sat	49	964	1013	1062	1111	1160	1209	1258	1307	1356	1405	1454	1503	1552	1601	1650	1699	1748	1797	1846	1895	1944	1993	

NOTES

NOTES

NOTES

NOTES

NOTES

NOTES

Supplemental Bible Study Helps

Bible Study Helps - Audio/Video Tapes

Revelation Tapes The following is a list of current seminar studies on Revelation. Video tapes may be purchased separately or the entire set of 21 tapes may be purchased at a reduced price. Keep in mind that each tape is a building block therefore, no presentation is complete within itself. For best results, they should be viewed in the order listed below.

1. The wrath of God and the full cup principle
2. The purpose and process of Bible prophecy
3. Who is Jesus? Why did He die for man?
4. Michael and Lucifer, the origin of sin
5. The Plan of Salvation - 2 tapes
6. The wonderful prophecies of Daniel - 3 tapes
7. Judgment day is almost here - 2 tapes
8. Introduction to Revelation / Rules of Interpretation
9. The seven seals - 2 tapes
10. The seven trumpets - 2 tapes
11. The two beasts of Revelation - 2 tapes
12. The man of sin and the 144,000
13. The two witnesses
14. The mark of the beast and God's everlasting covenant

continued on next page

Other Bible Study Helps by Larry Wilson

1. *The Revelation of Jesus* (Second edition available October, 1992) This new book of 300+ pages is an update and compilation of the three volume series first published in 1990. Also, the price has been greatly reduced due to volume printing. This book serves as an important companion to this volume by containing detail studies on five essential doctrines. These include: salvation by faith, Christ's ministry in the heavenly sanctuary, the nature and events surrounding the second coming, the condition of man in life and death, and the perpetuity and authority of God's law.

2. **Day Star Newsletter** Monthly issues. The newsletter usually contains one or two Bible studies on topics that relate to current issues and/or the prophetic stories found in Daniel and Revelation. Some remaining back issues are available.

3. *Warning! Revelation is about to be fulfilled* This book describes coming events in a story-like format. It is a must for anyone interested in a quick survey of coming events. A very handy book for sharing with friends and family. For quantity pricing on this book, give us a call. (Spanish version also available.)